Supply Chain Management

Supply Chain Management

by Daniel Stanton
Certified Supply Chain Professional

A Wiley Brand

Supply Chain Management For Dummies®

Published by: **John Wiley & Sons, Inc.,** 111 River Street, Hoboken, NJ 07030-5774, www.wiley.com

Copyright © 2018 by John Wiley & Sons, Inc., Hoboken, New Jersey

Published simultaneously in Canada

For general information on our other products and services, please contact our Customer Care Department within the U.S. at 877-762-2974, outside the U.S. at 317-572-3993, or fax 317-572-4002. For technical support, please visit https://hub.wiley.com/community/support/dummies.

Wiley publishes in a variety of print and electronic formats and by print-on-demand. Some material included with standard print versions of this book may not be included in e-books or in print-on-demand. If this book refers to media such as a CD or DVD that is not included in the version you purchased, you may download this material at http://booksupport.wiley.com. For more information about Wiley products, visit www.wiley.com.

Library of Congress Control Number: 2017958142

ISBN: 978-1-119-41019-5 (pbk); 978-1-119-41020-1 (ebk); 978-1-119-41021-8 (ebk)

Manufactured in the United States of America

C10011788_062719

Contents at a Glance

Table of Contents

Introduction

Supply chain management is about seeing your business as an interconnected system. *Supply Chain Management For Dummies* covers the tools, rules, and language that you need to understand how the parts of your company's supply chain fit together. The book also shows you how to plan and manage your supply chain in ways that reduce costs, increase profits, and minimize risks.

About This Book

Many books treat supply chain management as part of operations, logistics, or procurement, but this book takes a broader approach, showing that those functions are interconnected parts of a system.

I include lots of everyday examples that make it easy to understand each step in any supply chain, and that show how virtually any company can employ supply chain principles.

Most people get to see only a small part of the supply chains that they work in. This book helps you understand all the other processes and systems that feed into your supply chain, as well as how decisions that you make affect others up and down the supply chain, including your customers and suppliers. The book uses language that's easy to understand and is organized in a way that makes access to specific topics easy.

Foolish Assumptions

In writing this book, I assumed that supply chain management is important to you because

>> You need to understand it for your current job.

>> You need to understand it for a future job.

>> You need to explain it to other people so that they can do their jobs better.

I assume that you have some connection to supply chain management, probably because you've studied or worked in logistics, operations, or procurement. I assume that you may have been taught to see supply chain management from a narrow, functional perspective rather than as an end-to-end, integrated system.

I assume that you want to understand how decisions made in one part of a supply chain can influence the results in another part. Many companies have made bad choices with expensive consequences simply because they didn't recognize the effects of those choices on their supply chains. In most companies, more than 70 percent of costs and 100 percent of revenues depend on supply decisions. It's definitely worth the time and energy to understand how to efficiently manage a supply chain.

Icons Used in This Book

Icons emphasize a point to remember, a danger to be aware of, or information that you may find helpful.

The Tip icon marks tips (duh!) and shortcuts that you can use to make supply chain management easier.

Remember icons mark information that's especially important to know. To siphon off the most important information in each chapter, skim the paragraphs that have these icons.

The Technical Stuff icon marks information of a highly technical nature that you can normally skip.

The Warning icon tells you to watch out! It marks important information that may save you headaches.

Where to Go from Here

You can read this book in different ways, depending on why you're reading it. You can certainly start at the beginning and skip the things you already know, but I've written the book so that you can start reading anywhere that catches your eye and then hunt for additional bits that sound interesting.

If your goal is to discover what supply chain management is, start with Part 1. If you're trying to get a sense for how the pieces of a supply chain fit together in a framework, read about the Supply Chain Operations Reference (SCOR) model in Part 2. If you need to get a handle on the technologies that are key to supply chain management, check out Part 3. If you're looking for ways to drive strategic value for your company by using supply chain management tools, jump into Part 4. Finally, Part 5 is packed with information that can help you grow your career in supply chain management.

TIP

Some of the material in this book will be useful if you're preparing for a supply chain certification such as Certified Supply Chain Professional or SCPro (see Chapter 20), but you shouldn't use it as a substitute for the official study guides.

No matter how you go through the book, you'll eventually want to read all the chapters. Each chapter is useful on its own, but the book as a whole helps you see how interconnected the parts of a supply chain are and why you need to think about all of them when you make decisions that affect your business, your customers, and your suppliers.

TIP

For some helpful information about how to describe supply chain management, how to lead supply chain projects, and how to use the Supply Chain Operations Reference model, check out the Cheat Sheet for this book by visiting www. dummies.com and entering the book's title in the search field.

1

Getting Started with Supply Chain Management

Simplify the concept of supply chain management by breaking it into pieces.

Analyze supply chain management from different perspectives to see why it is important.

Align supply chain management with the goals of your business.

Optimize supply chain performance to drive better results for you, your suppliers, and your customers.

Chapter **1**

The Growing Demand for Supply Chain Management

These days, it's hard to find a copy of *The Wall Street Journal* that doesn't have the phrase *supply chain* somewhere on the first page. You hear about supply chains everywhere: in company reports, on the news, and even in casual conversation. But it hasn't always been that way. Only in the past 30 years has supply chain management gone from being a vague academic concept to a critical business capability. This chapter covers why supply chain management has become so important and explains the process for building best-in-class supply chain management into your company.

Defining Supply Chain Management

In spite of the current hype, supply chains aren't really that new. Entrepreneurs have been buying things from suppliers and selling products to customers for almost as long as people have inhabited the earth. However, supply chain *management* is new. In fact, the basic principles of supply chain management only began to take shape in the 1980s, at about the same time that personal computers came onto the business scene. You can see the trend clearly by using Google's N-Gram Viewer, shown in Figure 1-1, which shows how often the term "supply chain" has been used in book titles.

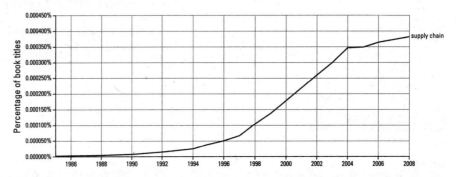

FIGURE 1-1:
Frequency that
"supply chain"
has appeared in
book titles.

Supply chain management is the planning and coordination of all of the people, processes, and technology involved in creating value for a company. Managing a supply chain effectively involves coordinating all of the work inside of your company with the things that are happening outside of your company. In other words, it means looking at your business as a single link in a long, end-to-end chain that supplies something of value to a customer.

TIP

The word "value" shows up a lot when people talk about supply chain management. Basically, value means "money." If a customer is willing to pay for something then it has value.

Negotiating prices, scheduling manufacturing, and managing logistics all impact the value equation for a company, and they are critical to a supply chain, but because they are so interdependent, it's a bad idea to manage them separately, in silos. As companies grow larger, supply chains get longer, and the pace of business gets faster, which means it becomes more important to keep the various functions in a supply chain aligned. Ironically, many of the strategies and metrics that businesses relied on in the past, and that managers have been taught to use, can actually drive the wrong behaviors. For example, a sales rep might hit her quota by landing a huge deal with a customer, but the deal might be unprofitable for the company because of the costs it will drive for the logistics and manufacturing functions. So sales, logistics, manufacturing, procurement, and all of your other functions need to be aligned to ensure that the business is pursuing profitable deals.

TIP

The difference between the amount of money your company brings in (revenue) and the amount of money that you spend (costs) is your profit. In other words, your profit is simply the amount of value that you have captured from your supply chain.

On the other hand, companies that do a good job of managing their supply chain are better able to take advantage of value-creation opportunities that their competitors might miss. For example, by implementing lean manufacturing, companies can reduce inventories. By being responsive to customer needs, they can build stronger relationships with their customers and grow their sales. By collaborating closely with their suppliers, they can get access to the materials they need, when they need them, at a reasonable cost.

TIP

Part 4 of this book is all about ways you can use supply chain management to create more value.

In most companies today, more than 70 percent of the costs and 100 percent of the revenues are dependent on how the supply chain is managed. So keeping all of the parts of the supply chain aligned is key to running any business successfully. That is why supply chain management has become so important, so quickly.

Exploring Complex Business Challenges

Managing a business is like playing a full-contact sport: So many moving pieces are involved, and so many things can change in an instant, that making long-term plans is virtually impossible. How can you really plan for commodity price swings, natural disasters, and financial meltdowns? You can't. You can't ignore those possibilities, either. Instead, you need to think about them and design your business so that it can function well under a range of scenarios. In other words, you need to think about the many different possibilities that the future holds, try to imagine them as a series of events, and then think about how each of them would affect your business.

To use scenario planning to prepare for the unknown and the unknowable, you need to know three really important things:

>> Which scenarios are most important to you.

>> What you'll do — and how — in each scenario. (In other words, each scenario calls for a different plan.)

>> How you can tell when a scenario is becoming reality. (In other words, as Yossi Sheffi, the Elisha Gray Professor of Engineering Systems at the Massachusetts Institute of Technology says, you need to have "sensors in the ground" to help you decide when to implement which plan. Then the job of supply chain management becomes a process of sensing and responding.)

You need to determine how your business will sense what is happening and how it will respond. Figure 1-2 shows how your sensors help you recognize which scenario is unfolding so that you can implement the proper plan.

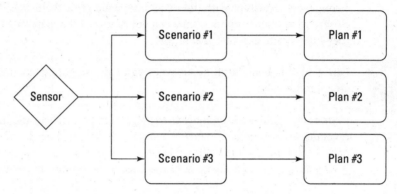

FIGURE 1-2:
Scenario-planning
model.

I can explain this concept with a few practical examples:

TECHNICAL STUFF

>> You run a manufacturing company that imports products from overseas, so you need to consider what you'd do if one of your inbound shipments is lost at sea, impounded by customs, captured by pirates, or caught in a port strike. Options might include shutting down your factory until the issue is resolved. You might also consider placing a new order with a different supplier so that you don't have to close the factory. In an extreme case, you might even declare *force majeure* and tell your customers that you won't be able fulfill your commitments to them.

   Force majeure is a legal concept that is used in contracts to justify why someone is unable to meet their obligations. Basically, it means that there was a problem that they could not have predicted, prepared for, or prevented.

>> You work for a wholesaler that has been selling a product at a steady rate for months, and one month, the company sells twice as much as normal. You don't have enough inventory to fill all your customer orders, and now you also have back orders to fill. You may even be at risk of losing some big sales and big customers. You might decide to place bigger orders in the future and keep more inventory on hand. That means you'll be investing more working capital into inventory. If sales drop off in the future, you'll have to figure out what to do with that extra inventory.

>> You work for a transportation company. The company's customers pay you to deliver their products around the world, and they count on your deliveries to help them meet their commitments to their own customers, so your ability to deliver on time is essential to them. Suddenly, a volcano in a distant part of

the world spews ash far into the sky, making it dangerous for airplanes to fly on a heavily traveled flight path. You could reroute your planes, but this is an expensive process that involves developing flight plans, scheduling airplanes, and finding available crews. Alternatively, you could tell your customers that their deliveries are on hold until normal operations can resume.

Thousands of companies have had to face every one of these scenarios in the past few years. In every case, making the right decision about how to respond requires understanding supply chains and supply chain management.

TIP

There's more information about supply chain scenario planning, and a link to the MIT Scenario Planning Toolkit, in Chapter 18.

Some supply chain management professionals are generalists and others are specialists. Supply chain experts who are generalists look at the big picture, whereas the specialists focus on a particular step in the supply chain. A good way for you to start learning about supply chain management is to take a look at some of the general principles.

The next sections cover ten supply chain management principles, five supply chain tasks, and the five steps to implement a new supply chain agenda. Each of these sections provides a slightly different perspective on supply chain management, but you'll see that they are really just different ways of describing the same challenge. The supply chain management principles are a way of describing the essence of supply chain management. The five supply chain tasks are more like the job description for a supply chain manager. And the new supply chain agenda is a strategy for helping a company to plan and implement effective supply chain management practices.

Operating Under Supply Chain Management Principles

Many people try to describe supply chain management by talking about what they do, which is a bit like describing a cake by giving someone a recipe. A different approach is to describe what supply chain management actually creates. To continue the cake example, that means describing how the finished cake tastes and what it looks like.

The ten principles illustrated in Figure 1-3 do a good job of describing supply chain management.

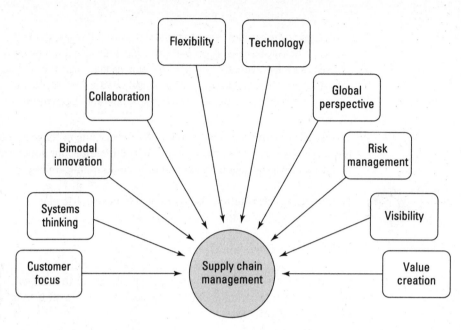

FIGURE 1-3:
Supply chain
management
principles.

The diagram shows the following principles pointing to "Supply chain management": Flexibility, Technology, Collaboration, Global perspective, Bimodal innovation, Risk management, Systems thinking, Visibility, Customer focus, Value creation.

Customer focus

Supply chain management starts with understanding who your customers are and why they're buying your product or service. Any time customers buy your stuff, they're solving a problem or filling a need. Supply chain managers must understand the customer's problem or need and make sure that their companies can satisfy it better, faster, and cheaper than any competitors can.

Systems thinking

Supply chain management requires an understanding of the end-to-end system — the combination of people, processes, and technologies — that must work together so that you can provide your product or service. Systems thinking involves an appreciation for the series of cause–and–effect relationships that occur within a supply chain. Because they are complex systems, supply chains often behave in unpredictable ways, and small changes in one part of the system can have major effects somewhere else.

Bimodal innovation

The world of business is changing quickly, and supply chains need to keep up by innovating. Supply chains need continuous process improvement, or sustaining innovation, to keep pace with competitors. Lean, Six Sigma, and the Theory of

Constraints (see Chapter 4) are process improvement methods that can help with this task. Continuous process improvement isn't sufficient, though, because new technologies can disrupt industries. This effect is called *disruptive innovation.* When a new solution for a customer's needs emerges and becomes accepted, this solution becomes the new dominant paradigm. In other words, if you're in the business of making buggy whips, you need to figure out how to make buggy whips better, faster, and cheaper than your competitors do, and at the same time, you need to figure out what the new dominant paradigm is going to be so that you know what you're going to make when buggy whips are replaced by a different technology.

Collaboration

Supply chain management can't be done in a vacuum. People need to work across silos inside an organization, and they need to work with suppliers and customers outside the organization. A "me, me, me" mentality leads to transactional relationships where people focus on short-term opportunities while ignoring the long-term results. This actually costs more money in the long run because it creates a lack of trust and an unwillingness to compromise among the players in the supply chain. An environment in which people trust one another and collaborate for shared success is much more profitable for everyone than an environment in which each person is concerned only with his or her own success. If you believe that you'll be doing more business together in the future, and that the business with a particular customer will be profitable, then you are more likely to give them a deal on the products they are buying from you today. Also, a collaborative type of environment makes working together a lot more fun.

Flexibility

Because surprises happen, supply chains need to be flexible. Flexibility is a measurement of how quickly your supply chain can respond to changes, such as an increase or decrease in sales or a disruption in supplies. This flexibility often comes in the form of extra capacity, multiple sources of supply, and alternative forms or transportation. Usually, flexibility costs money, but it also has value. The key is understanding when the cost of flexibility is a good investment.

Suppose that only two companies in the world make widgets, and you need to buy 1,000 widgets per month. You may get a better price on widgets if you buy all of them from a single supplier, which would lower your supply chain costs. But you'd have a problem if that supplier experiences a flood, fire, or bankruptcy and can't make widgets for a while. You may save on your purchase price for the widgets, but you're stuck if anything goes wrong with that supplier.

If you bought some of your widgets from the other supplier — even at a higher cost — you wouldn't be hurt as badly if the first supplier stopped making widgets. In other words, having a second supplier provides flexibility.

Think of the extra cost that you pay to the second supplier as a kind of insurance policy. You're paying more up front to have that insurance policy, but in return, you're increasing the flexibility of your supply chain.

Technology

The rapid evolution of technology, for moving physical products and for processing information, has transformed the way that supply chains work. A few years ago, we ordered things from a catalog, mailed in checks, and waited for our packages to be delivered. Today, we order products on our phones, pay for them with credit cards, and expect real-time updates until those packages are delivered to our doorsteps. Supply chain management requires understanding how technologies work and how to use them to create value at each step in the supply chain.

Global perspective

The ability to share information instantly and to move products around the world cheaply means that every company today operates in a global marketplace. No matter what product or service you provide, your company is global. As a supply chain manager, you must recognize that how your business depends on global factors to supply inputs and drive demand for outputs. You also need to think globally about the competition. After all, your company's real competitive threat could be a company you've never heard on the other side of the planet.

Risk management

When you combine high performance requirements with complicated technologies and dependence on global customers and suppliers, you have a recipe for chaos. There are lots variables, and lots of things can go wrong. Even a small disturbance, like a shipment that gets delayed, can lead to a series of problems further down the supply chain, such as stockouts, shutdowns, and penalties. Supply chain management means being aware of risks and implementing processes to detect and mitigate threats. Stability may be the key to making supply chains work smoothly, but risk management is the key to avoiding or minimizing the costs of dealing with surprises. Done well, risk management can provide opportunities to capture value during times of uncertainty.

Visibility

You can't manage what you can't see, so supply chain management makes visibility a priority. Knowing what's happening in real time (or close to real time) lets you make better decisions faster. Visibility comes at a cost, however: You have to build your supply chain in a way that lets you capture data about key steps in the process. The value of visibility is that it lets you make decisions based on facts rather than on intuition or uncertainty. Having better visibility into supply and demand allows you to optimize the amount of inventory that you hold throughout the supply chain.

Value creation

Supply chain management is about creating value — meeting your customers' needs in the right place, at the right time, at the right level of quality, for the lowest cost. This value is the heart of supply chain management. If I had to pick just one principle to describe the whole process of supply chain management, it would be value creation.

Introducing Five Supply Chain Tasks

James B. Ayers is a well-known supply chain management expert who works with manufacturers, service companies, and government agencies. In *Handbook of Supply Chain Management*, 2nd Edition (Auerbach Publications, 2006), Ayers says that supply chain management should concentrate on five tasks:

» **Designing supply chains for strategic advantage:** Consider how your supply chain can help you create value. You want to plan to operate your supply chain better, faster, and cheaper than your competitors. You need to think beyond just lowering costs. Also consider ways in which your supply chain can help you grow revenue, innovate your products, and even create new markets.

» **Implementing collaborative relationships:** Consider how you can get teams to work together toward a common goal rather than competing for conflicting goals. If your sales team is trying to improve customer service by making sure that you have plenty of inventory available, for example, and your logistics team is trying to reduce inventory to lower costs, both teams are probably going to waste a lot of energy without achieving their goals. Supply chain management can help them align their objectives.

>> **Forging supply chain partnerships:** Consider how you can build and sustain strong relationships with customers and suppliers. When companies understand that they depend on one another for their success — and perhaps their survival — working well together becomes a priority. Companies that don't do a good job of forming and sustaining supply chain partnerships end up at a competitive disadvantage.

>> **Managing supply chain information:** Consider how you can make sure that information is shared with others in the supply chain in ways that create value for everyone. When retailers share sales data with their upstream partners, the manufacturers and distributors do a better job of scheduling production and managing inventory. When manufacturers share data about commodity prices and capacity constraints with their downstream supply chain partners, the retailers do a better job of managing pricing and promotions. Sharing the right information up and down the supply chain helps everyone create more value.

>> **Making money from the supply chain:** Consider how you can leverage your supply chain design, relationships, partnerships, and information to capture value for your company. At the end of the day, businesses are sustainable only if they're able to capture value and generate a profit. In supply chains, a process change for one part often creates value for someone else. Find ways to share this value so that everyone has an incentive to work toward optimizing the value of the entire supply chain and ensuring that all the participants make a profit along the way.

Implementing the New Supply Chain Agenda

One of my favorite books about supply chain management is *The New Supply Chain Agenda,* by Reuben E. Slone, J. Paul Dittmann, and John T. Mentzer (Harvard Business Review Press, 2010). It's a business book — the kind that you'd find in an airport bookstore — that breaks down the challenge of supply chain management in a way that focuses on senior executives. The authors talk about working capital and liquidity, strategy, and alignment, and they lay out a five-step system for making a company better at supply chain management. The five steps of the New Supply Chain Agenda are shown in Figure 1-4.

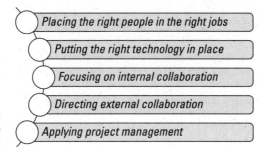

FIGURE 1-4:
The New Supply
Chain Agenda

- Placing the right people in the right jobs
- Putting the right technology in place
- Focusing on internal collaboration
- Directing external collaboration
- Applying project management

Placing the right people in the right jobs

Implementing supply chain management requires understanding how your job affects other people inside your company, as well as the people up and down the supply chain. If people don't understand the true effect of the jobs that they do, they need to learn so that they can do their jobs better. If someone is unable to learn or doesn't want to learn, he or she isn't the right person for that job. Getting the right people in the right jobs is the first step in implementing an effective supply chain strategy.

Putting the right technology in place

Supply chains depend on technology. The technology may be something simple, such as a whiteboard with sticky notes that gets updated daily, or it may be something as complicated as an enterprise resource planning system. Each business, and each function within each business, has different technology needs. Figuring out how technology can enable your supply chain to create and capture value and then implementing the right technologies at the right time is the second step in the New Supply Chain Agenda.

Focusing on internal collaboration

When you look at a company's organization chart, it's easy to see how traditional business structures create silos within a company, with divisions competing for limited resources and often working toward conflicting goals. Managing from a supply chain perspective helps you break down the silos that keep the divisions within a company from working together effectively. By changing the focus from the performance of the separate divisions to looking instead at the performance of the company's supply chain, each division becomes more dependent on the others for their own success. Sales teams need to collaborate with operations teams. Logistics teams need to collaborate with procurement teams. Everyone needs to understand the company's strategy and work toward common goals that support that strategy.

Directing external collaboration

Traditional business relationships are transactional and often self-centered. Buyers and suppliers approach each deal as a win-lose game: The suppliers are trying to inflate their profits, and the buyers are trying to squeeze them on price. Over the long run, this approach can damage both parties because it destroys value rather than creating it.

To build sustainable supply chain relationships, each partner needs to look for opportunities to contribute value to the relationship. In return for their contributions, buyers and suppliers develop systems for sharing the value in sustainable ways. The goal is for every partner in the supply chain to be successful over the long term and to maximize total value. This approach is very different from a transactional approach, in which each party is trying to squeeze every penny from each deal even if it means causing harm in the long run.

Applying project management

Supply chains are dynamic. Companies respond to changes with projects, so the last step in the New Supply Chain Agenda is implementing strong project management capabilities. Teaching people how to manage projects well and having professional project managers involved are the keys to ensuring that your supply chain evolves as your customers, suppliers, and company change.

TIP

I provide a whole section about leading supply chain projects in Chapter 4.

Chapter **2**

Understanding Supply Chains from Different Perspectives

There are several different ways to analyze what's happening in a supply chain. Each of these different perspectives can help you understand how your supply chain really works and reveals opportunities for improvement. Because there are *so many* different ways to look at the same issue, supply chain managers can encounter confusion and miscommunication about which options are the best. In this chapter, you get to see several of these approaches and examples that illustrate how all of them can actually be very useful when it comes to managing your own supply chain.

Managing Supply Chain Flows

One great way to explain a supply a chain is to think of it as three rivers that flow from a customer all the way back to the source of raw materials. These rivers, or *flows*, are materials, money, and information, as shown in Figure 2-1. Materials flow downstream in the supply chain, starting with raw materials and flowing through value-added steps until a product finally ends up in the hands of a customer. Money flows upstream from the customer through all the supply chain partners that provide goods and services along the way. Information flows both upstream and downstream as customers place orders and suppliers provide information about the products and when they will be delivered.

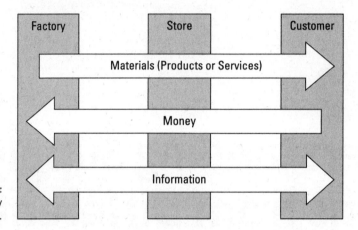

FIGURE 2-1: Three supply chain flows.

Managing a supply chain effectively involves synchronizing these three flows. You have to determine, for example, how long you can wait between the time when you send a physical product to your customer and the time when the customer pays you for the product. You also have to determine what information needs to be sent each way — and when — to keep the supply chain working the way you want it to.

REMEMBER

Every dollar that flows into a supply chain comes from a customer and then moves upstream. The companies in the supply chain have to work together to capture that dollar, but these companies are also competing to see how much of that dollar they get to keep as their own profit.

Synchronizing Supply Chain Functions

Supply chain management can also be described as integrating three of the functions inside an organization: purchasing, logistics, and operations. Each of these functions is critical in any company, and each of them has its own metrics. But these functions are interdependent (see Figure 2-2), so making good decisions in any of these areas requires coordination with the other two.

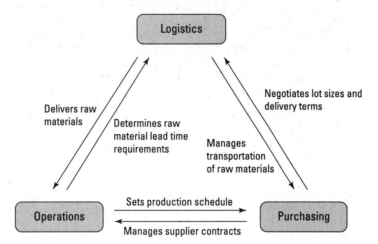

Logistics

Delivers raw materials

Determines raw material lead time requirements

Negotiates lot sizes and delivery terms

Manages transportation of raw materials

Sets production schedule

Operations

Manages supplier contracts

Purchasing

REMEMBER

The purchasing, logistics, and operations teams often have conflicting goals without realizing it. Managing these functions independently leads to poor overall performance for your company. Supply chain managers need to make sure that the objectives of these groups are aligned in order for the company to meet its top-level goals.

TIP

The simplest top-level goal for many supply chain decisions is return on investment. Focusing on this one objective can often help everyone see the big picture, and look beyond the functional supply chain metrics such as capacity utilization or transportation cost.

Purchasing

Purchasing (or *procurement*) is the function that buys the materials and services that a company uses to produce its own products and services. The basic goal of the purchasing function is to get the stuff that the company needs at the lowest cost possible; the purchasing department is always looking for ways to get a better deal from suppliers. Some of the most common cost-reduction strategies for a purchasing manager are

>> Negotiating with a supplier to reduce the supplier's profit margin

>> Buying in larger quantities to get a volume discount

>> Switching to a supplier that charges less for the same product

>> Switching to a lower-quality product that's less expensive

On the surface, any of these four options looks like a simple, effective way to reduce costs and therefore increase profitability. But each of these options can have negative long-term effects, too. For example, driving a supplier's profit margin too low could make it hard for them to pay their bills — or even force them out of business. While you might save money in the short term, you may have to end up spending even more time and money to find a new supplier in the future. In other words, it would actually increase your total cost. Many purchasing decisions can also have direct effects on the costs for other functions within your company. For example, sourcing lower-quality raw materials might lead to higher costs for quality assurance. Buying in larger quantities might lead to an increase in inventory costs.

TIP

Your total costs include all of the investments and expenses that are required to deliver a product or service to your customer.

Logistics

Logistics covers everything related to moving and storing products. This function can go by different names, such as physical distribution, warehousing, transportation, or traffic.

Inbound logistics refers to the products that are being shipped to your company by your suppliers. *Outbound logistics* refers to the products that you ship to your customers.

Logistics adds value because it gets a product where a customer needs it when the customer wants it. Logistics costs money, too. Transporting products on ships, trucks, trains, and airplanes has a price tag. Also, whether a product is sitting on a truck or gathering dust in a distribution center, the product is an asset that ties up working capital and probably depreciates quickly. The goals of the logistics function are to move things faster, reduce transportation costs, and decrease inventory. Following are some ways that a logistics department might try to achieve these goals:

>> Consolidating many small shipments into one large shipment to lower shipping costs

>> Breaking large shipments into smaller ones to increase velocity

>> Switching from one mode of transportation to another, either to lower costs or increase velocity

>> Increasing or decreasing the number of distribution centers to increase velocity or lower costs

>> Outsourcing logistics services to a third-party logistics (3PL) company

You can see an example of the conflicts that can occur between logistics and purchasing: Logistics wants to decrease inventory, which may mean ordering in smaller quantities, but purchasing wants to lower the price of the purchased materials, which may mean buying in larger quantities. Unless purchasing and logistics coordinate their decision-making and align their goals with what is best for the bottom line, the two functions often end up working against each other and against the best interests of your company, your customers, and your suppliers.

Operations

The third function that is key to supply chain management is operations. *Operations* is in charge of the processes that your company focuses on to create value. Here are some examples:

>> In a manufacturing company, operations manages the production processes.

>> In a retailing company, operations focuses on managing stores.

>> In an e-commerce company or a 3PL, the operations team may also be the logistics team.

Operations managers usually focus on capacity utilization, which means asking "How much can we do with the resources we have?" Resources can be human resources (people) or land and equipment (capital). The operations department is measured by how effectively and efficiently it uses available capacity to produce the products and services that your customers buy. Some common goals for operations teams include

>> Reducing the amount of capacity wasted due to changeovers and maintenance

>> Reducing shutdowns for any reason, including those caused by running out of raw materials

>> Aligning production schedules and orders for raw materials with forecasts received from customers

Although increasing operations efficiency sounds like a great idea, sometime it actually creates supply chain problems and does more harm than good. Companies may invest in increasing their capacity only to find out that their suppliers or logistics infrastructure can't support the higher production levels.

Connecting Supply Chain Communities

If you've ever taken a personality test, such as the Myers-Briggs Type Indicator, then you know that these tests can reveal important differences in the way that people approach problems and make decisions. It turns out that groups of people have "personalities," too. These personalities form the culture of a group, and culture matters a lot when it comes to managing a supply chain.

Suppose that one of your customers is a company that really values reliability. That company considers it important for a supplier to deliver exactly what was ordered, exactly the same way, every time. The culture of that group — the things that the company values — determines how it judges its suppliers. Now suppose that this customer has a choice of working with two suppliers: one that's known for consistent quality and another that's known for flexibility and innovation. Naturally, the first supplier would be a better cultural fit for this particular supply chain because of the value that the customer places on reliability.

The impact of culture can also apply to the functions within your organization. Different departments — such as purchasing, logistics, and operations — often develop cultures of their own. If the values of these departments clash, it's difficult for the company to manage its supply chain effectively.

One useful way to think about the culture of a company or a department is to use a framework that was developed by professor and thought leader Dr. John Gattorna in *Dynamic Supply Chains: Delivering Value through People*, 2nd Edition (FT Press, 2010). Gattorna says that four major behavioral forces (see Figure 2-3) determine the culture of a group. These forces are often related to the style of a group's leader and the norms for a particular industry.

>> **Integrator:** Force for cohesion, cooperation, and relationships

>> **Developer:** Force for creativity, change, and flexibility

>> **Administrator:** Force for analysis, systems, and control

>> **Producer:** Force for energy, action, and results

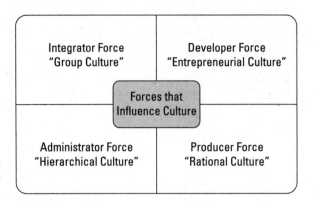

FIGURE 2-3:
Dominant group
personalities.

The strength of these personality forces lead to differences in the culture for a team or organization. The most accurate way to measure culture is to formally interview people on a team and then analyze their responses. But in many cases, you can get a good sense for a team's culture simply by working with them for a little while.

Teams that are driven by the Integrator force tend to have a "group" culture, where everyone on the team is encouraged to develop personal relationships and informal communications. In a group culture, people feel like they are part of a family. But a group culture also tends to be exclusive — it's their team against everyone else.

Teams that are driven by the Developer force form an "entrepreneurial" culture, where everyone is focused on achieving a common vision. Communications are informal and ideas are exchanged with people inside and outside of the group. An entrepreneurial culture may tolerate "bad" behaviors, as long as they doesn't interfere with achieving the shared goal.

Teams that are driven by the Administrator force create a "hierarchical" culture, where communication is formal and shared through official channels. Hierarchical cultures are good at developing processes and ensuring consistency, but they're often slow and inflexible.

Teams that are driven by the Producer force develop a "rational" culture, where communications are concise and fast. Plans are made, plans are executed, and updates are sent out to keep stakeholders in the loop. Rational cultures are good at keeping teams focused and delivering results. But these cultures often find it hard to deviate from a plan, even when the circumstances around them change.

A useful exercise when analyzing your supply chain is to list the groups that work together, and try to determine the dominant culture for each of them. This can often help you anticipate conflicts that can emerge when these groups interact. And, it can help you find ways to use these differences to your advantage. Here are some common examples that illustrate how this can work:

» Purchasing departments often have an hierarchical culture whereas operations departments have a rational culture. In this situation, the purchasing department may feel frustrated because operations doesn't follow the rules. Operations may be frustrated because purchasing is slowing them down. So you could create a small team of expeditors, with members from both operations and purchasing, to manage urgent orders while assuring that all of the proper policies are followed.

» Large companies often have strict rules that lead to a hierarchical culture. Technology companies that focus on innovation have an entrepreneurial culture. In order for big bureaucracies to take advantage of the latest technologies, they may need to start new programs that respond faster and have more flexibility for their suppliers.

» Human resources teams often have an group culture, whereas consultants may have a rational culture. The human resources team may find the consultants to be rude and disinterested, and the consultants may view the human resources team as nosey and unprofessional. In order for these groups to work effectively through a corporate merger, for example, you may need to schedule time for them to interact in a social setting such as a kickoff celebration.

You can also use an understanding of group personalities to help you choose teams to partner with in your supply chain. If your priority is creativity and innovation, for example, you're likely to work best with supply chain partners that are driven by an entrepreneurial culture, and you're probably going to be disappointed by a supply chain partner with a hierarchical culture.

Gattorna makes the point that supply chains are dynamic, so balancing these forces is an ongoing process. One way to create balance is to build teams of people with each of these tendencies. If the team has a diverse set of personalities, the team is more likely to appreciate the strengths of diverse supply chain partners and to find ways to build effective relationships with other teams that emphasize any one of the forces.

Designing Supply Chain Systems

The most complicated way to look at a supply chain is to look at it as a system. (I think that this perspective is often the most useful.) Like many other systems that we encounter every day, supply chains are made up of many interconnected components that can behave in unpredictable ways.

Your car is a good example of a system that you depend on every day. You expect your car to move you from Point A to Point B. In fact, you probably take for granted that your car will take you to Point B any time you want to go. Your car is actually a system, though, and it can perform the way you expect it to only if all the components are operating correctly. A dead battery, a broken fuel pump, or worn-out brakes could bring the whole system to a halt (or, in the case of the worn-out brakes, not bring the system to a halt!).

Supply chains are systems, too. The components that make up supply chains are people, processes, and technologies. Each of these components needs to be organized and managed correctly for the system to operate as expected.

When you look at them as systems, you begin to see that supply chains have underlying rules and patterns that are key to understanding how they work. A good example of one of these patterns is when a company experiences wild swings in inventory levels. It can be hard for people in the company to understand why these swings occur until you look at the supply chain as a system. Then you can recognize a pattern called the *Bullwhip Effect*, in which inventory peaks and valleys are amplified as they move upstream from one step to the next in a supply chain. The Bullwhip Effect is a problem that frequently occurs in supply chain systems, and it is a normal, predictable result of everyone in the supply chain making decisions that seem logical. To fix the problem, you need to change the system, and that means you need to understand what is really happening. Here's a scenario that explains how a Bullwhip Effect can occur:

A customer comes in to buy a widget, which turns out to be the last widget in the store, so the store needs to order more inventory from its wholesaler. But the wholesaler doesn't sell individual widgets; it sells widgets in cases of 100 units. Now the store has to buy a full case — 100 widgets — even though it sold only one. If that was the last case in their warehouse, then the wholesaler will replenish its inventory by ordering more widgets from the factory. The factory, however, sells widgets in batches of 100 cases, so the wholesaler has to buy 100 cases of 100 widgets each. The wholesaler just bought 10,000 widgets even though it only sold 100.

How many widgets did the factory sell? 10,000. How many did the wholesaler sell? 100. And how many did the customer buy? Yep. . . just 1. A small demand signal at the end of the supply chain became amplified at every step, creating a Bullwhip Effect on inventory. The store may never sell another widget, so it would still be stuck with 99 widgets in inventory. The wholesaler may never sell another case of widgets, so it may be stuck with 99 cases of widgets. All that extra inventory costs money for everyone in the supply chain without adding any value.

Here are three ways that you can change the system that can reduce and even eliminate the Bullwhip Effect:

>> **Make batches smaller.** The fewer of widgets that the store and the whole-saler need to buy, the less amplification occurs when orders move up the supply chain.

>> **Improve forecasting.** If all the partners in the supply chain have a better forecast, there's less chance of ordering widgets that no one will buy.

>> **Improve communications.** If the store, the wholesaler, and the manufac-turer know exactly how many widgets are being sold, they can do a better job of managing their inventories.

An important point to notice is that some of the things you should do to reduce the Bullwhip Effect might seem odd to a functional manager. In fact, they might even interfere with the objectives of your functional teams. For example, smaller batch sizes are likely to increase costs for both purchasing and logistics. To understand many of the challenges that occur every day, your team needs to recognize that supply chains are systems, and that the people, processes, and technologies inter-act in ways that aren't always obvious.

Supply chains are really systems, where the people, processes, and technologies interact in complex ways. Managing your supply chain as a system may require a different approach to measuring success than what functional teams normally use.

In some cases, it helps to build a model of your supply chain to show how the parts of the system interact. These models can show cause and effect relationships — how one thing affects another, which then causes something to happen, which causes something else to happen, and so forth. In other words, these models can show causal relationships. Very often, systems models reveal *reinforcing loops*, where a series of events repeats over and over, getting stronger each time. Or, they can show *balancing loops* that have the opposite effect in which a series of events gets weaker over time.

Figure 2-4 is an example of a causal loop diagram, one of the most common tools for modeling the dynamics of a system. In this example you can see how two important supply chain dynamics both affect the market share for a company. As the number of customers increases, the market share grows higher. But as the market share goes up, the number of prospective customers gets smaller. That's because the prospects have now become customers. As the number of prospects gets smaller, the increase in market share slows down and eventually stop growing. There's more information about supply chain modeling and simulation in Chapter 18.

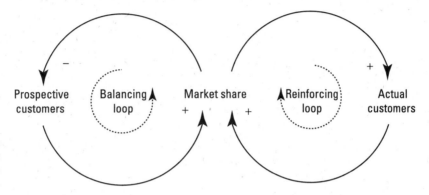

FIGURE 2-4:
Example of a causal loop diagram.

TECHNICAL STUFF

A few universities now require their supply chain management students to take classes in system dynamics, which includes a whole set of tools for predicting how supply chains behave over time. System dynamics was originally developed in the 1950s by MIT professor Jay Forrester.

TIP

System dynamics modeling usually requires special software. You'll find reviews of several different options at https://en.wikipedia.org/wiki/Comparison_of_system_dynamics_software, but if you are looking for a simple tool that gives you a chance to see some examples and try building your own system dynamics model for free, check out Insight Maker at www.insightmaker.com.

Measuring Supply Chain Processes

You can look at a supply chain in terms of flows, functions, communities, or systems. But in order to manage a supply chain, you need to be able to measure what's happening. Virtually every process in a supply chain can be measured with quantitative metrics or qualitative metrics.

Quantitative metrics are objective, numerical indicators. *Qualitative metrics* describe intangible characteristics. For example, quantitative metrics might include things like current inventory levels or the amount of money spent on transportation. Qualitative metrics could describe the level of engagement of your employees or how satisfied your customers are with your service. Table 2-1 lists some common types of qualitative and quantitative metrics.

TABLE 2-1

Quantitative Metrics versus Qualitative Metrics

Quantitative	Qualitative
Times	Degree of satisfaction
Rates	Likelihood of doing something
Values	Perceptions
Amounts	Desire or need
Frequencies	Level of agreement

Collecting measurements costs money and takes time, so it is important to decide which metrics you really need. The key is to identify the steps in each supply chain process that will be most useful in understanding how things are working and what decisions you need to make. The metrics that give you this insight are called **key performance indicators** (KPIs). The KPIs in one business or facility can be very different from the KPIs in another — it just depends on which processes are most important in each. More information about metrics is in Chapter 16.

A good way to look for improvement opportunities in any process is by comparing your own performance to that of someone else. For example, you can compare the KPIs from one facility to the KPIs at another facility. Comparing KPIs between facilities, and even between companies, is an example of *benchmarking*. Companies can benchmark their supply chain KPIs using the SCOR Model, which is covered in Chapter 5. Benchmarking has become so popular that there are many companies whose entire business is built on collecting supply chain KPIs from each of the firms in an industry and then providing all the companies with benchmarking reports.

TIP

Companies (even competitors!) share benchmarking data all the time. But sharing business information can also lead to problems if it violates laws such as the Clayton Anti-Trust Act. Before you start benchmarking with other companies, it's a good idea to talk your plans over with a corporate attorney so that you are sure it's okay.

There are lots of different ways to look at a supply chain. In order to manage a supply chain well, you need to understand each of these perspectives, and use them to select the KPIs that give you visibility into how your supply chain is performing. Benchmarking those KPIs against other facilities, and other companies, can reveal both the areas where you are doing well and opportunities for improvement.

S&OP steps

1. Choose a planning horizon
2. Develop a sales forecast or demand plan
3. Create a supply plan
4. Identify constraints
5. Resolve constraints
   i.e., give up demand or install capacity or improve throughput
6. Revise
   Update plan on regular cycle. The more volitile supply and demand the more frequent the update.

Chapter 3

Digging into Your Supply Chain

Before you can manage something, you have to understand how it works and what you want it to do. A supply chain is no exception. Many kinds of supply chains exist, and each of them needs to deliver a different kind of product or service to meet customers' needs. This chapter covers the factors that define how a supply chain needs to perform and how each factor affects costs. Then the chapter discusses trade-offs are being managed in every supply chain.

Prioritizing Supply Chain Goals

A friend of mine has a sign on her desk that reads "Good, Fast, Cheap . . . Pick Any Two." The message is relevant for supply chain management because you often have to figure out what's most important to you and be willing to compromise on the rest.

Step 1: Understand what customers value

To make good decisions about what to prioritize in a supply chain, start with your customers. Because the purpose of a supply chain is to deliver value to a customer, the first step in engineering and managing a supply chain is understanding exactly what your customers value. They may value having a wide selection of products to choose among, for example, or they might prefer to have a smaller number of options at a lower price. Alternatively, your customers may value having products available immediately for pickup, or they might prefer to have products delivered to their homes at a time that they choose.

The answers may be "all of the above," but each of these choices creates different requirements for a supply chain, and they may be contradictory. It often helps to choose a particular customer, a **key customer**, and focus in on their specific preferences.

Some great techniques are available to help with identifying what customers value the most. One of the most popular is called *quality functional design (QFD)* or the *house of quality (HOQ)*. Figure 3-1 shows an example of a HOQ, which looks like a bunch of boxes with a roof on top. To build an HOQ, first you interview customers to determine which characteristics or features they value the most. Then, you match those features with your design to ensure that you're focusing on delivering products and services that genuinely meet your customers' needs. For more information on how to build an HOQ, visit https://hbr.org/1988/05/the-house-of-quality.

Another common technique for determining customer preferences is called *A-B Testing.* To perform an A-B Test, you give your customer a choice between two options: Option A and Option B. Online shopping sites frequently use A-B Testing to see which products or ads are most attractive to customers, but A-B Testing can also be used in face-to-face experiments.

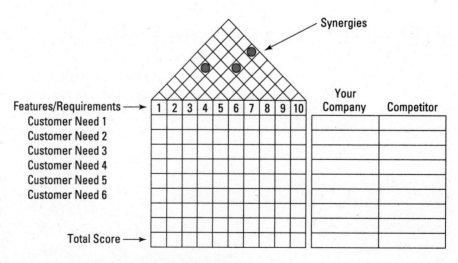

FIGURE 3-1:
Example of
an HOQ.

WHAT JOB DOES A MILKSHAKE DO?

Dr. Clayton Christensen gives a great example of his Jobs To Be Done Theory by telling a story about the managers of a fast-food restaurant who wanted to analyze their sales of milkshakes. The restaurant was selling lots of milkshakes early in the morning, and the managers couldn't understand why. After interviewing their customers, they discovered that people were buying milkshakes at the beginning of their commute because it gave them something to do while they were stuck in traffic. In other words, the milkshake wasn't just food; it was also entertainment! Understanding what their customers truly valued about the product helped the managers of the fast-food restaurant think differently about how to package the product, manage their business, and design their supply chain.

Step 2: Recognize your competitors

The next step in prioritizing your supply chain goals is recognizing your competitors. In the age of e-commerce, your competitors may not be who you think they are. Many traditional retail stores, for example, have been slow to realize that their most aggressive competitor is not another brick-and-mortar store, but a website: Amazon.com. Amazon.com isn't competing only with retailers, however; it's also competing with trucking companies, warehousing and distribution companies, and even technology companies such as Apple and Microsoft.

To understand who your real competitors are, you need to stop thinking about the product or service that you sell and start thinking about the problem that it solves. Dr. Clayton Christensen of Harvard Business School calls this approach to matching your product with a customer's problem the Jobs to Be Done Theory. Think about what "job" your product or service does for your customers and what other products or services might be able to do that same job better, faster, or cheaper. These alternative products (or services) are your product's real competitors, and you need to design and manage your supply chain so that your product can do that same job better than its competitors.

Step 3: Understand your products or services

The next step in prioritizing your supply chain goals is understanding the characteristics of your products or services. The easiest way to illustrate this step is to show how different kinds of products need to achieve different goals to deliver the greatest value to their customers.

Table 3-1 and the sections that follow describe supply chain priorities for different kinds of products. These examples are definitely not an exhaustive list of supply chains, but they illustrate why the supply chain for corn, for example, has different priorities from the supply chain for computers.

TABLE 3-1

Supply Chain Priorities

Product Type	Supply Chain Priorities
Commodities	Low price, high availability, minimum quality standards
Luxury goods	High quality, uniqueness
Fashion goods	Fast throughput, low inventory, wide variety
Durable goods	Balance between transportation/inventory cost and customer needs
Technology	Speed, flexibility, security

Commodities

Commodities are things that are easy to find and easy to substitute. Common examples are food crops, metal ores, and gasoline. Because it's so easy to substitute commodities from one supplier for commodities from another supplier, most people buy commodities wherever they can get what they need for the lowest price. Therefore, commodity supply chains need to have high availability, meet minimum quality standards, and be cheap.

Luxury goods

Luxury goods like high-end cars and jewelry are all about quality and variety. When customers are purchasing luxury goods, they want something in just the right size and color, and they don't want everyone else to have the same item. Also, ensuring that luxury goods are free of defects and damage is essential. The supply chains for luxury goods need to accommodate a wide assortment of products with plenty of protection to keep them safe.

Fashion goods

Fashion goods like shoes and purses are all about selection and timing. Because styles change quickly, fashion supply chains need to transform ideas into products and get them sold to customers before the products become passé. Keeping the right amount of inventory is a delicate balance for fashion: If you don't have products in stock, you can't sell them. But if an item sits around in inventory for too long, it may fall out of style. Supply chains for fashion need to focus on speed and flexibility.

Durable goods

Durable goods, like household appliances, are heavy, and they need to last a long time. They're also expensive, so they consume capital when they're sitting in inventory. Making durable goods takes a long time, however, and customers usually don't want to wait a long time for them. (If your refrigerator goes out, you want to have a new one delivered right away.) Durable goods can also face tough competition for pricing, and shipping big, heavy items can get expensive. Supply chains for durable goods need to balance the cost of keeping inventory available close to where the customers will want it with the cost of transporting the products and keeping them in inventory.

Technology

Technology products — such as computers, television sets, and electronics equipment — tend to be light and expensive. They also tend to become obsolete quickly. Technology products tend to be sensitive to moisture damage and are vulnerable to theft. Supply chains for technology products need to be fast, flexible, and secure.

Looking at Cost Drivers

Most supply chain managers spend a lot of their time looking for ways to reduce costs. But one of the big challenges with supply chains is that things are often interconnected, so making a change in one area to lower costs can cause a change somewhere else that actually increases the cost. That's not to say that you shouldn't look for cost-savings opportunities, but you need to understand how the system works to ensure that you aren't creating new problems in the process.

There are four decisions areas that drive most of the costs in any supply chain, and I describe them in the following sections. Thinking about all these items together can help you find true opportunities for savings.

Procurement costs

One of the most obvious costs for any supply chain is the amount that you pay for the products you buy. Some common ways to reduce procurement costs are to negotiate better prices from your suppliers, agree to buy larger quantities over a longer period or switch to a supplier that agrees to accept lower prices. Also, each supplier that you maintain a relationship with costs you money, because someone has to find the supplier, sign all the contracts, keep track of the supplier's performance, and make sure the supplier gets paid. So the cost for procurement also includes the salaries and overhead for your procurement team and the information systems that they use. Reducing the number of suppliers and streamlining your procurement processes can often reduce procurement costs.

Transportation costs

Moving a product from one place to another costs money, and different modes of transportation have different costs. These modes have different speeds, which can be just as important as transportation cost. For example, a faster and more expensive transportation mode might actually save you money by decreasing the amount of inventory that you have in transit. It is also common to use more than one mode of transportation to move a single product through a supply chain. Changing from one mode to another using multi-modal transportation can optimize transportation costs. Another common way to reduce transportation costs is to pack more products into each load, thereby improving capacity utilization. The important thing to remember is that choosing a transportation mode that is slower and less reliable may reduce transportation costs, but it will increase your inventory and consume working capital.

Generally, when you rank transportation methods from least expensive to most expensive, the order is this: pipeline, sea container, full truckload, less-than-truckload, and parcel.

Inventory costs

Keeping products in inventory costs money. Of course, the products that you are storing in inventory cost money. If you're borrowing money from the bank to pay for that inventory (which is often the case), your inventory costs you whatever interest rate you're paying to the bank. Other costs include paying for a building to keep the inventory safe and paying people to move the inventory around inside the building. You also run the risk that products could be lost, damaged, or stolen. This problem, often called *shrinkage,* also incurs a cost to your company. Finally, products can expire or become obsolete if they sit in a warehouse for too long.

Quality costs

Any time you buy a product, you expect it to meet a certain level of quality. In some cases, you may need to have formal inspection and quality assurance processes in place to make sure that the products you receive from suppliers, and the products that you send to your customers, meet these requirements. Any product that doesn't meet these standards costs you money, and the more closely you have to look for quality problems, the more money you spend. Reducing the variation in manufacturing and distribution processes through techniques such as Lean and Six Sigma, which are discussed in Chapter 4, can reduce the quality costs in a supply chain.

You can see in Figure 3-2 how these four supply chain cost drivers are interdependent, and how changes in any one of the buckets can affect the others.

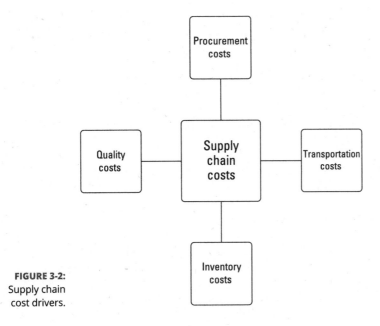

FIGURE 3-2:
Supply chain
cost drivers.

Dealing with Trade-Offs

Supply chain management involves making choices and trade-offs that help you maximize your profits over the long term. When you get right down to it, conflicts occur between any two functions in a business, as well as between any two businesses that work together as a part of a supply chain. Six conflicts, or trade-offs, are so common that every supply chain management professional needs to understand them and know how to manage them effectively (see Table 3-2). I discuss these trade-offs separately in the following sections.

TABLE 3-2

Common Supply Chain Management Trade-Offs and Solutions

Conflicts and Trade-Offs	Solutions
Sales versus operations	Sales and operations planning (S&OP)
Customer versus supplier	Collaborative planning, forecasting, and replenishment (CPFR)
Engineering versus procurement	Cross-functional teams
Inventory versus customer service (wholesale/retail)	Forecasting
Inventory versus downtime (manufacturing)	Lean manufacturing
Procurement versus logistics	Total cost analysis

Sales versus operations

Salespeople often say that you can't sell a product you don't have, and if you ask them how much product the company should make, the number is high. In other words, the salespeople want to make sure that you have enough product to meet all the customer demand that they can possibly generate, plus a little bit more. That scenario is seldom realistic.

Meanwhile, the operations and logistics people are responsible for the costs of making, moving, and storing products. They also understand that variations in your supply chain flow cost money because you need to pay for the space and the people to meet your peak demand, even if you aren't using that space and those people the rest of the time. Operations people want to make and store only as many products as are needed in order to keep manufacturing and logistics costs low.

This trade-off between sales and operations can lead to major conflicts in a company. In many cases, a sales department creates an unrealistic forecast, and the operations department is blamed for having too much inventory. In other cases, the sales department can't meet its revenue targets because the operations team was too conservative in its planning.

A common solution for this problem is a process called sales and operations planning (S&OP), which forces the sales and operations teams to coordinate and agree on their goals and targets.

S&OP usually starts with a sales forecast for a certain planning horizon. For example, the sales team might estimate that they could sell 1,000 widgets per month for the next 12 months. This is called an *unconstrained forecast* because it is based on a best-case scenario.

Once the forecast has been established, the operations team looks at the forecast and decides whether the numbers are reasonable and what it would take to manufacture that many products. In some cases, operations may not have the staffing, the equipment, or the raw materials to make all of the widgets that are called for in the unconstrained forecast. In that case, the operations team would ask the sales team to reduce their forecast based on all of the constraints that have been identified. Or, the operations team may need to make changes or investments that will enable them to meet the sales forecast.

S&OP is an iterative process that needs to be repeated so that the constrained sales forecast and the manufacturing production plan stay in sync. In many cases, the S&OP process involves senior executives from a company to ensure that trade-offs are understood and aligned with the corporate strategy.

S&OP may sound simple, but many companies struggle to make it work. Dr. Larry Lapide from MIT is one of the leading experts on S&OP. In his article "Sales and Operations Planning Part I: The Process" in *The Journal of Business Forecasting*, Dr. Lapide says that there are 10 factors that are required for S&OP success:

>> Ongoing, routine S&OP meetings

>> Structured meeting agendas

>> Pre-work to support meeting inputs

>> Cross-functional participation

>> Participants empowered to make decisions

>> An unbiased, responsible organization that can run a disciplined process

>> Internal collaborative process leading to consensus and accountability

>> An unbiased baseline forecast to start the process

>> Joint supply and demand planning to ensure balance

>> Support from an integrated supply-demand planning technology

>> External inputs to the process

TIP

To read more about details about the S&OP process, visit http://ctl.mit.edu/ sites/ctl.mit.edu/files/library/public/article_jbf_soplanningi_ lapide.pdf.

Fundamentally, S&OP is about sharing information and getting people to agree on a plan. There are a number of software companies that offer S&OP tools to help the sales and operations teams automate workflows and streamline the process.

Before making an investment in S&OP software, it's a good idea to get input from consultants who specialize in S&OP and to check out the latest product reviews from software analyst firms. Companies whose products get high marks will often provide you with copies of these reports for free.

Customer versus supplier

Each company in a supply chain has an effect on all the others. If your company surprises one of your suppliers with a big order, that order is likely to create problems — and cost the supplier money. But if your supplier has a pretty good idea of what you're going to buy and when you're going to buy it, the supplier can plan in such a way to meet your needs while keeping its own inventory and transportation costs low. In other words, everyone wins when supply chain partners collaborate and share information.

One way for supply chain partners to help each other is through a process called collaborative planning, forecasting, and replenishment (CPFR). In the CPFR process, companies share information about how much they expect their customers to buy and how much inventory they have on hand so that they can help each other achieve high service levels with lower amounts of inventory. You can download a very good overview of CPFR from GS-1 here:

```
www.gs1us.org/DesktopModules/Bring2mind/DMX/Download.aspx?
Command=Core_Download&EntryId=492&language=en-US&PortalId=
0&TabId=134
```

CPFR is a registered trademark of GS-1, a not-for-profit association that maintains supply chain communication standards.

Engineering versus procurement

Engineering teams are always looking for ways to innovate, make changes, and improve products. For their innovation processes to work well, engineers often develop relationships with suppliers that can be flexible and collaborative, but this flexibility and the time invested in understanding the engineers' needs have a cost. Typically, the suppliers that are best at innovating and collaborating are the most expensive. Meanwhile, the procurement team is always looking for ways to get products that meet the minimum specifications at the most favorable price. The lowest prices typically come from suppliers that produce at the minimum quality level with highly standardized systems and processes. The conflicting goals between engineering and procurement can lead to tension within a company.

One of the best ways to manage this tension is to create cross-functional product teams. Engaging procurement professionals during the design phase of a product can help you ensure that you're considering the costs of each step in a product's life cycle. Likewise, engaging engineering teams throughout the procurement process can help you ensure that lower-cost options that meet the needs of your company and your customers are properly vetted.

Another way to manage the trade-off between engineering and purchasing is to use a *design-build* strategy. With design-build, there is a single contract awarded to a supplier who both designs and makes a product. That way, the designer has an incentive to keep manufacturing costs low, and the manufacturer has an incentive to pursue innovative design options.

Inventory versus customer service

Inventory costs money because it ties up working capital, eats up labor and real estate, and depreciates quickly. Many supply chain professionals and business analysts will even tell you that inventory is the enemy. You may wonder why everyone doesn't immediately eliminate all inventory. Wouldn't supply chain management be a whole lot easier if you didn't have to deal with warehouses, distribution centers, and stock rooms?

That approach has one major problem: Companies make money by selling products to their customers, and if they have no product to sell, they earn no revenue. When you think about what customers value — what they're willing to pay for — the product itself is only part of the equation. You have to consider, for example, whether customers would be willing to pay the same amount for your product if they had to pick it up 100 miles away or if they had to wait for it for a year. In other words, the placement and availability of a product actually have a big impact on its value to your customers and on your revenues! Inventory acts as a buffer against uncertainty about who's going to buy your product, how much they're going to buy, when they're going to buy it, and where they're going to want it.

Whether your customers buy your product in a store or through a website, your ability to provide them with all of the products they want when they order them is called your *service level*. High service levels are good for business. Customers tend to buy from suppliers that meet their needs quickly, so high service levels can increase revenue and grow market share. Achieving a high service level typically requires you to have inventory on hand. To maintain a 100 percent service level, you'd actually need to have an infinite amount of inventory, which is unrealistic, so you need to find ways to manage the tension between reducing inventories to lower costs and increasing inventories to maintain acceptable service levels.

Companies balance inventory levels and service levels by optimizing their inventory. Inventory optimization is a process of reducing inventories to the minimum level necessary to maintain the desired service level. Inventory optimization starts with *forecasting*, the process in which you try to guess how much product you're going to sell and when you're going to sell it. Companies have many ways to generate forecasts, ranging from rules of thumb to sophisticated statistical modeling. No matter what forecasting method you use, the truth is that your forecast is still a guess. A common joke among supply chain professionals is that the first law of forecasting is that the forecast is always wrong.

The way to deal with potential errors in a forecast is to keep extra inventory on hand. The better the forecast is — the more confidence you have in it — the less extra inventory you need to keep to meet your desired customer service levels. If you don't trust your forecast and want to make sure that you have products to sell when customers want them, you need to carry extra inventory.

The degree to which a forecast is wrong is called the error. Improving your forecasts involves reducing this error as much as possible. There are two kinds of errors that can occur in a forecast:

>> An unbiased error is random and is generally a result of imperfect information.

>> A biased error is an error that occurs in a pattern. For example, a forecast might always be higher than actual sales, or it might always be lower.

Figure 3-3 shows an example of a forecast that is biased — it is always higher than the actual sales. If you can measure the amount of bias then you can take the bias into account to create a new *adjusted forecast*.

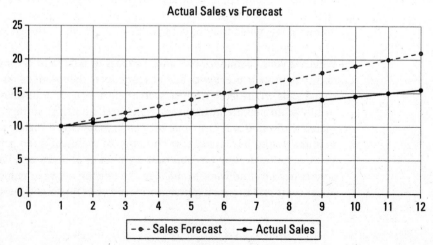

FIGURE 3-3: Illustration of a biased forecast.

It is often easy to spot forecast bias visually by creating a graph that compares forecast data to actual data.

The degree of forecast accuracy is usually measured as the mean absolute percentage error (MAPE).

When everything is said and done, the real way that most companies deal with the potential for errors in a forecast is by increasing their inventory. So the better the forecast is — the more confidence that you have in it — the less extra inventory you need to keep in order to meet your desired customer service levels. But if you don't trust your forecast, and you want to make sure that you have products to sell when customers want them, then you need to invest in extra inventory.

Inventory that provides you with protection from a stockout is called *safety stock*.

Inventory versus downtime

Manufacturing operations focus on maximizing the amount of product that they're able to make in a given period. Sometimes, manufacturing processes need to be shut down. Planned shutdown times typically are based on the shifts that people work. Planned shutdowns may also occur so that the company can perform maintenance or change equipment to make different products.

Unplanned shutdowns also happen for a variety of reasons, all of which are bad. An unplanned shutdown could be caused by a power outage, a broken piece of equipment, a strike, or a new government regulation. An unplanned shutdown also can be the result of running out of inventory. You can't make a product unless you have the raw materials and components that go into it.

While the other kinds of unplanned shutdowns are often hard to predict and control, you can prevent shutdowns due to a lack of materials by maintaining inventory. Unplanned shutdowns can be hard to predict and control, but inventory is one part of the process that's relatively easy to control. As a result, manufacturing operations managers tend to prefer to have extra inventory as an insurance policy — to make sure that they never run out of materials that would cause an unplanned shutdown. That extra inventory, of course, ties up working capital and eats up space.

Lean techniques help manufacturers minimize the number of unplanned shutdowns caused by inventory stockouts while minimizing the amount of inventory in a supply chain.

One of the key elements of Lean Manufacturing is the use of a *kanban* or *pull strategy* for inventory replenishment. A kanban is basically a container for inventory. With Lean Manufacturing, empty kanbans are used to trigger inventory replenishment at each step in a supply chain. This provides for a smooth flow, step by step, of inventory. When you use a kanban system there is no way for inventory to be "pushed" down to the next step in a supply chain. It can only be "pulled" by the downstream kanban.

Lean Manufacturing techniques have become popular because they help to minimize the number of unplanned shutdowns that are caused by inventory stockouts while also minimizing the amount of inventory in a supply chain.

TECHNICAL
STUFF

Toyota developed a unique approach to managing the flow of products through its manufacturing process, allowing the company to minimize inventory costs and unplanned shutdowns. This approach involves tools and techniques that are collectively known as the Toyota Production System. As other companies adopted this approach, it became known as the Lean method because it reduces the inventory "fat" in a supply chain. Chapter 4 includes more information about Lean.

Procurement versus logistics

Procurement teams look for ways to get the same materials at lower cost. Two common ways reduce costs are to buy in larger quantities and to buy from a supplier in a low-cost region. Both of these options are likely to provide lower cost per item, but they also can have the unintended result of increasing logistics costs.

For one thing, increasing the amount of material that you order each time, called the *lot size*, also increases the amount of inventory that you have. You start with no inventory; then you receive a shipment of whatever lot size you agreed to purchase from your supplier. You gradually sell that inventory to customers until you have no inventory left. Eventually, you run out of inventory again. Over that period, how much inventory did you have on average? The answer is that the average amount of inventory — and the average amount of working capital that you had tied up in inventory — is half of your lot size. Therefore, on average, the more you order at one time, the more inventory you end up with. You can see how this works in Figure 3-4.

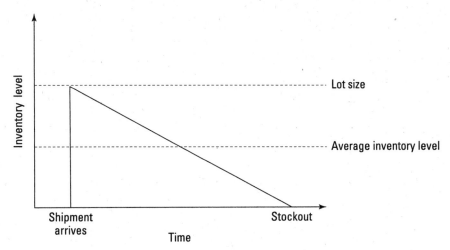

Ordering in larger quantities also means that you need to have extra space to store inventory and more people to manage it. Although increasing the lot sizes may get you a lower cost per unit, it could end up increasing your inventory costs even more.

A similar problem comes up when you consider suppliers located farther away. The price per unit may be lower, but the increased transportation costs can eat up all those savings and then some. Shipping items a longer distance can also force you to buy in larger quantities. The farther you have to move something, the more things can go wrong along the way. To compensate for this risk, you'll probably need to — yep, you guessed it — increase inventory.

The way to balance the priorities of purchasing and logistics is to take a total-cost analysis approach to sourcing decisions. Make sure that you're evaluating all the elements that will cost your supply chain money. You may find that a nearby supplier that can deliver in small batches and at a low transportation cost is a much better option than a lower-cost supplier in a distant location that would require you to spend more money on transportation and inventory.

Chapter **4**

Optimizing Your Supply Chain

D epending on the product or service that you're selling, you probably have many alternatives to choose from when designing your supply chain. You may have choices of how and where to buy your materials or make your products. Perhaps you can even choose different ways to deliver your products to your customers. This chapter discusses techniques to optimize your supply chain to ensure that you're creating the most value, in the most sustainable way, for you and your customers. Then, it talks about how to implement improvements to your supply chain through cross-functional projects.

Designing Your Network

It's often useful to think about your supply chain as a network. Networks are made up of nodes and links. As Figure 4-1 shows, every stop that a product makes between raw materials and a customer is a *node* of the network. A factory is a node; so is a warehouse, a distribution center, and a retail store. Nodes are connected by links. Generally speaking, *links* are forms of transportation, such as a ship, a railroad, a truck, or a drone. Products move through a supply chain, flowing through links and stopping at nodes.

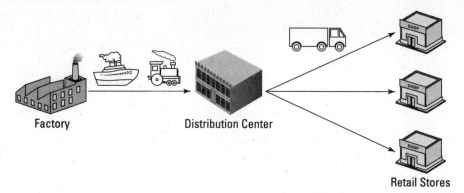

FIGURE 4-1:
Nodes and links
in a supply chain.

Factory

Distribution Center

Retail Stores

Your goal for any supply chain is to deliver maximum value at the lowest cost. One way to achieve this goal is to change the nodes and the links. Perhaps you can lower the costs of your raw materials by sourcing them from a different supplier, which means you'd be changing one of your nodes. Changing a node also means changing the links that connect that node to the rest of your supply chain.

Making changes in the links and nodes is called *network optimization*. One approach to network optimization is called *value-stream mapping* (VSM). Figure 4-2 shows a simple example of a VSM. The more of your supply chain that you're trying to optimize, the larger — and more complex — your VSM becomes.

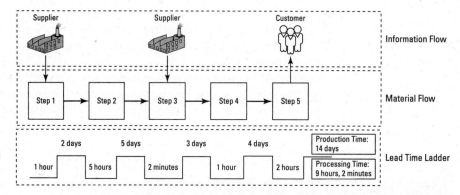

FIGURE 4-2:
Example of a
VSM.

Value stream mapping is an important part of a Lean professional's tool kit, as you'll see in the next section. However, network optimization can be done on a larger scale using sophisticated mathematical analysis. Several supply chain software platforms are available to help with analyzing supply chain flows, starting with spreadsheets and moving up to complex supply chain modeling tools. For example, in addition to factoring in the costs for buying materials and transporting them between nodes, some network optimization tools can factor in variables such as supplier performance and the effects of tariffs and taxes. The sections on supply chain modeling software and business intelligence software in Chapter 12 discuss this in more detail.

Improving and Innovating Processes

Supply chains are made up of people, processes, and technologies. All three components need to improve over time for a supply chain to remain competitive. People get better through education, training, and experience. Technology gets better through improvements in hardware and software. Processes get better through innovation and . . . well, process improvement.

Three approaches to process improvement are particularly useful in supply chain management: Lean, Theory of Constraints, and Six Sigma. These approaches share a goal — process improvement — but achieve it by focusing on different aspects of a process. Table 4-1 highlights the primary focus of each method.

TABLE 4-1

Three Approaches to Process Improvement

Method	Focus
Lean	Reducing waste
Six Sigma	Reducing variability
Theory of Constraints	Relieving bottlenecks

Lean

Lean is an approach to supply chain management that originated with Toyota, which is why you may hear it referred to as the Toyota Production System (TPS). The idea behind Lean is that you use the least amount of time, effort, and resources by maintaining smooth and balanced flow in a supply chain. The best way to accomplish this is by having logical, disciplined processes and excellent communications.

TIP

Because Lean originated in a Japanese company, many of the principles of Lean manufacturing are described using Japanese names.

Many people make the mistake of thinking about Lean as a training program or a set of tools that a company can buy. However, Lean is really a philosophy — a different way of looking at how businesses create value. In order for Lean to work properly, everyone in the company needs to be working together to eliminate three things that cause inefficiency:

>> **Muda:** Waste

>> **Mura:** Unevenness in operations

>> **Muri:** Overburdening of people and equipment

When someone identifies a need to innovate or improve a process, the key stakeholders are brought together for a *kaizen* event. (*Kaizen* is pronounced to rhyme with "Hi Ben.") During a kaizen, the stakeholders form a team and look at how the process is working, come up with ideas for how to make it better, and then implement changes. That sounds simple, and it should be. Because business cultures often make it hard for people to speak up or be heard, a formal approach like Lean helps to get everyone involved.

TIP

A core value of TPS is that people must be treated with respect because all of the workers have ideas to contribute that could benefit the company.

In the Lean approach there are eight kinds of Muda, or waste, that companies should be constantly driving out of their processes and their supply chains:

>> **Transportation**: Any time that you ship something from one place to another, you are consuming time and money. The less you need to ship a product, the better.

>> **Inventory:** Any time that you have products sitting around in inventory, you are wasting money by tying up space and working capital.

>> **Motion:** Any time that you move something when it isn't necessary, or when it isn't somehow making your product more valuable to a customer, you are wasting time and money.

>> **Waiting:** Any time that you have to wait for one thing to happen before you can do something else, you are wasting time and money.

>> **Overproduction:** Any time that you make too much of a product, or make a product before you can sell it or use it, you've wasted time and money.

>> **Overprocessing:** Any time that you do something that doesn't add value — that a customer won't pay for — you are wasting time and money.

>> **Defects:** Any time that you make a product that you can't use or sell, you've wasted time and money. This also includes wastes such as scrap and rework.

>> **Untapped skills and employee creativity:** Any time that you fail to engage and inspire your employees to offer ideas, implement improvements, or identify waste, you are wasting an asset that you are already paying for — their brains.

TIP

An easy way to remember the eight wastes is with the acronym "TIM WOODS." (The S at the end comes from *skills* in the last item.)

Toyota originally identified seven kinds of waste, but as Lean has been adopted in other companies, most of the experts have come to agree that untapped human creativity is so important that it needs to be included as an eighth form of waste.

TPS originated in the manufacturing world, so it is often called Lean manufacturing, but the principles have gradually been adopted in retail, distribution, and even service-based organizations. These days, you can find Lean initiatives in virtually every industry.

Six Sigma

Six Sigma is a process improvement method that's built on statistics. The basic idea is that variation is bad. When you're running a manufacturing process or a supply chain, you need consistency and predictability. If you don't have consistency, some percentage of the things that you make probably isn't useful for your customers. If you do have consistency — that is, if you have a process under control — there's a much better chance that the products you make are useful. Consistent processes lead to a high quality level for products.

Statisticians describe the variation of a process in terms of the amount of deviation from an average value. The symbol that is used to represent deviation in a mathematical equation is the Greek letter sigma (σ). Any set of data about a process has some deviation, but the more sigmas you have, the more stable your process is. So the statistical basis for Six Sigma is to reduce process variability so much that defects occur only at the sixth sigma (6σ), or 3.4 times per million.

I don't want to get too deep into the math here; you can find plenty of other books that do. The important thing to understand about Six Sigma is that the goal is to have a very small number of defects — that is, improved quality — as a result of decreased process variation. You get there by measuring processes and using mathematical tools to improve consistency.

You follow five steps to apply the Six Sigma as a process improvement methodology. These steps create the acronym DMAIC (pronounced "duh-may-ick").

1. Define
2. Measure
3. Analyze
4. Improve
5. Control

Another Six Sigma approach called DMEDI (Define, Measure, Explore, Develop, Implement) is used to design new processes.

Step 1: Define

The first step is to clearly define the process that you're trying to improve and why you want to improve it. During this phase, you need to build a business case for why the project is important and what resources you need to complete it. An important part of building the business case is to get feedback from the people who deal with the outputs of a process: the customers. This feedback is called the *Voice of Customer (VOC)*. The overview of the project, including the VOC, should be summarized in a Six Sigma project charter.

Writing up the project charter can be harder than people expect. Don't get hung up worrying about making the charter perfect. Instead, just create a rough draft that explains what you are trying to do. That will make it easier to clarify your thinking and to get input from other people. The charter is just your starting point. It is okay to make changes and improve it as the project moves forward.

Step 2: Measure

The second step is measuring the process that you're trying to improve. Because Six Sigma is a mathematical approach, you need to collect data so that you can measure how the process is working and calculate the amount of variation. Taking good measurements is critical so that you can calculate benefits during the next steps in a project. If your measurements aren't accurate then your improvement efforts are probably going to be misguided.

Step 3: Analyze

After you collect data about the process, you analyze the data. In the world of Six Sigma, this analysis often requires a solid understanding of statistics and the use of some statistical analysis software. Generally speaking, the data helps you iden-tify variations in a process and shows how those variations affect the quality of your products. Data analysis can help you understand what things are causing the variability — the root causes — so that you can look for ways to improve the process.

Step 4: Improve

The next step is putting the knowledge you gained from data analysis into action by making changes to improve the process. These changes can happen at the same time, or they can be phased in over time. Commonly, this phase includes some pilot studies to provide confirmation that the changes provide the expected benefits before you implement them throughout a process. If you decide that there are several improvements that will need to be brought online over time, you can sequence them in a *Multi-Generational Project Plan (MGPP)*. An MGPP is like a roadmap that shows the order in which you will implement improvements.

Step 5: Control

The funny thing about improving a process is that sometimes, when you stop paying attention to it, the process goes right back to working the way it did before you improved it. In Six Sigma, the final step is establishing a system to ensure that the improvements you made become permanent. Control often involves performing ongoing measurements and reporting to show that the improvements remain in place and continue to provide consistency over time.

REMEMBER

The DMAIC approach is used for improving an existing process. DMEDI is used for designing new processes.

There are lots of educational programs available to help people learn about Six Sigma, and many of them will even grant you a certificate when you're done. Generally, there are four levels for Six Sigma training and certification:

>> Yellow belts understand the basic concepts and terminology of Six Sigma and can contribute as a member of a process improvement project.

>> Green belts have a solid understanding of Six Sigma and can lead process improvement projects on their own.

>> Black belts have mastered Six Sigma and can teach other people how to manage process improvement projects.

>> Master Black Belts have such a high level of mastery that they can train and supervise Black belts.

TIP

There is so much overlap between Lean and Six Sigma that some people combine them into a single discipline called Lean Six Sigma.

Theory of Constraints

The Theory of Constraints (TOC) is one of the simplest, most powerful supply chain concepts. The basic idea is that every process is limited by some kind of *constraint* (think of the saying, "A chain is only as strong as its weakest link").

TOC is really about tuning an entire supply chain to run at the same pace as the slowest step in the process. There are many examples of how constraints actually control all of the processes around us. In the world of auto racing, there are times when you need to limit the speed at which cars travel around the track, so you send out a pace car that no one is allowed to pass. When you're draining a bathtub, the rate at which water flows out is constrained by the size of your drain. In other words, the most restrictive step in a process is the one that constrains the entire system. TOC helps you focus improvement efforts on the constraints because that is where you can have the greatest effect on the supply chain.

After you find the constraint, you have two choices:

>> Slow all the other steps down so that they run at the same speed as the constraining step. This will prevent the buildup of inventory between the steps in your process.

>> Improve the constraint so that the entire system moves faster. As you continue to improve the constraint (perhaps by using Six Sigma), eventually, it reaches the point where it's no longer the slowest step in your process. In other words, it stops being your constraint. Some other step becomes the constraint that's limiting your process, and the cycle starts again.

TECHNICAL
STUFF

The Theory of Constraints was made popular with a novel called *The Goal* by Eliyahu M. Goldratt (North River Press, 2014). Herbie was one of the fictional characters in the book, and his name has since been adopted into the jargon of TOC as a way of describing the constraining step in any process. Although looking for a constraint may sound obvious, the problem is that constraints are often hard to find. When a constraint is at the beginning of a process (like a pace car) or at the end of a process (like a bath drain) then the process is probably stable. When a constraint occurs in the middle of a process, the constraint can cause chaos. For example, a machine in the middle of an assembly line that breaks down might be a Herbie. But until you look at it from the perspective of TOC, people might not see how the starts and stops of that one machine actually cause inefficiencies throughout the whole supply chain and lower the company's overall capacity.

REAL-LIFE EXAMPLE

Let's say that you have a supply chain that involves several steps. Your customers, at the end of the supply chain, want to buy 1,000 widgets each month. But you can only manage to deliver 750. So how do you find the problems and fix them so that you can increase the capacity of your supply chain and sell your customers the products they want?

Because of TOC, you know that the entire process is limited by a single constraint — in this case, the slowest step in the process. So instead of trying to fix everything, you need to start by figuring out which step is slowing down the rest of the system.

After you have found the constraint you have two choices. First, you can slow down all of the other steps so that the entire system is running at the same speed. In this case, you would tune each step to only produce 750 widgets per month. That way, you won't have inventory building up in between the steps of your process. But you also wouldn't be meeting all of your customer's needs.

The second option is to improve the constraint which allows the entire supply chain to move faster. As you continue to make improvements, eventually the constraint will reach a point where it is no longer limiting the process. At that point, some other step has become the constraint on the process. Then you need to shift your focus to the new constraint.

Structuring Supply Chain Projects

Projects are the way that companies make changes. Because supply chains need to adapt to changes all the time, project management has become an important part of supply chain management. One common characteristic of supply chain projects is that they tend to be cross-functional. You may need to have logisticians and operations managers, human-resources professionals, information technology experts, and accountants working together. This can create challenges in terms of communication and workload. First, you need to look at the common characteristics of supply chain projects and how they can create challenges. Then you need to have a set of principles that help you lead cross-functional projects and navigate these challenges effectively.

Managing Cross-Functional Project Teams

Supply chains connect companies and cut across the silos within a company. As a result, supply chain projects commonly involve team members from many functions. A supply chain project team might include people from business development, customer services, shipping, receiving, manufacturing, information technology, accounting, and human resources. Managing cross-functional supply chain projects is a great way to develop a broad network and a deep understanding of the complexity of supply chains. The project manager must master the use of influence, pay careful attention to communica-tions, and help team members manage their priorities for the benefit of the team.

Bringing people with diverse skill sets together as a project team can be a great way to stimulate innovation and accelerate change. Cross-functional project teams have some major challenges, too. Three of the most common challenges for cross-functional project managers are authority, communication, and prioritization.

Managing cross-functional supply chain projects is a great way to develop a broad network and a deep understanding of the complexity of supply chains. The project manager must master the use of influence, pay careful attention to communications, and help team members manage their priorities for the benefit of the team.

Authority

Authority means that you have the ability to hire, fire, reward, and correct someone. Often, key team members report to managers in another division in the company and are only loaned to the project, so it can be difficult for the supply chain project manager to address performance issues directly because they do not have the authority to do so. If the project manager doesn't have the authority to manage the team members, she will need to rely on influence to keep all the team members pulling in the same direction.

Communication

Experts in any field have their own tools, rules, and language. In supply chain management, the same word can mean something different things depending on the context. For example, transportation companies (such as steamship lines and trucking companies) refer to their customer as the *shipper*, whereas their customers often use the term *shipper* to describe the transportation company. The project manager needs to be able to provide translation among functions and encourage people to explain what they're trying to say without using jargon.

Priorities

When someone is asked to work on a project, that person may not get to stop working on other things; he or she may be working on several projects. If one of the other projects requires more time and attention, you must make sure that your project gets enough support to avoid getting into trouble. Anticipate potential problems so that you can make formal arrangements. You might make an agreement with the team member's boss to ensure that your project has priority, for example. Or perhaps the team member's boss may promise that the team member needs to commit a certain number of hours each week to your project.

Creating Cross-Functional Project Plans

One of the best ways to deal with the challenge of leading a cross-functional project is to have a solid project plan. Building the plan gives everyone a chance to provide input and catch interdependencies. Human resources, for example, may not be able to start training employees in a new process until the necessary equipment has been delivered and installed. An integrated, cross-functional project plan makes it easy to see these connections and provides a clearer picture of the time required to complete a project. Creating an integrated plan also provides a natural opportunity for anyone on the team to ask for clarification on unusual words or jargon.

You can use many approaches to build an integrated project plan, but the following system works best for me:

1. **Bring representatives from all the necessary functions together for a planning meeting.**

Representatives may include people from logistics, operations, information technology, human resources, and accounting.

2. **Ask the team to come up with a list of deliverables.**

Deliverables are clearly defined results that the project must produce.

TIP

To tell whether a deliverable is a good one, use the Done/Not Done test. You should be able to ask whether a deliverable is done or not. The answer shouldn't be "Almost," "Mostly," or "It's 64.67 percent done." The answer should be "Yes, it's done" or "No, it's not done."

3. **Ask the team to create ten tasks for each deliverable.**

You might ask the team members, "If you were to summarize what it takes to complete this deliverable in ten steps, what would those steps be?" Each step is a task. A structured list of tasks, like the one in Figure 4-3, is called a *work breakdown structure (WBS)*.

ID	Name	Accountable Owner
1	Select location for distribution center	Sue
1.1	Complete network design study	Bob
1.2	Select three regions for potential site studies	Jim
1.3	Complete site studies	Dean
1.4	Submit site studies to VP for review	Sue
1.5	Schedule visits	Dean
1.6	Conduct negotiations with developers	Jill
1.7	Select final site	Sue
1.8	Sign contract	Sue
2	Select real estate broker	Dean
2.1	Acquire list of licensed brokers	Jim
2.2	Interview reference clients	Dean
2.3	Interview broker candidates	Dean

Deliverable →

Tasks

FIGURE 4-3:
Sample work breakdown structure.

TIP

I prefer that deliverables and tasks start with verbs, which makes it easy to tell what needs to be done. "Design receiving process" is more descriptive than simply "Receiving process," for example.

4. **Ask the team to decide which tasks have to be completed before another task can begin.**

   Relationships among tasks are called *dependencies*. The task that needs to happen first is called a *predecessor*. The task that has to wait is called a *successor*. For small, simple projects, you may be able to track dependencies manually, but in most supply chain projects, the dependencies make the projects complicated. Figure 4-4 shows a *network diagram* that illustrates the predecessor and successor relationships between tasks.

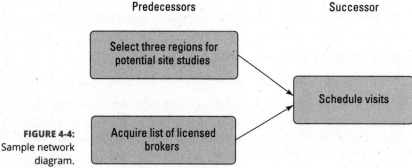

FIGURE 4-4:
Sample network diagram.

TIP

Using project management software to track tasks and dependencies can help you avoid mistakes and save a lot of time.

5. **Evaluate the timeline, and crash the plan.**

Dependencies often mean that it takes longer to complete a project than anyone expected or considered to be reasonable. At that point, you need to look for logical ways to shorten the timeline. This process is called *crashing* the project plan.

Start by looking at the tasks that are driving your schedule — the ones that are taking the longest time to complete. The longest series of tasks is called the *critical path*. The only way to shorten a project is to change the tasks on the critical path. Perhaps some tasks don't need to occur in sequence or in series. Instead, those tasks could run at the same time or in parallel, or they could be independent of one another. Continue analyzing the tasks on the critical path until you have a timeline that seems reasonable to the team and to your sponsor.

TIP

Creating a list of project deliverables and tasks is relatively easy and can be done with a word processing or spreadsheet program, but calculating project timelines and the critical path are cumbersome work. Project management software does this work automatically, which saves a lot of time when you are crashing a project plan.

Creating a RACI Matrix

When there are lots of people working on a project, they often have different opinions about their roles and responsibilities. You need to establish a clear understanding of what everyone is doing to make sure that all of the tasks are completed. It is much easier to set expectations up front than to confront misunderstandings later on.

For any task in a project, there are really only five different roles that a team member can have:

>> **No role:** The team member has no connection to the task.

>> **Inform:** The team member needs to be notified that a task is occurring, or that it has been completed.

>> **Consult:** The team member should be asked to provide input for a task, but he isn't the one doing the task, and he isn't making decisions.

>> **Responsible:** The team member is responsible for helping to complete a task. If the task requires someone to do work or make a decision, then that person is responsible for working on that task until it is complete.

>> **Accountable:** The team member is the one, and the only, person who is ultimately accountable for getting the task done. The accountable owner may need to make the decisions and do the work. Or she may need to prod and poke her team members to do the work. When it comes time to ask the question, "Is this task complete?" the accountable owner is the person whose career and credibility are on the line.

Assigning people to these five different roles makes it easier to communicate what each team member has to do for your project to be successful. You can document the roles with a RACI Matrix (pronounced like *race see* and short for Responsible – Accountable – Consult – Inform).

Using a RACI matrix like the one in Figure 4-5, you list all the tasks in your project and define the role for each of your team members in supporting each task. If there is a disagreement about someone's role on a task then you have a chance to resolve it on paper before it creates a problem for your project. Reading it horizontally, a RACI matrix makes it very easy for the project manager to know who needs to be involved in order for each task to get done. Reading it vertically, you can easily see what each person's role is, and exactly which tasks they are involved in.

Task	Sue	Bob	Jim	Dean	Jill
Complete network design study	I	A	R	R	
Select three regions for potential site studies	I	C	A	R	
Complete site studies		R	R	A	
Submit site studies to VP for review	A	R	R	R	I
Schedule visits	C	C	C	A	C
Conduct negotiations with developers	C			R	A
Select final site	A	R	R	R	R
Sign contract	A	I	I	I	I

FIGURE 4-5: Sample RACI matrix.

TIP

It can sometimes be hard to convince team members that only one person should be accountable for every task. However, I've found that when more than one person is accountable it is more difficult to manage the project. If two people insist that they are both accountable for a task, consider breaking that task into two smaller tasks and making each person accountable for one of these two tasks.

Designing Project Scorecards

Tracking the progress of a project is the key to figuring out what's working, what's not working, and where you need to focus resources in order to keep a project on track. One of the most effective ways to track a project is to use a scorecard and update it on a regular basis. For most projects, I recommend doing weekly updates at the same time every week; for slower-moving projects, monthly or quarterly updates are fine. In some cases, things change so fast that you need daily — or even hourly — updates.

The project scorecard should make it easy for anyone to tell at a glance how a project is doing — whether it's ahead of schedule and under budget or behind schedule and over budget; whether things are going as planned, or whether unplanned risks are putting the project in jeopardy. Following are the items I like to include in a scorecard and update every week:

>> **Status of major deliverables:** Which deliverables have been completed, and whether they were on time, early, or late.

>> **Recent accomplishments:** New things that have been completed since the last time the scorecard was updated.

>> **Upcoming tasks:** Things that the team will be working on between now and when the scorecard is updated in the future.

>> **Risks and concerns:** Unexpected challenges and issues that are causing problems or that could interfere with the project.

Having this information at your fingertips in a scorecard makes it much easier to manage well, reward people for their accomplishments, and help them deal with challenges. If you understand what is happening, what should be happening, and what might happen, then you can make better decisions, faster. However, there are other pieces of information that sometimes add value to a scorecard, such as information about budget performance, quality ratings, and employee engagement. To build a good scorecard, understand what information you need to track to keep everyone on the same page and ensure the success of your cross-functional supply chain projects.

Figure 4-6 is an example of a scorecard that makes it easy to communicate four essential pieces of information about the status of a project.

Project Scorecard for the Week of January 21

Status of major deliverables	Upcoming tasks
Recent accomplishments	Risks and concerns

Using the DIRECT Model

Over the years, I've developed an approach to leading cross-functional teams called the DIRECT project leadership model. The idea for this approach came from the realization that every movie — no matter how great the actors are — needs a director who can keep everyone working on the right things at the right time, and a cross-functional project in a company is no different.

The DIRECT model is built around the six things that a leader needs to focus on in order to help their team complete a project successfully (see Figure 4-7):

>> Define the objective.

>> Investigate the options.

>> Resolve to a course of action.

>> Execute the plan.

>> Change the system.

>> Transition the people.

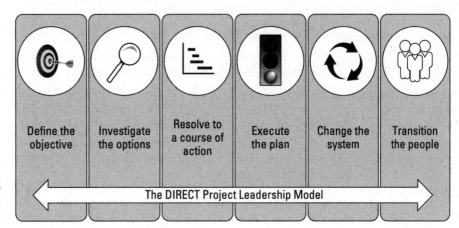

FIGURE 4-7:
The six
responsibilities of
a leader in the
DIRECT model.

| Define the objective | Investigate the options | Resolve to a course of action | Execute the plan | Change the system | Transition the people |

The DIRECT Project Leadership Model

Define the objective

Every project should start with a charter that clearly describes the scope, schedule, and budget of the project; identifies the project sponsor; and explains why the project is important. The charter helps ensure that everyone has similar expectations for the project and can prevent *scope creep* (new work added to the project later).

Investigate the options

Before running down the path of a particular solution, it's usually a good idea to consider other ways to accomplish your goal. Investigating your options early reduces the chances that you'll suffer buyer's remorse and ensures that you take into account the many points of view that can affect decisions in the supply chain.

Resolve to a course of action

When the options are clear, the team needs to make a decision and move forward. Supply chain projects can be stalled by *analysis paralysis* when teams get bogged down trying to collect data rather than making decisions and taking action. On the other hand, supply chain projects can also collapse because the team gets busy working too soon — before they properly understand all of the interdependencies and risks.

TIP

Resolving to a course of action is a leadership art that involves probing and listening to ensure that you truly understand the priorities and concerns of your team members, as well as helping them accept the need to compromise. The best way to resolve to a course of action is to have the team build a single project plan that shows the dependencies among all their tasks.

Execute the plan

When the plan is in place, the team needs to focus on executing the plan. Moving projects forward, keeping them on schedule, and keeping them on budget require special skills. Surprises will always occur, and surprises take time and money to address, but the credibility of the team and the value of the project depend on getting the work done on time. Executing the plan takes focus, a sense of urgency, and good communication among team members.

Change the system

Projects are about changing the way that the supply chain — the system — works. You must understand how a system works, the current state, before you change it. That understanding comes from the work that your team does to define and investigate the project. You also need to know how you expect the system to perform when the change is complete — the future state — which comes from the work the team does to resolve and execute. The change from the current state to the future state doesn't happen instantly or by magic. The implementation of the change needs to be planned, too. If you're starting a new distribution center on Monday, for example, consider whether you should shut down the old one the Friday before or run both centers in parallel for six months to make sure that the new one is working properly. You should also plan for the issues that are likely to come up during the change, such as shipments that get misrouted or equipment that doesn't work as expected.

Transition the people

You need to think about the people who operate the system and how your changes will affect the routines of your customers, your employees, and your other stakeholders. If your project is going to affect those people's experience, you need to help them prepare for the change. Any time something changes, people need to process and accept that change. Organizational behavior expert Dr. William Bridges studied the process that people go through when responding to a change in their environment, and he called this process *transitioning*. The key point is that managing the transition is just as important as managing the change. Whereas the change is about the system, the transition is about the people.

2
Managing Supply Chain Processes

Break your supply chain into high-level processes using the SCOR Model.

Look at the how different kinds of supply chains plan, source, make, and deliver products and services.

Explore opportunities for capturing value and reducing waste with reverse supply chains.

Think about the range of other processes that enable a supply chain to operate efficiently.

Chapter **5**

Connecting Supply Chain Processes

C hapter 2 covers several different ways that you can describe a supply chain, and one of the options was to look at it as a series of processes. This chapter goes deeper into that process-focused perspective and shows how to set targets, measure performance, and make better management decisions.

Supply chain management is such a new field that there aren't official rules or standards for many of these processes. A consortium of companies has been working together in the last few years to develop a shared framework called the Supply Chain Operations Reference Model (SCOR Model). As these companies have begun to incorporate the SCOR Model into their management systems, it has become easier for all of us to communicate more effectively about what's really happening in our supply chains.

Understanding Supply Chain Processes

I define a *supply chain process* as any activity or series of activities that adds value to a product or service. Making a hamburger is a supply chain process, for example, because customers are willing to pay more for a cooked patty with lettuce and tomato inside of a sliced bun than they are for the individual ingredients. Serving a hamburger is a supply chain process, too; customers who eat a hamburger in a restaurant, with a server carrying it to their table, will pay more than when they purchase the same burger at a drive-through. Anything that adds value — anything that moves or changes a product or service in some way that a customer is willing to pay for — is a supply chain process.

When you start thinking about supply chains in terms of processes, you begin to see more clearly how all of the pieces fit together. You have a process to order the components before you can make your products. Then you have manufacturing processes, sales processes, and delivery processes. Each of the processes in a supply chain depends on, and connects with, other processes. Supply chain processes never exist in a vacuum or a silo; they are all interdependent.

Although the details of most supply chain processes vary wildly among industries and companies, it turns out that they can be lumped into a surprisingly small number of categories. In fact, most supply chain processes fall into one of these six categories:

>> Plan

>> Source

>> Make

>> Deliver

>> Return

>> Enable

These high-level process categories don't address absolutely everything that's done in a supply chain, but they do cover most of the important steps necessary for creating and delivering value.

Introducing the SCOR Model

The SCOR Model is a framework that you can use to map out the processes in any supply chain. It contains six top-level processes — the key activities that are involved in creating and delivering value to a customer. Because each of these processes contains many levels of sub-processes, they are sometimes called *process groups*. The six processes are

>> Plan

>> Source

>> Make

>> Deliver

>> Return

>> Enable

All supply chain activities should be planned, so the Plan process connects with all of the others. Then, there is a logical sequence from Source, where you buy materials, to Make, where you manufacture products, to Deliver, where you get those products to your customers. At any point in the Source, Make, or Deliver processes you may need to send some of your products back up the chain, so the Return process sits underneath all of them. And because the SCOR Model is designed to describe a supply chain, not just an individual company, these processes also have to link to your customers and suppliers. So the Source process for *your company* connects to the Deliver process for *your suppliers*. And the Deliver process for *your company* connects to the Source process for *your customers*. In order to make all of that work, you need to have the right talent and information technology in place to Enable these processes. Figure 5-1 shows how these processes connect within your company, and how they connect your company to the rest of your supply chain.

Supply Chain Operations Reference Model

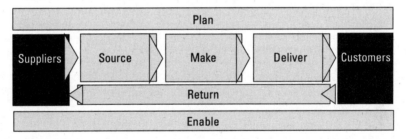

FIGURE 5-1:
The six top-level supply chain processes in the SCOR framework.

TECHNICAL
STUFF

Consulting companies, analysts, and various industries have developed their own supply chain process models over the years. These frameworks may use different words, but they encompass the same concepts as SCOR. For example, analyst firm Gartner includes similar process steps in their Supply Chain Talent Attribute Model, but they have added New Product Development and Customer Management as processes. And the U.S. Department of Defense replaces Make with Repair in its process framework. So when you understand the principles of the SCOR Model, then understanding the other models should be easy.

A good way to illustrate how the SCOR Model works is by looking at how it would apply to a supply chain that you already know. For example, imagine that you are suddenly in charge of the supply chain for a hamburger restaurant. Table 5-1 shows how the top-level processes of the SCOR framework could help you think through issues that you'd need to address.

TABLE 5-1   **Example Top-Level SCOR Processes**

Process	Description
Plan	You need to estimate how many hamburgers you going to make, decide where you are going to make them, and determine what your supply chain priorities are. You may need to choose whether to focus on quality and freshness, customer service and convenience, or low cost. These choices will influence the other decisions and trade-offs that you make throughout the supply chain.
Source	You need to decide where you will buy your ingredients and supplies. You need to negotiate with your suppliers in order to get the best prices, along with the best quality and service. It might be better to have suppliers that are close by, so that transporting products is fast and cheap. Or it might make sense to choose suppliers that are farther away but can provide the products at a lower cost or in larger quantities.
Make	You need to manage the process of making your hamburgers. It will help if you can define the stages of your manufacturing process, and how long each of them will take. You may also need to decide whether you should make the hamburgers by hand, or if you can buy a machine that can make them better, faster, and cheaper than a person.
Deliver	You need to manage the logistics of getting your hamburgers into your customers' hands. That means you'll need to decide whether you want customers to pick up their hamburgers at a counter, or whether a server will carry the hamburgers to their table. Or perhaps you need to have a drive-through window, or deliver your hamburgers to your customers' homes or offices.
Return	For many products, it's important to think about what will happen to them after your customer is finished using them. In the case of hamburgers, you may need to think about washing the plates and recycling napkins.
Enable	Last but not least, you need to decide what else you need in order to make the supply chain work. You may need to hire people with specific skills, which means you need to think about how you will find them, and how you will measure their performance. And there may be other processes that you need to have in place for your supply chain to achieve its goals, such as marketing programs or accounting policies.

You can see from this example how the SCOR Model can help you drill down into choices that you need to make and how these choices will affect the design of your supply chain.

Each of these processes is broken down in more detail in Chapters 6 through 11.

TIP   Using a process framework like the SCOR Model is a good way to analyze the steps involved in making a supply chain work. A framework can help you pinpoint the trade-offs in your supply chain and ensure that your decisions align with the results that your customers value. But most importantly, using a process framework gives you the ability to identify and focus on the metrics that are critical for managing your supply chain effectively.

SIPOC

When analyzing what a supply chain process really does, it is often useful to identify five key attributes that are referred to by their acronym, SIPOC:

- *Suppliers* are people, groups, or systems that provide you with inputs to a process. This could include companies that you buy supplies from, but it could also include a computer system that provides you with necessary data.

- *Inputs* include anything that goes into a process, a system, or a machine. Inputs could include raw materials, components, packaging materials, information, and instructions.

- *Process* is the step in a supply chain that you are trying to analyze. The process could be a planning process (like setting inventory targets) or an execution process (like picking an item in a fulfillment center).

- *Outputs* are what a process produces. Outputs include the product or service that the process is supposed to deliver and may also include information. In many processes, the outputs also include waste.

- *Customers* are people, groups, or systems that use the outputs of a process. The customer in a SIPOC doesn't have to be the customer that buys your finished product.

A SIPOC analysis helps to show the dependencies between each of the processes in a supply chain. A good way to illustrate a SIPOC analysis is by looking at the process of picking orders in a fulfillment center:

- *Suppliers* include the receiving department that is responsible for putting inventory into the warehouse, and the warehouse management system that is responsible for keeping track of inventory.

- *Inputs* include the products that are stored in inventory along with instructions about where to find the products in the warehouse.

- *Process* in this case could be "pick item from inventory." Or you could break the process down into more detailed steps such as "print pick sheet, travel to first pick location, place item on cart," and so on.

(continued)

(continued)

- *Outputs* are the item that is picked, where it is delivered, and how long it takes to complete the process. The outputs could also include updating the warehouse management system when the pick is complete and creating a packing list for the shipment.

- *Customers* in this case will be the shipping department, which is responsible for the next process in the supply chain.

This example shows that you can think about a supply chain as being a series of SIPOCs. The customer from one process is the supplier for the next process. For example, the shipping department is the customer of the picking process, but in the next process — shipping — the shipping department is the supplier and the transportation provider is the customer.

Clearly articulating SIPOCs is important when looking at the impacts of automating a process, because you need to consider how suppliers and customers of the process could be affected by a change. A useful tool for communicating this information is a SIPOC diagram, like the one shown in the figure.

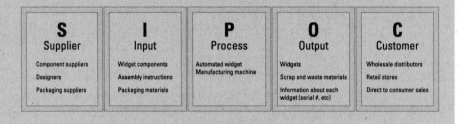

Establishing Process Metrics

After you define the processes in a supply chain, the next step is deciding how to measure them. Metrics reduce the subjectivity of a process and bring everyone's focus to the things that really matter.

In many cases, metrics are *quantitative,* which means that they represent objective data that's easy to measure and verify. The amount of time that a process takes to complete, the number of units that it produces, and the amount of money that it costs are examples of quantitative metrics.

In other cases, metrics are qualitative. How satisfied your customers are with a process, how convenient is it, or how likely customers are to recommend it could be important metrics, but they're difficult to measure. Metrics that rely on someone's judgment or opinion are *qualitative.*

Some supply chain processes are best measured quantitatively, some qualitatively, and some both quantitatively and qualitatively. The key is to choose metrics that help you understand how well a process is functioning and whether it provides opportunities to add value or decrease waste.

In a fast-food restaurant, the following three metrics could be very useful:

» **Order-to-delivery-cycle:** How long it takes from the time a customer places an order until he or she receives the food

» **Perfect order proficiency:** What percentage of orders are delivered on time and exactly as the customer asked (and paid) for them

» **Net promoter score:** What percentage of customers were so pleased with their experience that they would recommend the restaurant to someone else

Notice that order-to-delivery-cycle and perfect order proficiency are quantitative metrics; they're based on objective data. The net promoter score, however, is a qualitative metric; it measures how people feel and, therefore, is based on subjective data.

It's usually best to use a combination of quantitative and qualitative metrics to understand how your supply chain is performing and where you have opportunities for improvement.

Building the Right Supply Chain

There's really no such thing as a "perfect supply chain" because supply chain performance depends on so many factors. But there are clear differences between a good supply chain, and a bad one. A good supply chain will always give your customers what they want for a price that they're willing to pay, while leaving a sufficient profit margin for your company.

That definition may sound simple, but actually designing and managing a supply chain that can profitably meet your customers' expectations is tricky for a couple of reasons. First, the real world is full of surprises that force you to choose whether to spend more money to fill an order or take a chance on disappointing your customers. Second, over time, your customers' priorities will change, and your business will evolve, so your supply chain will need to adapt to those changes.

Four goals can help you evaluate how your supply chain should be designed: capacity, responsiveness, flexibility, and cost. All of these goals are important, but many supply chain decisions will require you to make trade-offs between them.

To understand how important each of these factors is for your supply chain, it may help to rank them. For example, you can create a chart, like the one in Figure 5-2, that shows how important each of these factors is for your customers. In this chart, the farther to the right a star is, the more important that supply chain attribute is to your customers. Prioritizing your supply chain goals in this way can help everyone on your team understand what it will take for your supply chain to meet your customers' needs while enabling your company to make a profit.

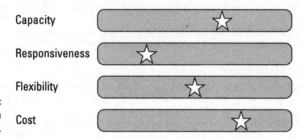

REMEMBER

>> **Capacity:** *Capacity* refers to how much product or service your supply chain can produce in a given period of time. One of the main goals of supply chain management is to provide your customers with as much of your products or services as they are willing to buy. If you don't have enough capacity, your customers will have go without the products they want, or they will buy from your competitors because you aren't meeting their demand. But if you have too much capacity, you're tying up capital without generating a return. So maintaining the proper amount of capacity is an important balance.

Closely related to capacity is the concept of *availability*, which is the capability of a system to provide products or services when customers want them. Customers don't really care about your supply chain's capacity; what matters to them is product or service availability. But companies often focus on capacity because the more capacity you have, the easier it is to maintain high availability. When you don't have enough capacity, or when you don't manage your capacity well, then your availability becomes low, and that means customers can't get your products or services when they need them.

>> **Responsiveness:** *Responsiveness* is the measure of how quickly your supply chain can provide a product or service to a customer. Basically, you measure responsiveness from the time that your customer places an order, to the time when you deliver it to them. Some products, such as ships, can take years to design and build. Those products' supply chains aren't very responsive. Other products, such as pizza, can be made and delivered to a customer's doorstep in 30 minutes. So responsiveness obviously varies a lot depending on the kind of product that your supply chain is delivering. But within a particular industry,

responsiveness is often a key differentiator between competitors. Customers usually go shopping when they need something, so the most responsive company — the one that can deliver their product the fastest — has a better chance of getting the order.

Supply chain responsiveness is important for driving top-line revenue, because it is often a critical factor in a customer's purchasing decision.

» **Flexibility:** *Flexibility* is the measurement of how well your supply chain scales up or ramps down in response to change. If customers always wanted the same stuff in the same quantities and at regular intervals, then supply chain management would be a whole lot simpler. But that's not the way it works in the real world. One week, everyone is buying doughnuts, and no one is buying ice cream. The next week, everyone is buying ice cream, and no one is buying doughnuts. So supply chains must have the flexibility to respond to changes in demand — whether those changes are increases or decreases.

Supply chains also need to have flexibility when it comes to supply. In other words, your supply chain has to be able to deliver value to your customers even if your suppliers have low availability.

» **Cost:** *Cost,* of course, is the amount of money it takes to operate your supply chain. Supply chain management needs to provide the capacity, responsiveness, and flexibility that your customers need at the lowest possible cost. The cost metric is the ultimate test of supply chain management. You have a goal of delivering value to your customers; the less you spend to achieve that goal, the bigger your monetary reward is.

Chapter **6**

Planning the Supply Chain

B efore you can engineer and manage a supply chain, you need to plan what it's supposed to do. Planning gives you an opportunity to set goals, evaluate options, and make decisions; it also helps ensure that you invest your time and money wisely.

Supply chain planning is not a one-time event; planning is an ongoing and iterative process that ensures your supply chain adapts to changes in your business.

This chapter covers how to plan a supply chain by looking at it as a complete system, which means thinking about it from several angles: what your resources, requirements, customers, and products are; how you'll make and deliver your products; and how you'll handle returns of used or defective products.

Balancing Supply and Demand

The fundamental question at the heart of every supply chain plan is "How are we going to balance supply with demand?" There are three main approaches to balancing supply and demand:

>> Make-to-stock

>> Make-to-order

>> Engineer-to-order

When your supply chain plan is based on a *make-to-stock* approach, you start by forecasting how much you think customers are going to buy. This forecast drives all your manufacturing and distribution planning. The work is done and the products are ready to go before you receive an order from a customer. This approach is sometimes called a *push system* because you're pushing products out toward your customers even though they haven't yet placed orders.

When your supply chain plan is built on a *make-to-order* approach, all your manufacturing and distribution services are standing by, waiting for an order to come in. The product design work is complete, but you don't make or move a product until you get the order for it. This approach is an example of a *pull system* because an order has to pull the products through the supply chain.

When your supply chain plan uses an *engineer-to-order* approach, you are making a customized product for each order, so you can't finish the product design until your customer gives you the specifications. The final engineering work, manufacturing, and distribution are triggered by the customer order. Like make-to-order, engineer-to-order is a pull system.

TIP

You'll find more details about implementing make-to-stock, make-to-order, and engineer-to-order in Chapter 8.

Make-to-stock, make-to-order, and engineer-to-order are different ways to plan a supply chain. A company can have more than one supply chain, and many companies operate all three types of supply chains while using many of the same supply chain assets.

A good way to see how these three approaches work is with the example of buying a new car. You could drive to your local car dealership and buy any of the cars on the lot. Each car was manufactured based on a forecast; the manufacturer guessed that someone would want to buy it. After the manufacturer forecasted the demand, they pushed inventory into the dealer's supply chain to meet that demand. All those cars, therefore, came from a make-to-stock supply chain.

You may not like any of the cars that the dealer has in stock, however. Maybe you want a car with a specific combination of features, such as red paint, tan interior, and the high-end entertainment package. The dealership will be delighted to get you that car, but it needs to order it from the factory. The supply chain for a car you order this way is a make-to-order supply chain. The flow of material, information, and money is quite different from the flow in a make-to-stock supply chain.

Suddenly, one of your friends hears about your new car and gets jealous. She wants a similar car, but she wants the rear seat to be converted to a kennel for her Newfoundland. The factory doesn't offer this configuration as a standard feature, but (for a price) has agreed to do it. The manufacturer has to design the kennel compartment and source all the materials, so the process takes a while. The manufacturer wouldn't have designed the kennel until a customer had ordered it and provided her requirements. Now that it has an order and knows exactly what the customer wants, the factory can produce a car that meets the customer's needs perfectly. This system is an engineer-to-order supply chain.

To a customer, the finished cars may look similar, but in terms of the supply chain, the processes to make them are very different. Making sure that those processes are aligned for your products and your customers is the result of supply chain planning.

Aligning Resources with Requirements

Supply chain plans are built around goals, or *requirements*. Whether your plan is based on a make-to-stock, make-to-order, or engineer-to-order process, planning always starts by identifying a requirement. The plan you create explains how you intend to meet that requirement while taking all your resources and constraints into account.

Anything you use to make a supply chain work is a *resource*. People are resources. Facilities are resources. Machines are resources. Inventory is a resource.

Every resource has constraints — things it can do and things it can't do. The constraints may be physical limitations, or they may be limits imposed on the supply chain by financial, safety, and policy rules. Here are some examples of constraints that may exist for your supply chain resources:

>> Employees can work only 40 hours per week unless you pay overtime.

>> A machine can operate for only 1,000 hours before it needs to be serviced.

» Operators must be certified on a piece of equipment before they can use it.

» Finished-goods inventory can't be stored outside during the winter.

The connection among the items in this list is that each item limits the capacity of your supply chain resources. So your supply chain plan needs to take all these constraints into account. A plan that assumes a 45-hour work week but doesn't include the additional cost of overtime may cause you to miss your financial targets. A plan that involves storing inventory outside while you wait for customers to pick it up may work during the summer but not during the winter. Constraints are not always obvious; it takes research and judgement to understand all of the constraints that affect a supply chain's performance. Identifying and managing hidden constraints is critical for effective planning.

Suppose that your requirement is to make 100 widgets per day. You need to figure out what resources are required to meet that requirement and what constraints exist for those resources. You will need manufacturing equipment, skilled employees, raw materials from your suppliers, and many other resources. Each of these resources is subject to constraints; perhaps the manufacturing equipment can only produce 10 widgets per hour, the raw materials won't be delivered for five weeks, and your employees are only available on Tuesdays. Your supply chain plan needs to explain how you will meet your requirements with the resources you have available.

The supply chain planning model shown in Figure 6-1 illustrates the factors involved in aligning resources with requirements and shows that all those factors are subject to constraints.

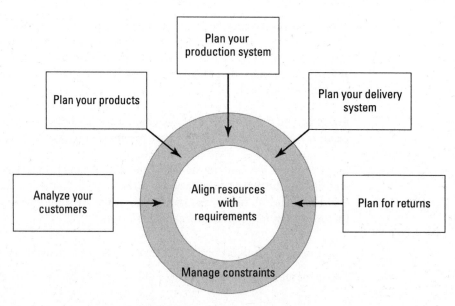

FIGURE 6-1:
Supply chain
planning model.

Analyzing Your Customers

I define a supply chain as "a complex system made up of people, processes, and technologies that is engineered and managed to deliver value to a customer." Supply chain planners tend to focus on the people, processes, and technologies. But good supply chain planning also requires that you align plans with the needs of your customers, who are the source of every dollar that flows into your supply chain. Each customer is unique, with specific needs, preferences, and constraints. The better you understand your customers, the better chance you have of ensuring that your supply chain delivers the value they expect.

Some customers have specific needs or tastes and are willing to wait — and pay — for a custom product that's just perfect for them. These customers would be dissatisfied with a generic product, even if it were cheaper and immediately available. If you have customers like these, you probably need to have an engineer-to-order supply chain. Other customers are more interested in getting the lowest cost, which might lead you to implement a make-to-order supply chain because it minimizes inventory cost. Still other customers need to have your product immediately, which forces you to implement a make-to-stock supply chain. Understanding your customers' needs helps you make better decisions about your supply chain.

There are three common ways to analyze customers and their needs:

>> Market segmentation

>> Persona development

>> Key customer analysis

You can create groups of customers by segmenting them based on demographic characteristics. If your customers are people, their demographics may include where they live, how much money they make, and how old their children are. If your customers are businesses, their demographics may include their industry classification, annual revenue, and the number of employees. Once you have defined your customer segments, you can check to ensure that your supply chain plan will align with each segment's needs.

Another way to get to know customers is to create personas for them. A *persona* (or customer profile) is a description of an imaginary customer that represents key characteristics of many of your real customers. The following example is a persona that a consumer products company might create to describe a target customer for its new laundry soap:

> Bob is a single man who works 60 hours a week and has an active social life outside work. He's short on time, so he's drawn to hacks that can solve problems quickly and easily. For him, washing clothes is a chore, but a necessary one. He buys his laundry soap in a drugstore near his urban apartment.

A persona can be useful for marketing, and it can be useful for planning your supply chain, too. Understanding the personas of your customers helps you understand what they value so that you can make a supply chain that meets their needs.

A third way to define customer requirements is to identify the actual customers who are most likely to buy your products, your *key customers*. By studying your key customers you can get a better idea of what they want or need, how much they will buy, and how much they are willing to pay.

A Customer Relationship Management (CRM) system can provide useful data for studying your customers by tracking purchases and other interactions with customers. CRM data can be used to create personas, to analyze market segments, or to study key customer behaviors. (See Chapter 12 for more information about CRM systems.) Additionally, many CRM systems allow you to run experiments that provide insights into customers' preferences. For example, you could gather data through A/B tests where you try offering two versions of a promotion to see which one is more likely to encourage a customer to place an order.

Planning Your Products

Part of supply chain planning is being clear about what you are going to make and how you'll make it. The supply chain for a product can change based on demand-related factors. For example, product designs often change based on customer feedback. Supply chains can also be changed based on supply-related factors. For example, resources and constraints may dictate that you make changes to your product. Knowing which materials are readily available, where to get them, and how much they cost are important factors in making design decisions for many products. Product characteristics often evolve over time, and those characteristics should be incorporated into your supply chain planning.

A good example of how product characteristics need to be considered during supply chain planning comes from the catalytic converter that goes into the exhaust system of a car. There are two metals that can be used as the catalyst in a catalytic converter: platinum and palladium. When platinum becomes expensive, automakers opt for catalytic convertors that are made from palladium. When palladium becomes expensive, automakers switch to platinum catalytic convertors. In other words, as the prices for platinum and palladium fluctuate, automakers change the design of their cars and re-plan the supply chain for their catalytic convertors.

Another good example of how product characteristics can influence supply chain requirements occurs in the fast-food business. The seasonings used by national fast-food chains sometimes differ depending on where each restaurant is located. Although the logo, uniforms, and menus may look exactly the same wherever you go, there is a supply chain for the seasonings used in restaurants in different regions.

TIP

A bill of material lists all the parts that go into a product, and can help you identify many of the resources that should be included in your supply chain plan.

Yet another example of how products affect the supply chain is package size and quantity. Knowing whether you're going to be packaging a box of crayons for individual sale or shipping them in huge tubs can be an important factor in determining the requirements of your supply chain and defining the resources you need. Small boxes need to be easy for store associates to handle. Large tubs need to be compatible with the material handling equipment at each step in the downstream supply chain.

Planning Your Production Systems

Your production plan determines when, where, and how to make products so that you can meet your requirements without violating your production constraints.

You could plan to ship all the raw materials to a single facility and manufacture your products there, for example. This is an example of centralized production. When manufacturing requires large investments in capital equipment (such as expensive factories), a plan for centralized production may make sense. Centralized production tends to make manufacturing more efficient but often leads to long delivery times and high transportation costs

When customer or product requirements demand short lead times and low transportation costs, a distributed production plan may make more sense. Distributed production involves manufacturing products at multiple sites to satisfy demand in each region.

TIP

3D printing (see Chapter 13) has the potential to make distributed production a good option for many products that are manufactured centrally today.

If one of your manufacturing facilities does not have the capacity to manufacture your entire product, you could split the manufacturing process among several factories. Splitting manufacturing steps across multiple factories can be a good way to increase your access to resources and overcome constraints (such as not having enough space or enough people) in each production facility. Splitting manufacturing can also give you access to local expertise and lower-cost resources.

One of the issues to consider when splitting up the steps in a manufacturing process is the impact it will have on inventory. Partially assembled products in between manufacturing steps are called work-in-process inventory, or WIP (pronounced like "whip"). The further one manufacturing step is from the next one, the more WIP you are likely to accumulate between the steps. So the benefits that come from dividing a manufacturing process need to be weighed against the potential that it creates for increasing WIP.

Planning Your Delivery Systems

Making your products is one thing; getting them to your customers is quite another. Factors such as the locations involved, the characteristics of your product, and the needs of your customers can constrain your delivery system. The work of delivery (which includes moving and storing products) is called *logistics*. The collection of resources that you use to do this work is a logistics (or distribution) network.

Logistics networks come in many shapes and sizes. If you're making small widgets and selling them directly to consumers via the Internet, for example, you might put an e-commerce fulfillment center next to your factory. That arrangement makes it easy to ship products to your customers when they place an order. In this case, your logistics network starts at your suppliers, flows through your factory to your fulfillment center, and ends with your customers. Any resource that you use along the way to move or store the products is part of your logistics network.

But if you're selling your widgets through a big-box store, your factory probably needs to ship them by the truckload to your stores. If you're sending widgets to stores internationally, you may need to ship them by the containerload. Depending on where you ship the products, you may need to think about issues such as tariffs and international trade rules. In each case, you have a different logistics network and need different resources to support your logistics processes.

TIP

Chapter 9 provides more information about what's involved in delivering a product. This material can be useful for defining the resources and constraints that need to be addressed in a supply chain plan.

Planning for Returns

When you plan your supply chain, you need to account for returns. Returns are normal in most businesses, but they're often overlooked during the planning process. Depending on the industry, 5 to 10 percent of all the products sold may be returned by customers, and in e-commerce, this figure can be 30 percent or higher.

TIP

Many e-commerce retailers go out of their way to make it easy for customers to return products because they believe that doing so will increase sales (and profitability) in the long run.

The network for returned products is called a *reverse supply chain* because the flow goes from the customer back to your company. Reverse supply chains, however, involve more than just customers returning products they don't need, don't want, or are dissatisfied with. Reverse supply chains can also be used to repair, remanufacture, or recycle products, as well as ensure that hazardous products are disposed of safely. As in any other supply chain, the goals of a reverse supply chain include minimizing costs and maximizing the value; the value of a reverse supply chain is often the amount of money that is recovered from returned products.

Companies that make computers, for example, have reverse supply chains. If you buy a computer that stops working during the warranty period, you can usually send it back to the manufacturer. The manufacturer wants to make the return fast and easy for you as a customer so that you buy more of its products in the future. It may even send you a new replacement computer. But now the company has an almost-new computer that doesn't work. If it does nothing with the returned computer, the defective computer is a write-off. The company, however, may be able to recover most of the value of the returned asset by planning the reverse supply chain properly. It can run a series of tests, repair the defects, and then resell the computer as a refurbished unit, for example.

REMEMBER

A well-planned reverse supply chain for returned products creates value in two ways: It keeps customers happy, and it reduces losses from disposing of damaged or defective products.

Another strategy for reverse supply chains focuses on recycling. Many products contain valuable materials that can be recovered when the product is no longer needed or when it reaches the end of its life. Electronics devices, for example, often contain precious metals such as silver and gold. A common reverse supply chain is the network of junkyards and scrap recyclers that collect everything from old cans to old cars to be melted down and turned into new products.

In some industries, a well-planned reverse supply chain can create new business opportunities. Automobiles, airplanes, and heavy equipment have many components that can be remanufactured. These used components, called *cores*, become raw materials for a remanufacturing process that makes like-new parts. Remanufactured parts typically are much cheaper to make than new parts, even though they usually meet the same technical specifications. The savings can be passed along to customers, who get discounts for buying remanufactured parts.

In addition to being good for business, reverse supply chains can benefit the environment, especially for products that contain harmful chemicals (as batteries and some electronics devices do). Given the opportunity to recapture value from used products and the environmental benefits, many companies are striving to design closed-loop supply chains, which means that all their products can be recycled.

By planning your returns properly, you can minimize the amount of waste created throughout the life cycles of your products.

TIP

A properly planned reverse supply chain can actually create an additional source of supply and, at the same time, increase profits.

Chapter **7**

Sourcing, Purchasing, and Procurement

For your company to sell things to your customers, you first need to buy things from other companies. The process of buying things for your company has many names, but the three most common are *sourcing, purchasing,* and *procurement.* The companies that sell you goods and services are your *suppliers* or *vendors.* Since supply chains flow from raw materials down to a customer, your suppliers are *upstream* in your supply chain.

Procurement professionals add value to the supply chain by constantly evaluating the marketplace and selecting sourcing strategies that minimize risk and cost for their companies. One of their responsibilities should include calculating the total cost of each option because the upfront savings from any one change is often offset by additional costs down the road.

This chapter discusses the issues that you need to consider as a part of your purchasing process. Supply chain management includes decisions about what to buy, who to buy it from, when to buy it, and how much to purchase at one time. These choices have a big effect on the cost of providing your customers with the products and services they need. The money that you save by making good decisions about purchasing allows you to lower the prices you charge customers and to increase profits for your business.

Understanding Strategic Sourcing

Not long ago, purchasing departments focused on buying stuff as cheaply as possible. As executives have come to understand the effect that purchasing has on supply chains, awareness has grown that the procurement process needs to be strategic. Companies now compile their purchasing data to evaluate what they buy, who they buy it from, and what they could change to drive additional value to their supply chain. This process is called *strategic sourcing*.

Every consulting company has its own model for strategic sourcing, but all these models have some basic steps in common:

1. Collect and analyze data about what you bought in the past.
2. Collect and analyze forecasts about what you'll buy in the future.
3. Evaluate how past suppliers have performed in terms of cost and quality.
4. Investigate whether other suppliers could provide the same products and services at better prices or higher quality levels.
5. Consider opportunities to outsource or insource the products or services.
6. Determine how important the product or service is, and how available it is in the marketplace.
7. Evaluate the impact of payment terms on your working capital.
8. Assess risks associated with each supplier.
9. Make changes.
10. Repeat Steps 1–9.

The value that the purchasing process adds to your company can be measured by looking for costs — and missed revenue opportunities — that resulted from a poor alignment with the rest of the supply chain. Applying the principles of strategic sourcing helps to ensure that you are optimizing the performance of your entire supply chain.

Segmenting Your Supply Chain

It is easier to analyze purchasing data when you segment your supply chain based on the characteristics of suppliers. One way to segment suppliers is by placing them into *tiers* based on how far upstream they are in your supply chain. The companies that you buy from are your Tier 1 suppliers; the companies from which your

Tier 1 suppliers buy goods and services are your Tier 2 suppliers, and so on, as shown in Figure 7-1. The company that makes the final product, at the end of all of the tiers, is called the *original equipment manufacturer (OEM)*.

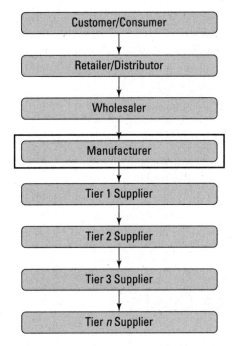

Customer/Consumer

Retailer/Distributor

Wholesaler

Manufacturer

Tier 1 Supplier

Tier 2 Supplier

Tier 3 Supplier

Tier *n* Supplier

Suppliers can also be placed in *spend categories* based on how your company uses the goods and services that they provide. If a supplier is providing you things that get included in your own products, this company is a *direct supplier*. The things that you buy from that supplier are *direct materials* and *direct services*. If a supplier is providing you things that aren't necessarily going to be included in the goods and services you sell, it's categorized as an *indirect supplier*.

Imagine that you have a fast-food restaurant. The companies that sell you hamburger patties, lettuce, and buns are Tier 1 direct suppliers. You buy things from those suppliers that go directly into your products. The company that sells your supplier flour for the buns is one of your Tier 2 suppliers. You may have no idea what company is that Tier 2 supplier, but it plays an important role in keeping your supply chain working correctly.

On the other hand, the companies that sell you napkins, hand soap, and floor wax are Tier 1 indirect suppliers because their products aren't actually incorporated into the products and services you sell. These suppliers are still necessary, and they're still part of your supply chain, but the connection is indirect.

Figure 7-2 shows part of an automotive OEM supply chain. The suppliers are categorized as either direct or indirect and are organized into tiers for each category.

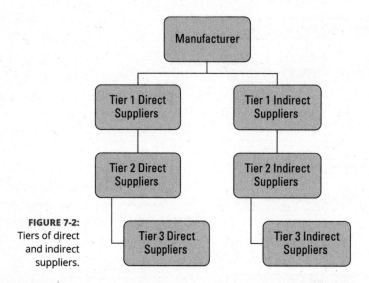

FIGURE 7-2: Tiers of direct and indirect suppliers.

Managing Life Cycle Costs

An important part of purchasing is analyzing and understanding the total cost of everything you buy. The total cost is almost always much higher than the price that people expect to pay. Following are some of the costs that factor in to the total cost, and which have a financial effect on your company:

» Purchase price

» Transportation

» Inventory holding costs

» Quality inspection and defect resolution costs

» Insurance

» Shrinkage, security, and loss prevention

» Duties, tariffs, and taxes

» Permits

» Licensing fees

- » Maintenance costs

- » Disposal costs and recoverable value

- » Product liability, recalls, and warranty risks

In other words, the purchase price is one of many variables to consider when you calculate how much something is really going to cost. This big-picture view of how much something really costs is often called the *total cost of ownership* (TCO) or the life cycle cost. Understanding TCO can help you ensure that you make purchasing decisions that deliver the greatest value, rather than just the lowest purchase cost.

Minimizing input costs

A business is sustainable only if it makes a profit. Purchasing can have a huge effect on the profitability of any company. The products and services that your purchasing department buys are the inputs for your company, and every dollar you save by reducing input costs is pure profit. Purchasing professionals are always looking for ways to reduce costs.

These common options are good starting points when you look for ways to reduce costs:

- » Negotiating a long-term agreement in exchange for lower costs

- » Increasing order quantities in exchange for a volume discount

- » Accepting lower-quality products in exchange for a price reduction

- » Requesting new price quotations from lower-cost suppliers

More creative purchasing managers might explore additional alternatives that could translate into savings:

- » Extending the lead time that suppliers have to fill an order

- » Sharing information with suppliers that allows them to plan farther ahead

- » Changing product or packaging designs to use less-expensive inputs

- » Providing financial guarantees to support a supplier's investment in facilities and equipment

Minimizing input costs is an ongoing process. Purchasing managers should constantly analyze the input costs of your products and services and collaborate with your suppliers (and your internal teams) to find new ways to reduce input costs and increase profits.

Sourcing your inputs

A single link in a supply chain usually has five components: suppliers, inputs, processes, outputs, and customers (SIPOC). A SIPOC diagram is handy way to illustrate this concept (see Figure 7-3; see Chapter 5 for more information about SIPOC).

Supplier	Inputs	Process	Outputs	Customers
Acme Meat Processors	Hamburger	Make hamburgers and deliver to customers	Finished hamburgers, properly cooked and packaged for sale	Walk-in Drive-through
Best Bread Bakery	Buns			
Condiments Central	Ketchup Mustard Mayonnaise			
Paper Supply Warehouse	Napkins and bags			

FIGURE 7-3: SIPOC diagram.

If you look at the process of making a hamburger, for example, your primary inputs are the ingredients: meat, bun, and toppings. You need a stove to cook the hamburger on, so a stove might be listed as an input. You also need wax paper to wrap the burger in, along with napkins and a paper bag. All these items are inputs to your process, and each input comes from a supplier.

Choosing where to buy your inputs can have a great effect on the quality of your products and services and on the profitability of your company. You don't want to pay more than you need to for any of your inputs; doing so would be a waste of money. On the other hand, sometimes, you truly do get what you pay for. The money you try to save by choosing a low-cost supplier can lead to higher transportation costs, unreliable deliveries, increases in inventory, or quality problems.

One way to approach this challenge is to segment your inputs into spend categories. You can segment inputs in lots of ways, but the most common way is to create a chart that compares how important or risky each input is with how much money you spend on it. Figure 7-4 shows an example of this kind of segmentation diagram.

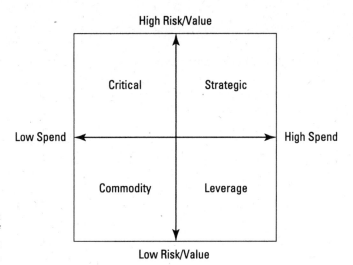

High Risk/Value

Critical   Strategic

Low Spend ←————————→ High Spend

Commodity   Leverage

Low Risk/Value

FIGURE 7-4:
Segmentation of inputs to a process.

Understanding which spend category an input falls into can help you make smarter decisions about where to source the products and services you need to support your supply chain. Here are some guidelines for the best way to manage procurement of goods and services in each category:

» **Leverage:** If you spend a lot of money on a particular input, but you can buy it from lots of places and have it delivered quickly, this input is an opportunity for leverage. In other words, this item is a negotiating chip that you can use to get better prices for other things.

» **Commodity:** If you don't spend a lot of money on an input, and the item is easy to get when you need it, it's really just a commodity. Get the best deal you can, and keep moving. Make sure that you aren't overpaying, of course, but don't worry too much about where the item comes from.

» **Critical:** If you don't spend a lot of money on a particular input, but the item is hard to get when you need it, it's a critical component with a high chance of creating bottlenecks. The same applies if your quality standards for an input are especially high. For critical components, you need to build and maintain strong relationships with your suppliers to make sure you always have supply available.

» **Strategic:** If you spend a lot of money on an input, and that item is hard to get, it's a strategic input. Managing strategic inputs properly can be one of your biggest opportunities to increase profitability and reduce the risk in your company's supply chain. In addition to building strong relationships, you should think about the suppliers of strategic products and services as candidates for a merger, acquisition, or joint venture.

Forecasting your demand

To make smart decisions about buying your inputs, you need to understand what you're going to need. The difference between buying 1 piece per week and buying 100 pieces per day could have a huge effect on which supplier you should be buying from and how much you should pay.

Estimating how much of an item that you're going to need is called *demand forecasting.* The challenge with demand forecasting is that you almost never know exactly how much you're going to need and when you're going to need it. Your needs depend on many factors, such as how many finished products your customers decide to buy. Even so, you need to make some educated guesses about how much you expect to buy so that you choose the right suppliers and negotiate the right terms.

Insourcing, outsourcing, and offshoring

It's hard for a company to be successful when it tries to be a jack of all trades. Instead, each company needs to figure out which characteristics make it truly valuable in a supply chain. In the context of supply chain management, your *core competencies* are the things that your company can do better than others, and for a lower cost.

Core competencies are key to maintaining your competitive position in a supply chain. Companies usually focus on building their core competencies through research and development and through continuous process improvement. Generally speaking, the source of any work that's directly related to your core competencies should come from people working inside the company, meaning employees. In other words, this work should be *insourced.*

Some work is important for your company but isn't a core competency, which means that other companies can do that same work better, faster, and cheaper than your company can. Because this work isn't your core competency, and because it isn't important for maintaining your competitive position, it doesn't make sense for you to pay more to do this work yourself. Instead, you may be better off *outsourcing* that work to another company.

In some cases, there are good business reasons to *offshore* work — take work that's being done in one country and move it to a different country. Although it's controversial, offshoring can reduce costs and improve quality, as well as allow your company to access talent and open new markets. In the information technology world, many companies have found that it makes sense to move programming and technical support functions to India. In the manufacturing world, many global companies have built factories in China.

Offshoring can also create some real risks, though. For example, a challenge with offshoring manufacturing is that longer supply chains lead to higher transportation costs and the need to carry more inventory. Two other risks in offshoring are (1) communicating and coordinating supply chain activities with people who are separated by distance and time zones and (2) dealing with problems related to intellectual property.

Your company may have decided a few years ago that offshoring made sense, but because of changes in the market, offshoring no longer provides benefits to your supply chain. In that case, you may decide to move the work from a foreign source to a domestic source, which is called *reshoring* or *nearshoring*.

A good example of an industry that does a lot of insourcing, outsourcing, and offshoring is automotive manufacturing. Most of the big auto brands see the design, assembly, and marketing of cars as being their core competencies, which are critical to their strategic role in the supply chain. Many of the parts that go into their cars, however, are made by other companies. In other words, the automakers outsource the manufacturing of their components to third-party suppliers. It might make sense for these companies to purchase those components from suppliers that are close to the automotive assembly facilities, because they'd have low transportation costs and short lead times. But in some cases, it's much cheaper to manufacture components or even entire cars in another country, so the companies offshore some or all of these processes. Later, they may decide that it's better to do manufacturing in their home country and reshore some of their processes.

Managing Supplier Relationships

From the standpoint of your suppliers, you're the customer. That fact may be obvious, but it's amazing how often people forget it. Think about all the things your customers do that make your life easier — or harder. Good customers give you plenty of notice when they want to buy something; they buy in predictable quantities; and they're willing to pay you a reasonable amount of money. Difficult customers order everything at the last minute, place huge orders, and fight you over every penny. What kind of customer are you for your suppliers?

You might expect your suppliers to live by the saying "The customer is always right," but you need to balance that with the saying "You get what you pay for." As a customer, your purchasing behaviors affect both the costs that your supplier has to pay and your supplier's willingness to negotiate with you. For example, if you can share an accurate forecast with your supplier far enough in advance, then the supplier can safely reduce the amount of inventory it carries without concern about whether it can fill your orders — a definite win-win situation. If you understand this dynamic and use it to your advantage, your suppliers may pass some of their savings along to you. This scenario requires both sides to share some information, which requires trust.

Building and maintaining good relationships with suppliers can be a strategy for getting market intelligence and early access to new innovations. Your suppliers probably sell the same stuff to your competitors that they sell to you. So they may know a lot more about trends and new technologies in the industry than you do, but they'll only share that information if they trust you.

Here are four things that you should focus on to build trust with your suppliers:

>> **Be honest:** Share information that will help your suppliers be more successful. If there's information that you can't share, just say so. But never lie to them.

>> **Be reasonable:** Your suppliers need to make money, so try to be reasonable when negotiating prices. Make it clear that you want your suppliers to be successful, but they need to help you be successful, too.

>> **WIIFM:** Ask yourself "What's In It For Me?" (WIIFM). Be clear about what you are getting out of the relationship with a supplier and what you would like to get. The more that you benefit from doing business with a supplier, the stronger your relationship will be.

>> **WIIFT:** Ask yourself "What's In It For Them"? (WIIFT). Understand how your supplier benefits from doing business with you and investigate what other options they have. Suppliers can refuse to do business with a customer they don't like; if that happens, it could disrupt your supply chain. The more that a supplier values your business, the stronger your relationship will be.

Eventually, every supplier relationship comes to an end. Sometimes it's because the suppliers turn out to be bad partners. Other times it is simply the result of changing markets and technologies. When you need to terminate a supplier relationship, make sure that you are following the terms and conditions of any contracts that you have in place. You should consider getting your attorney involved to make sure you aren't creating liability for your company.

REMEMBER

There are two very good reasons why you should try to end supplier relationships on the best note possible:

>> You may need that supplier again in the future.

>> You don't want other suppliers to think your company is difficult to do business with.

Establishing Supply Contracts

When you enter into an agreement with a supplier, you probably create a contract. This contract may take several forms, depending on what you're buying, how much of it you're buying, and where you're buying it from.

>> **Firm-fixed-priced contract:** A firm-fixed-price contract sets out the amount of products or services that will be purchased and how much they will cost. This type of contract can include adjustments for inflation and can include incentives for meeting goals.

>> **Cost-plus contract:** A cost-plus contract reimburses a supplier for their costs and allows them to charge an additional fee. The fee is often a fixed percentage of the costs.

>> **Time and materials contract:** A time and materials contract is often used for repairs. The buyer agrees to pay the supplier set rates for the parts and labor that they use on a project.

You probably sign a time and materials contract every time you take your car in for service.

>> **Indefinite delivery contract:** An indefinite delivery contract is used when the buyer doesn't know how much they are going to order or when they will need the materials delivered. These contracts usually provide minimum and maximum quantities for the supplier but give the buyer flexibility to purchase as much or little as she needs, as long as it falls within the agreed-upon range.

Indefinite delivery contracts are useful when your production schedule is likely to vary.

Selecting contract terms

From a supply chain perspective, keep in mind two questions any time you establish the terms and conditions of a supplier contract:

>> How do you want things to work if everything goes as planned?

>> How will you handle the issues that arise if surprises occur or circumstances change?

Addressing these issues in the contract at the beginning of a relationship benefits both you and your suppliers.

You can imagine the sorts of issues that a fast-food restaurant would need to consider when establishing contract terms with the company that supplies its hamburger buns:

>> How many buns does the supplier need to deliver?

>> How much will we pay for the buns?

>> How will we and the supplier measure quality?

>> How quickly does the supplier need to deliver orders?

>> How long will the contract last?

>> Can the supplier sell the same buns to other restaurants?

>> When will we pay for the buns?

>> How will we resolve issues and disagreements?

This list isn't complete, of course, but it gives you a sense of some of the issues you need to think about when developing the terms of a contract with your suppliers.

WARNING

I'm not a legal expert, so none of this information should be treated as legal advice. Any time you enter into a contract, you should get advice from a lawyer. Making sure that your contract is written properly can protect both you and your supplier if things don't go the way you planned.

Selecting payment terms

Negotiating when to pay a supplier for the products that you purchase is a powerful tool. Managing payment terms correctly can affect the financial performance of your supply chain. Payment terms come in three main types:

>> **Payment in advance:** Some companies expect their customers to pay in advance. They want to have the money in hand before they provide a product or service to ensure that their customers pay.

>> **Payment on delivery:** A company may ask its customers to pay as soon as it delivers a product or service. With payment on delivery, there's some risk that a customer won't pay, but at least the supplier will know right away and can take immediate action.

>> **Net payment terms:** Some suppliers sell products and services and then wait to get paid later. This is a form of credit called *net payment terms.* A supplier may ship an order to a customer with the understanding that the customer

will pay the invoice within 30 days, which is called a net 30 payment term. With net payment terms, there's a higher risk that customers may not pay their invoices, which is called a *default*.

Supplier payment terms greatly affect your cash flow and working capital. The time between when you collect money from your customers and the time when you pay your suppliers is called the *cash conversion cycle*. Following are three examples that show how payment terms and the cash conversion cycle can affect your business:

» **Zero cash conversion cycle:** Suppose that you charge your customers when they place an order and that you instantly place an order with your supplier and pay for it at the same time. In other words, you get paid, and your supplier gets paid, at the instant when your customer places the order. Many consignment relationships work this way. In this case, your cash conversion cycle is zero.

» **Positive cash conversion cycle**: Suppose that you buy products from suppliers on net 30 terms and sell to your customers on net 60 terms, which means that you pay your suppliers 30 days before you get paid by your customers. In this scenario, you need to have 30 days' worth of working capital to support your sales, which is a positive cash conversion cycle.

Positive cash conversion cycles are common in all kinds of businesses, but they're expensive. The working capital may need to be borrowed from a bank that charges interest. Supply chain managers can reduce the amount of working capital that the business needs to borrow and increase profitability by shortening the cash conversion cycle.

» **Negative cash conversion cycle:** Suppose that your customers pay you for a product today but you can wait 30 days to pay your suppliers. In other words, you get to hang on to that money for 30 days, for free. Rather than paying a bank to borrow money, you can have the same bank pay you interest. Negative cash conversion cycles are rare, but they can be powerful ways for supply chains to drive value to a business.

TECHNICAL STUFF

The negative cash conversion cycle was one of the secrets to success in the early days of Dell Computer. The company required customers to pay when they placed orders but negotiated with its vendors to delay payments. In effect, Dell Computer got to keep its customers' money sitting in the bank for a month or two before paying its suppliers and actually made money from the interest.

Figure 7-5 illustrates these cash conversion cycles.

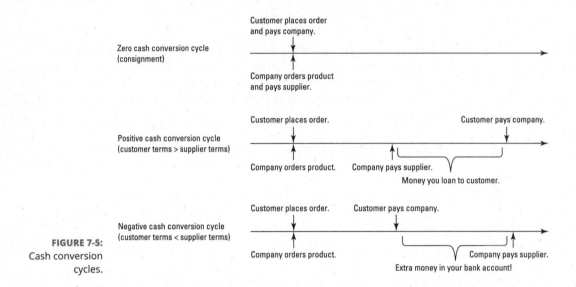

FIGURE 7-5:
Cash conversion
cycles.

At first glance, it seems obvious that you want to have short payment terms with your customers and long payment terms with your suppliers, but that strategy may not be the best choice in the long run. Extending credit to customers may be necessary for you to earn their business. If you insist on getting your customers' money up front, and your competitors offer them net 30 terms, you may lose business. On the back end, it costs your suppliers money to extend you credit, so it may look like you're getting free credit by asking your suppliers to extend their payment terms, but eventually, that cost will show up somewhere else on your income statement.

Mitigating Supplier Risks

One of the most challenging aspects of sourcing — and also one of the worst-managed — is dealing with risk. Telling whether one supplier is cheaper than another is easy, and so knowing which one costs you less money up front is also easy. But consider the cost of having a supplier that doesn't deliver on its promises and how that supplier will affect your bottom line if the materials you buy are damaged, low-quality, or counterfeit, or if they don't show up when you need them. In other words, consider the potential costs associated with supplier risk.

In general, you can think of *risk* as meaning *uncertainty*. Supply chains are full of uncertainty; an infinite number of things can happen to change the flow of money, material, and information. You're never going to identify and mitigate every risk. You can get a pretty good sense of what the most likely risks are, however, and develop strategies to minimize their effects on your supply chain.

You can easily create a good risk register (also called a risk scorecard) by using a spreadsheet program. Enter a name for the risk, the problem that it's likely to create, a number to indicate how severe that problem would be, and another number to indicate is the likelihood that the risk will occur. Given that information, the spreadsheet program can calculate a risk index so that you can focus on the risks that are most likely to occur and will have the biggest effect.

Dealing with risks

For each risk, decide how you're going to deal with it. You may think that there are lots of ways to handle a risk, but all the options fall into just four buckets. In the following list, I describe each option in terms of the risks that you encounter when you drive a car:

>> **Accepting the risk:** If you accept the risk, you know that it exists, but you're willing and prepared to live with the consequences if it occurs. There's a risk that a rock will fly up from the road and chip the paint, but you can't do much to prevent that risk, its probability is fairly small, and the cost of repairing the paint chip is fairly low. You'd probably accept that risk.

>> **Avoiding the risk:** Sometimes, you can make a choice to avoid the risk. There's a risk that if you drive through an area with road construction, you'll get caught in a traffic jam. The delay would make it take longer to get where you're going, and you'd probably burn more gasoline. Rather than deal with this risk, you probably want to choose a route that doesn't have construction, so you avoid the risk of being delayed by road construction.

>> **Transferring the risk:** There are many risks that are unavoidable but potentially expensive, and you may want to transfer those risks to someone else. For example, you could hit another car, or another car could slam into you. The cost of repairing or replacing an entire car — or of paying for an injured person's medical treatment — can be thousands of dollars. If they had to shoulder those costs, most people wouldn't be able to drive at all. Instead, they transfer that risk by buying insurance. They pay a relatively small fee to an insurance company that accepts the risk on their behalf. If an accident occurs, the insurance company agrees to pay for it.

>> **Mitigating the risk:** In many cases there are things that you can do to mitigate a risk — to make it less severe or less probable. For example, you might stop to fill up the tank before the gas gauge drops below a quarter-tank because that mitigates the risk of running out of gas. Why? Because if you run out of gas, you could waste a lot of time trying to find a gas station, get there, and get back to your car. The cost of keeping gas in the tank — maintaining some inventory — is much lower than the cost you'd incur if you ran out of gas, so you mitigate this risk by maintaining some inventory of gasoline.

Deciding which risks to manage

When you know how you'll manage risks, you have to decide which risks you need to manage. Follow these steps:

1. **Identify the process, part, or supplier that you're concerned about.**

   Enter this in the heading for register.

2. **Think about the things that could go wrong with that part or supplier.**

   In other words, list all the sources of risk or uncertainty. Don't try to judge or filter the risks; put everything in the list. Enter each of them in the column labeled "Description of Risk."

3. **Think about how these risks would affect your supply chain.**

   You're likely to find that some risks have more than one effect. If you're driving through a construction zone, the risk of getting stuck in traffic has two effects: It increases the time it takes to get to your destination, and it increases the amount of gas you burn to get there. Enter each of these of the effects in the column labeled "Description of Impact."

TIP

   When you enter this information in your risk register (refer to "Mitigating supplier risks" earlier in this chapter), put each combination of risk and effect in a separate row. If one risk has two effects, enter the same risk in both rows. If two risks could cause the same effect, list the effect in both rows.

4. **Quantify the likelihood of each risk.**

   This step can be a bit tricky, but it becomes easier with practice. Think about the probability that each risk will occur, and rank it on a scale of 1 to 10. A risk that has a high probability of occurring — meaning that you're almost sure it will happen — gets a score of 10. A risk that has a low probability of occurring — meaning that it's very unlikely to occur — gets a score of 1. Enter the probability that a risk will occur in the column labeled "Likelihood of Risk."

Most risks fall between 1 and 10, and the discussions you have with a team about the right number tell you a lot about how your team members think (see the nearby sidebar "Brainstorming risks and effects").

If a risk has a probability of 0, it isn't a risk and shouldn't be in the list.

5. **Decide how severely each impact would disrupt your supply chain.**

   A risk that would have a catastrophic effect gets a score of 10. A risk that would have a relatively minor effect gets a score of 1. Most effects fall between 1 and 10. Enter the severity of each impact in the column labeled "Severity of Impact."

6. **Multiply the probability by the impact for each risk.**

   In the column labeled Risk Index, multiply the value from the Likelihood of Risk column by the value in the Severity of Impact column. The risk index makes it easy to figure out which risks pose the greatest threats to your supply chain and where you need to focus your attention and resources. If the risk is likely to occur, and the effect would be severe, the risk index is high. If the probability that the risk will occur is low, and the effect would be minor, the risk index is low.

Figure 7-6 shows a completed risk register. In this example, the machine failure risk has the highest risk index and should be addressed first.

Item #	Description of Risk	Description of Impact	Likelihood of Risk	Severity of Impact	Risk Index (Likelihood x Impact)
1	Tornado	Shut down factory until repaired	1	10	10
2	Supplier bankruptcy	Unable to buy components	3	7	21
3	Machine failure	Unable to manufacture products	6	5	30

FIGURE 7-6:
A risk register.

BRAINSTORMING RISKS AND EFFECTS

Getting started with a list of risks and effects can be a challenge. It's common for people to have writer's block, but one of the best ways to get past it is to start writing. Another good way to build the list is to bring a few people together to talk about risks. Ask one person to serve as the recorder. Start a conversation about things that could go wrong, and make sure that the recorder keeps a list of everything the group discusses. Brainstorm and come up with as many ideas as you can. Don't let someone in the group slow the process by challenging or discounting any of the potential risks and effects. Just add each one to the list and keep going.

As the list of risks and effects gets longer, you'll start thinking more broadly about how vulnerable your supply chain is, even to things over which you have virtually no control. At some point, though, you'll have a sense that your list is good enough. You'll never be able to list every possible risk and effect, but you'll have enough to paint a good picture of your vulnerabilities.

Establishing Purchasing Ethics

Because the purchasing process involves big decisions about large amounts of money, it's important to ensure that decisions are made in a fair and ethical way. People may not always recognize ethical dilemmas, however, or may have differing senses of right and wrong. To ensure that no confusion occurs about appropriate behavior in purchasing, create a formal, written code of ethics that everyone who makes purchasing decisions is required to follow.

Your purchasing ethics policy may include the following situations:

» Accepting gifts from suppliers

» Supporting small businesses

» Dealing honestly with suppliers

» Avoiding slave labor and child labor

» Complying with laws

» Encouraging competition

» Reporting conflicts of interest

» Complying with payment terms

» Evaluating how suppliers treat employees

» Examining suppliers' wages and working hours

TIP

To find guidance on creating and implementing a purchasing ethics policy, consult a professional organization such as the Institute for Supply Management (`https://www.instituteforsupplymanagement.org`) or the Chartered Institute of Procurement and Supply (`https://www.cips.org`).

Chapter **8**

Making Your Products or Services

E very business makes something — a product or a service — and every product or service has a supply chain. This chapter describes how the steps you follow to make *anything* can be broken down into a handful of subprocesses so that you can measure and manage them effectively. In terms of a process framework such as Supply Chain Operations Reference (SCOR; see Chapter 5), *Make* refers to the group of processes that transform components into a new product or service that has value for a customer. The job of overseeing these processes is often called *operations management*.

This chapter explains how to design your operations so that you make the right number of products at the right time. First, you'll look at planning a production schedule. Then you'll examine the two main environments for making products: *discrete manufacturing*, in which items are made individually or in batches, and *continuous manufacturing*, where items are made in a stream. After that, you'll consider whether to make products before or after a customer places an order. Finally, you'll look at some of the key elements of managing quality and sustainability because they are important strategic issues that are heavily influenced by your Make processes.

Honestly, a lot of the terminology related to the Make process can be tough for folks to wrap their heads around. And different companies use the same words to mean different things. I've kept the definitions simple and provided examples based on things in your daily life, like running a fast-food restaurant. But these exact same terms and concepts are used daily in the supply chains for cars, appliances, microwave dinners, and basically every other product and service that you buy. Of course, the same ideas apply to your supply chain, no matter what type of business you are managing. So throughout the chapter, try think about how each of the topics relates to some part of your own business and whether your Make processes are aligned with what your customers truly value.

Planning and Scheduling Production

The process of making anything really starts when you decide what to make, how much to make, and when to make it. In a manufacturing company, this is (conveniently) called *production planning and scheduling.* Service companies often make life more complicated by finding creative names for this process, but most of them sound a lot like "service planning and scheduling."

TIP

If you are working in a services supply chain, try not to get hung up on the word *Make.* Just remember that the point of any Make process is to transform inputs such as raw materials and technical skills into outputs for a customer. For a doctor, the Make process would be performing a surgical procedure. For an artist it would be creating a painting.

Planning production

Before you can create a good production plan you need to take a lot of factors into account. Here are 10 examples of the kinds of information that you really, truly need to consider before you can tell whether a production plan will actually work:

- » Determine when customers need the product and if they are waiting for it now.

- » Determine how long it will take you to make the product.

- » Determine the capacity of your manufacturing process.

- » Determine the setup time required to make the product and whether that affects the setup time for other products.

- » Determine how to prioritize the order in which you'll make products.

- » Determine what parts, components, or supplies you need to have on hand so that you can make a particular product.

- » Determine whether you have the parts you need already or if you have to order them.

- » If you must order parts, determine the supplier's lead time and the shelf life of the products.

- » Identify risks that could disrupt production.

- » Determine whether you need to schedule time for breaks, holidays, changeovers, and equipment maintenance.

This isn't a complete list, but it's enough to make the point. There are so many factors to consider that production planning can quickly become overwhelming. The only way to make this work is to develop a production planning process and set some rules. However, you also need to ensure that the rules give you enough flexibility to change the plan when needed. Figure 8-1 is a high-level view of the steps involved in creating a production schedule.

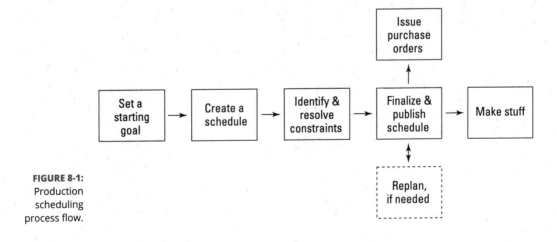

FIGURE 8-1: Production scheduling process flow.

Setting a demand goal

Production planning starts with a high-level goal: how much you want to sell. You can think of this as the "in a perfect world" scenario. If you think you'll have 1 million customers next month in your fast-food restaurant, you'd start with a demand goal of 1 million hamburgers. This high-level demand goal is called the Master Demand Schedule (MDS). It's okay if your MDS is optimistic, but try to keep it reasonable, too. There's no point in building a production plan for a sales target that you'd never be able to meet.

Creating a production schedule

After determining your demand goal, you break that sales goal down into a Master Production Schedule (MPS). In other words, building the MPS is how you to decide what you'll need to make each day to meet the MDS goal. Creating an MPS forces you to look more closely at the materials you need and when you need them. It also drives you to look at the people and equipment you have available to make your products.

As you build your MPS, you begin to uncover *production constraints,* which are bottlenecks or problems that may interfere with production. You may not be able to order as much of the raw materials as you want because your suppliers don't have enough capacity, for example. Or perhaps your manufacturing equipment can't produce the materials quickly enough. In the example of a fast-food restaurant, two obvious constraints that the MPS will need to address are space and time. There's a limited amount of room to store buns, meat patties, and lettuce, and these ingredients are perishable, so you need to use them before they spoil.

Each constraint that you find will require you to make some decisions. You need to consider whether you can do something to resolve or eliminate the constraint, such as find a new supplier or rent extra storage space. Or you may need to change your production schedule. It's common to repeat this constraint resolution process several times, because each time you change the MPS to resolve a constraint, you need to check to see whether that change affects other constraints. In other words, production scheduling is an iterative process.

Finalizing the production schedule

When you know what materials you need to order and you're confident that they can be delivered on time, you can finalize, publish, and execute your production schedule. The final production schedule gives your team their actual production targets — how much you expect to make and when you expect to make it. Your production schedule also drives purchase orders to authorize buying the components you need from your suppliers. The schedule may be broken down into jobs or batches of products that are similar or that are being made for the same customer. Once the jobs are scheduled, then you can sequence the delivery of parts so that they show up just in time (JIT) for you to use them.

TIP

Lean manufacturing often combines parts sequencing and JIT deliveries. For example, in an automotive assembly plant, there are many different kinds of upholstery for car seats. So the seats are sequenced to show up in a particular order and they are delivered to the assembly line JIT.

If everything works properly, then your production schedule won't change, and will be stable. But it doesn't always work that way. Even after the production schedule is published, there's a good chance that you may end up making changes if things don't go as you expect — if a shipment of supplies gets delayed or a machine breaks down, for example. When you revise the schedule, you may have to change the order of production jobs or adjust your production targets. Of course, this replanning also affects both your suppliers and your inventory levels, because it will change the order in which you use each component. Since so many activities are driven by the production schedule, frequent replanning can cause confusion and frustration. A production schedule that changes too often is called a nervous schedule.

TIP

Nervous production schedules create waste in a supply chain such as unnecessary work and excess inventory.

Most companies make a choice about how far in advance they can realistically change the production schedule without creating chaos for their supply chain. This threshold, usually measured in days or weeks, is called a *time fence*. For example, they might decide that it's okay to make a change to the production schedule with at least a one-week notice. In this case, it would be possible (but not desirable) to make changes to the production schedule outside of the one-week time fence. But once they cross over that time fence — once they are less than one week out from a production run — the schedule is frozen, and no more changes will be allowed.

REMEMBER

The earlier in the process you can identify a constraint and replan the production schedule, the better off you'll be. In most cases, changing the production schedule after you've already issued purchase orders for the supplies means that you'll end up with extra inventory, which increases your costs.

You can think about the challenge of production scheduling for a fast-food restaurant. Suppose that something unexpected happens: You sell fewer burgers than you expected, everyone asks for extra pickles, or there's a recall on lettuce.

In each case, you need to see whether these differences change your goals or create constraints; if they do, you'd need to replan your production schedule.

Your production targets should always be aligned with your sales goals to ensure that you aren't making too much or too little to satisfy your customers. This process is called sales and operations planning (S&OP), and it was discussed in Chapter 3.

In the old days, people prepared and updated production schedules manually, which was a complex, time-consuming process. Today, most companies update schedules automatically by using material requirements planning (MRP) software. See Chapter 12 for a more detailed explanation of MRP.

Considering capacity

Every person, every group of people, and every machine in the world has a limit to how much it can process or produce in a particular amount of time. Whether you're in the business of manufacturing bottles or delivering babies, you refer to this limit as your *capacity*. There are lots of ways to measure and define capacity, but when you strip away the fluff, there are three concepts that every supply chain manager needs to understand because they factor into your production plan: design capacity, operating capacity, and capacity utilization.

Design capacity

The *design capacity* (or *theoretical capacity*) is the maximum that a machine (or person) can possibly produce. The design capacity of your imaginary fast-food restaurant is the amount you could make if every person and every machine were running continuously, every minute of every day. That might be a whole lot of hamburgers and French fries, but it is still not infinite.

Operating capacity

Let's be real: Most processes don't actually run at their design capacity (at least not for very long!). People need to take breaks. Facilities shut down for shift changes. It takes time to perform equipment maintenance and software upgrades. When you take all these constraints into account, you end up with a new limit on how much you can make, which is much lower than your design capacity. This limit is called your *operating capacity* (or *effective capacity*).

Unless you're making only one product over and over, you probably need to shut down some machines and make changes between jobs, such as switching tools or bringing in different components. This setup time affects how much operating capacity is available for making products. And, of course, things can go wrong — a machine could break down, you could run out of inventory, or someone could be late for a shift. Any of these issues — and many others — can slow down a manufacturing process, and all of them eat away at your efficiency.

TIP

Because you could never possibly make more of a product than what your design capacity would allow, the design capacity is technically one of your production constraints. However, because operating capacity is almost always lower than design capacity, it is rare for a process to actually be constrained by the design capacity.

TIP

Operating capacity is one of the main constraints on production. In many cases there are things that you can do to increase the operating capacity, such as running extra shifts or changing your maintenance procedures. Therefore you may have some flexibility when managing the operating capacity for your production plan. A common goal for supply chain managers is to increase operating capacity, and get it as close as possible to the design capacity.

Capacity utilization

With all of the factors that can constrain production, the actual output of a manufacturing process is often just a fraction of how much you think it could make. A common way to measure production output, or **yield**, is the percentage of operating capacity that you actually use. This percentage is called *capacity utilization*. If your process is running at full speed, making as many widgets as it possibly can, then your capacity utilization is 100 percent.

TECHNICAL
STUFF

The U.S. Federal Reserve tracks industrial production and capacity utilization across various business sectors as a way to measure how well the economy is doing. You can find the latest capacity utilization rates at www.federalreserve.gov.

REMEMBER

A common goal of supply chain management is to increase capacity utilization. The more capacity you use, the more products you're producing and the more money you're able to make with the assets you have.

You can see how these concepts are related by looking at the fast-food restaurant example. The number of burgers that you actually make is your production output, which is a smaller quantity than your operating capacity, which in turn is smaller than your design capacity. Figure 8-2 illustrates the relationship of production output (capacity utilization) to operating capacity and design capacity.

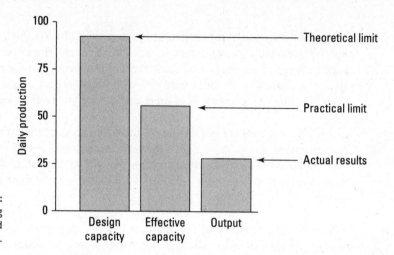

FIGURE 8-2:
Manufacturing
capacity and
output.

Increasing capacity utilization always sounds like a good idea, at first. But when you look at it more closely, sometimes it can actually increase your costs and decrease your efficiency. For example, your car probably has the capacity to drive at a 100 miles per hour. However, it gets much better gas mileage at closer to 50 miles per hour. (Let's ignore traffic laws for a second, and just focus on the mechanical issues.) In addition to burning more gas, driving your car at 100 miles per hour is going to cause many of the parts to wear out more quickly. And it gives you less time to react if there is a pothole in the road. So even though the car has the *capacity* to go faster if you need it to, you'll probably choose a slower pace for day-to-day commuting. In other words, you will decide that it is better overall to operate your car well below its design capacity.

In the same way, manufacturing processes often become less efficient when they get close to their capacity limits. One obvious reason is that equipment may wear out faster, which causes breakdowns. Also, increasing capacity utilization (in other words, making more products) can create an inventory problem if the rest of your supply chain can't keep up. (Refer to the Theory of Constraints in Chapter 4.) Your real goal as a supply chain manager is to make only as many products as your customers will buy — to provide enough supply to meet demand. If your output is high, but your sales are low, increasing manufacturing capacity utilization only means that you'll build up unneeded inventory and tie up your company's cash. And that is bad for the supply chain.

REMEMBER

The goal of production planning and scheduling is to make as many products as your customers will buy at the precise time that they need them. Building your production schedule around customers' demand and your supply chain's constraints ensures that you use your capacity efficiently while keeping your inventory as low as possible.

Identifying Manufacturing Process Types

The world of supply chain management has two types of processes for manufacturing products:

>> **Discrete:** Some products are manufactured as separate items or in batches. In other words, they're made by a *discrete* process.

>> **Continuous:** Other products can't be easily separated into individual units or batches, so they're made by a *continuous* process.

In your imaginary restaurant, for example, the burgers and fries are made with a discrete process, and the soft ice cream is made with a continuous process. Each burger and each French fry will be slightly different. But the ice cream is all mixed together. Understanding the basic differences between discrete and continuous manufacturing processes will help you think about how your supply chain operates and see ways to manage it more effectively.

Operating a discrete manufacturing process

You can find lots of examples of products manufactured with a discrete process, such as television sets, cars, guitars, furniture, and clothing. The output of a discrete manufacturing process typically is measured by the number of items produced during a certain period, usually per hour or per day. This metric is the *production rate*.

REMEMBER

Many principles of discrete manufacturing also apply to the supply chains of service companies. A call center may measure its production rate as the number of calls handled per day; a cleaning service may measure its production rate by the number of houses cleaned each week.

Discrete manufacturing usually is broken into steps that are repeated for each product. But there are two different ways to execute this work: by bringing the work to the workers (assembly line) or by bringing the workers to the work (cellular manufacturing). Figure 8-3 illustrates the difference.

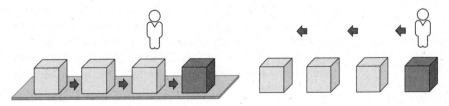

FIGURE 8-3: Assembly line vs. cellular manufacturing.

You can bring the work to the workers by using an assembly line. With an assembly line, the same production steps are repeated at each station while the products keep moving down the line from one station to the next. The time required for each step in an assembly line process is called *takt time* (pronounced *tacked time*).

Takt is the German word for the baton a symphony conductor waves around to set the tempo for an orchestra. So in the world of manufacturing, the takt time is the time required to complete each step in a process. In order to create a smooth flow on an assembly line, each of the process steps needs to have a similar takt time. Adjusting process steps to achieve consistent takt times is called *balancing* or *leveling* a line.

The time required for all the production steps to be completed, from beginning to end, is called the *cycle time.* In other words, the minimum amount of time required to make each product (or batch of products) is the cycle time. And the cycle time is calculated by adding up the takt times from all of the steps in the process.

For products that are bulky and difficult to move or that require a lot of time and customization, using an assembly line may not be the best approach. It may be easier to build the entire product in one place by bringing the tools and components to that spot. The place where these products are built is called a *manufacturing cell* (or *manufacturing stall*). so this approach is called *cellular manufacturing.* You'll find manufacturing cells in factories for big products like airplanes and mobile homes. But you may also see manufacturing cells in factories that produce small artistic items like jewelry or hand-painted crafts.

TECHNICAL
STUFF

The use of the word "cellular" in this case goes back to the days before cell phones. It's ironic, but you would never use a cellular manufacturing process for manufacturing a mass production product like a cellular phone.

Whether you're using cellular manufacturing or an assembly line, the capacity of discrete manufacturing is relatively flexible. You can operate a manufacturing line for a single shift (or even part of a shift) and then shut down the line. If you need more capacity, you can add a second or third shift to that same manufacturing line without buying new equipment or changing the manufacturing process.

On the down side, discrete manufacturing is inherently inefficient, because the equipment sits idle any time you aren't using it to make products. You pay to have the equipment 24/7, even if you only use it for part of a shift each day.

Another challenge in discrete manufacturing is that gaps occur between steps, and each step takes a different amount of time. It might take three minutes to cook a hamburger, but the next step — slapping it on a bun with ketchup and mustard — takes only a few seconds. So you could say that discrete manufacturing is "lumpy" and that the gaps in time between processes create waste and inefficiency. When applying Lean manufacturing principles, supply chain managers look for ways to reduce the gaps between process steps and even out the flow of products throughout the entire supply chain. (For more information on lean manufacturing, see Chapter 4.)

TIP

Many of the principles of Lean manufacturing can reduce the inefficiency of discrete manufacturing processes by making them behave more like continuous manufacturing processes.

Operating a continuous manufacturing process

Lots of manufacturing processes don't involve individual items. Breweries, chemical manufacturers, gasoline refineries, food-processing plants, and even electrical power plants that burn coal or natural gas are examples of businesses that use continuous processes. With a continuous process, you essentially feed material into one end and get a steady stream of product out the other end.

When they're running, continuous manufacturing processes tend to be highly efficient, because the capacity of each step in the process can be sized for the same rate of material flow, or *throughput*. Starting and stopping continuous processes, however, is often slower and more expensive than starting and stopping discrete processes.

Another common challenge in continuous manufacturing is that a there is a minimum amount of flow required for the process to work. It's like a car engine that stalls out if falls below a certain minimum speed. Also, with continuous manufacturing it is harder to switch from making one product to start making another. You probably need to shut the line down, clean out all of the equipment, and then restart the entire line. So even though they are generally more efficient when compared with discrete manufacturing, continuous manufacturing processes may not give you as much flexibility to adjust your production rate or change the types of products that you make.

Choosing Your Production Environment

The effectiveness of your supply chain ultimately determines the success of your business. In order to give customers what they want, when they want it, you need to decide whether you should make the product before customers are even ready to buy it or whether you should wait until they place an order. Choosing the right *production environment* is based on two factors: *what you're making* and *what your customers need*. There are three types of production environments to choose from:

» Make-to-stock

» Make-to-order

» Engineer-to-order

Figure 8-4 compares these three production environments and shows how each of them affects both the amount of customization that is possible and the lead time for your products.

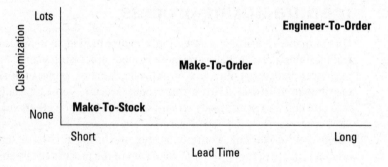

FIGURE 8-4:
Make-to-stock, make-to-order, and engineer-to-order production.

The *total lead time* for a product (also called customer response time) is the time between when a customer places an order and when you deliver the product to them. The total lead time is made up of several smaller chunks of lead time, including the time it takes to process an order, the time it takes to make a product, and the time it takes to deliver the product to the customer. In other words, total lead time includes order processing lead time, manufacturing lead time, and delivery lead time.

REMEMBER

When you decide which production environment to use, you need to consider how soon your customers need the product, how long will it take to make it, and how much customization will be required.

Make-to-stock

If your customers need a product right away, and the product doesn't require customization, you probably want to have some items premade and ready for them to buy. This approach is called *make-to-stock*. The stock — your inventory — ensures that you can fill customer orders quickly.

The biggest benefit of a make-to-stock strategy is that customers can get their orders filled immediately. Having a high level of product availability is important for keeping customers happy and growing your market share. If you don't have products available for a customer to buy, they may take their business to your competitors.

A make-to-stock strategy has some challenges, however:

» When you make a product before you receive an order, your customers need to take the product the way it is; you can't customize it for them.

» You need to forecast how much your customers will buy and when they'll buy it. In other words, you are taking a risk and speculating that there will be future demand.

» After you make products, they sit in inventory and tie up cash until they're sold, which costs your company money. (You also have to consider the costs of the warehouse space and the people required to move, manage, and maintain the inventory.)

» Inventory can be stolen or damaged, or it can become obsolete and unusable.

TECHNICAL STUFF

You'll often hear supply chain professionals talk about the amount of money lost due to shrinkage. This is a jargon term to describe products that are stolen, damaged, or wasted. These are called shrinkage because they lead to a reduction — or shrinking — of inventory.

REMEMBER

Inventory adds costs to the supply chain. But it also creates value by reducing lead times for your customer. In most cases, your goal is to maintain just enough inventory to meet your customers' needs, and nothing more.

Make-to-order

If your manufacturing lead time is shorter than your customer's required response time, you may not need to have any inventory. Instead, you can wait until an order comes in and then produce the product for your customer. This *make-to-order* strategy has many benefits over the make-to-stock approach. Make-to-order eliminates inventory and warehousing costs, thereby freeing up cash, which translates directly into increased profits.

Hamburgers are a good example of a make-to-order product. Your restaurant has all of the ingredients ready, but you wouldn't want to make hamburgers ahead of time and hope that someone will buy them. Instead, you'd wait for a customer to place an order and then cook it for them. Business cards are another good example of a make-to order environment; the printer has all of the materials ready, but they can't actually manufacture any business cards until they know what to print on them.

To apply a make-to-order approach successfully, you need to address three challenges:

>> You must know the expected customer response time.

>> Your manufacturing lead time must be shorter than your customer's requirement.

>> Your manufacturing process must be reliable and have sufficient capacity to meet customer demand.

If a customer wants orders filled in 48 hours, and making the product takes you two weeks, a make-to-order strategy clearly won't work. But if customers can wait two weeks after the order is placed, and you can make the product in 48 hours, then make-to-order is an attractive option. This strategy can reduce costs without affecting product availability.

Engineer-to-order

In some cases, customers want specific products and services that really can't be pre-planned, such as yachts, racing engines, or custom cabinets. When your customers want this type of customization, you must wait until they place an order before you even know what you'll be making. This production environment uses an *engineer-to-order* approach.

In an engineer-to-order approach, you usually don't have a lot of finished product inventory to worry about, and your customers get the product or service exactly as they want it. The bad news is that you have a longer lead time before delivering the product to the customer, and demand forecasting and production scheduling are very difficult.

PROCESS TYPES VERSUS PRODUCTION ENVIRONMENTS

You may be trying to sort out the differences between process types and production environments. *Process type* usually is determined by the type of product you're making. Discrete processes are used to make products that need to be assembled, and continuous processes are used to make products that need to be mixed, blended, or cooked. The type of production environment has to do with how much lead time your customers will accept and how much customization they require. If the lead time needs to be short, then you don't have time for customization. The production environment will be make-to-stock, and your customers will buy products from your inventory. If customers want some customization and can tolerate a longer lead time, then your production environment will be make-to-order. When your customers want something very unique and are willing to give you the time to design and make it then you'd choose an engineer-to-order production environment. The matrix in the figure gives examples of products that fit into each process type and each production environment.

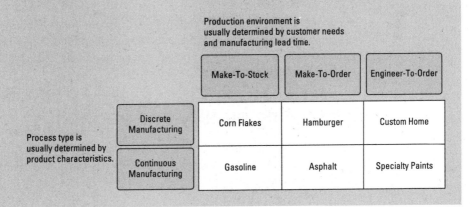

Production environment is usually determined by customer needs and manufacturing lead time.

	Make-To-Stock	Make-To-Order	Engineer-To-Order
Discrete Manufacturing	Corn Flakes	Hamburger	Custom Home
Continuous Manufacturing	Gasoline	Asphalt	Specialty Paints

Process type is usually determined by product characteristics.

Implementing Quality Control and Quality Assurance

Whether your process is continuous or discrete, and whether you operate a make-to-stock or make-to-order environment, your customers expect a certain level of quality. Ensuring that your supply chain produces high-quality products can have a big effect on the success of your business.

Considering the risks of poor quality

Here are a few examples of the potential costs of poor quality:

>> Repairing, reworking, and scrapping poor-quality products before they can be shipped

>> Returning, repairing, and replacing a defective product after it has been shipped

>> Refunding money to customers

Poor-quality products also create serious risks for your business:

>> Dissatisfied customers who won't buy your products in the future

>> Dissatisfied customers who share their negative experiences with other customers or potential customers

>> Liability for damages resulting from the performance of a defective product

You can probably think of many other ways that poor quality can suck profits from your company's bottom line. When you add together all of the costs of poor quality, you can easily see why companies are so interested in improving quality in their manufacturing processes.

Controlling quality and variability

Think about your imaginary fast-food restaurant and how your customers might describe the quality of your French fries. Here are a few things that your customers probably value:

>> Ingredients that are clean and safe to eat

>> Fully cooked

>> Portion sizes (neither too big nor too small)

>> Availability (prepared quickly and served hot)

To meet your customers' needs, you need to deliver high quality French fries every time someone places an order. Customers *might* forgive cold fries once or twice, but if they keep getting poor-quality products from you, they're going to stop coming to your restaurant.

You can measure the quality of a product — and how much variability you have in a process to make a product — through quality control (QC) and quality assurance (QA).

Quality control involves testing and measuring the outputs to make sure they are acceptable. For example, QC might involve pulling a few products off of the line every hour and taking them to the laboratory for testing, or you might test drive every new car to make sure that it works properly.

Quality assurance is about looking at each step in a production process and ensuring that things are working properly by measuring variability. QA starts with the realization that products are the output of a process. If the process is exactly the same all the time then the products will always be exactly the same. If a production process changes, even a little bit, this creates differences in the finished products.

TIP

Many companies use the terms *quality control* and *quality assurance* interchangeably, which can obviously be confusing. Strictly speaking, *quality control* is about *testing the products*, and *quality assurance* is about *managing the process*.

REMEMBER

In any manufacturing process, controlling variability is at the heart of quality assurance.

A small amount of variability in any process is natural and necessarily a problem. For example, none of the customers in a restaurant are likely to notice whether they receive their French fries in 3 minutes, or in 3 minutes and 10 seconds. There are lots of things in a production environment that can change throughout the day, such as temperature and humidity, and each of these changes results in small variations in a process. This is called *controlled variability*. The amount of variability that you choose to accept is called the *control limit* or the *tolerance*. As long as your process remains within its control limits, you can maintain a consistent level of quality for the products you make.

REMEMBER

Continuous process improvement methods like Six Sigma can help to tighten the tolerances for a process, which means that your outputs will be more consistent.

A little bit of variation may be okay, but variability becomes a problem when it is unexpected and your process exceeds your control limits. This type of variability is *random variability* (or *uncontrolled variability*). For example, a customer in your restaurant would definitely notice if everyone else got served in 3 minutes, but then it took an hour for them to get their food! If a process is generating random results, there's a good chance that many of the products won't meet your quality standards, or your customers' requirements. Investigating the root cause of uncontrolled variability often leads to the discovery of hidden risks or problems in a process. If it took an hour to cook a hamburger, then something probably went wrong in the process. Maybe the order got misplaced, or the chef took a break. You need to identify the root cause, and then you can change the process to prevent that issue from occurring in the future.

ISO 9001 CERTIFICATION

Companies that focus on implementing and managing quality in their processes often seek ISO 9001 certification. The International Organization for Standardization (ISO) manages this certification for quality management systems. Earning the ISO 9001 certification is a way to show your customers that you can make products consistently. Because quality issues have effects up and down the supply chain, many manufacturing companies also require their suppliers to be ISO 9001–certified.

The same root causes will often affect many points in a process. So identifying and eliminating the root causes of uncontrolled variability can help you fix problems throughout a supply chain.

Quality gurus also talk about common cause variability, which is similar to controlled variability, and special cause variability, which is similar to random variability. Common cause variability comes from something in the environment, like the temperature, whereas special cause variability can be assigned to a specific source or event, like a misplaced order.

Quality control and quality assurance cost money and take time, but they're insurance policies against defects that can lead to other costs. Understanding the true costs of poor quality such as rework, brand erosion, and warranty repairs, can help when calculating the benefits that can be achieved by investing in quality management.

Reducing Manufacturing Waste

When most people think about a manufacturing processes they focus on how to convert a set of inputs into a set of outputs. The important outputs, of course, are the products that you can sell to a customer. Manufacturing processes also have outputs that are not useful and end up being discarded. Anything that's left over at some point in the manufacturing process is *waste*. Whether it's metal shavings, carbon dioxide gas, used oil, or old packaging materials, this waste adds up, and it has to go somewhere. Often times, disposing of wastes is a hidden cost, but it is money that needs to be spent so that you can make your product. There are many choices that you can make when designing and managing a manufacturing process that will have a big effect on the kinds of waste that are produced, so it's best to consider this issue early on.

Here are two good reasons why you should always be looking for ways to reduce waste in your supply chain:

>> You had to pay for the materials that you're now throwing away.

>> Anything that's left over has to go somewhere. If it goes into the air, the water, or the soil, then it can be bad for the environment. And, you may need to pay someone to dispose of it.

Reducing waste can have a positive effect both on the planet and on your company's profits, because it's often the fastest, most effective way to make huge improvements. In many cases, it's as easy as looking at the waste from a manufacturing process, and asking "How could I produce the same results for my customer while eliminating this stuff from the process?"

Some supply chains use disposable corrugated packaging, for example. Replacing these cardboard boxes with reusable containers made of wood, metal, or plastic might eliminate a source of waste and save money, too. In other cases, corrugated cardboard might be a better choice because it is lighter to ship and easier to recycle.

You also can recycle some wastes by converting them into heat or electricity, which could reduce your facility's operating expenses. Some organic waste can be composted. Sometimes, water can be cleaned and recycled.

REMEMBER

The three options to keep in mind when looking at manufacturing waste are reduce, reuse, and recycle. If you can't reduce waste, maybe you can reuse it. And you should also look for ways to turn leftovers into cash. You can find companies that purchase used oil, cardboard, pallets, and scrap iron for recycling, for example. Every dollar that comes back to the company from monetizing your waste goes straight to your bottom line.

TIP

Companies sometimes overlook incredibly good opportunities to increase profits because they don't appreciate the value of reducing waste. If you want to increase profitability by $1 through sales, and your product only has a 10 percent profit margin, then you'd need to sell an extra $10 worth of products. But you could also get the same increase in profit by eliminating $10 f waste anywhere in your supply chain. Reducing waste is often a much easier answer than increasing sales.

When you're constantly looking for opportunities to reduce, reuse, and recycle throughout your supply chain, you can cut waste, save money, and minimize your impacts on the environment. That's why many companies have begun to change their management systems to look beyond just financial performance metrics. The most common approach, called *the triple bottom line*, measures the performance of a company based on social effects, financial performance, and environmental sustainability. This approach is also called the three Ps (people, profit, and planet). Some companies even publish sustainability reports along with their annual financial reports to investors.

Chapter **9**

Delivering Your Products or Services

When was the last time you picked up an item from a grocery-store shelf and asked, "How did this get here?" Most people never ask that question at all. If they did, the answer would give them a new perspective on the importance of logistics in their own supply chains.

Take the example of a simple tub of margarine. Margarine is made from vegetable oils. This complex supply chain starts with farms that harvest the vegetables and send them by truck or train to factories for processing. The oils are processed into margarine and then packaged in small containers that are placed in larger containers, which are placed on pallets. The pallets of margarine are shipped by truck or train, in refrigerated containers, to distribution centers. Then the distribution centers break the pallets apart and send smaller amounts of the margarine to the individual stores. Last but certainly not least, someone in the store unloads the truck, and the margarine is stocked on the store shelves.

Every step in this supply chain involves several players and many decisions. Every step needs to work properly; otherwise, customers won't get their margarine. Understanding how to coordinate all these logistics is a critical part of supply chain management.

This chapter examines the different kinds of transportation that you can use and explains the steps involved in moving products through a distribution center, including the different ways to replenish inventory. The end of the chapter discusses the important role that third-party logistics providers can play in your supply chain.

Understanding Modes of Transportation

Moving products from one place to another involves transportation. Products that are being transported are called cargo or freight. If you're the one sending the freight, you're the shipper. The place from which you ship the freight is the origin. If you're the one to whom the freight is being sent, you're the recipient. The place where you have the freight delivered is the destination. Each combination of an origin (O) and a destination (D) is a called an *O-D pair*, and the time that it takes cargo to get from its origin to its destination is the *transit time*.

The method you use to ship products from an origin to a destination is called the mode of transportation. When you choose a transportation mode for an O-D pair, you create a lane.

Many ways exist to ship cargo from one place to another, but seven primary modes of transportation cover the vast majority of logistics scenarios:

>> Pipeline

>> Ocean

>> Barge

>> Rail

>> Trucks

>> Parcel

>> Airplane

In addition to these seven transportation modes is *multimodal*, in which modes are combined to move a product from origin to destination. Moving a shipment from one mode to another is called *transloading*. A shipping container may be loaded onto a truck, transloaded to a ship, unloaded on a train, and delivered to its destination, for example.

Pipeline

For liquids and gases, pipelines are often the cheapest, safest, and most reliable form of transportation. Most people are familiar with the pipelines that deliver water and natural gas to homes. On a larger scale, pipelines are used around the world to transport huge amounts of water, petroleum, gasoline, and natural gas.

Ocean

For most products moving from one continent to another, cargo ships or freighters are likely to be the lowest-cost option. Even though most freighters are powered by diesel engines, they're still commonly called steamships. The companies that operate these cargo vessels are called steamship lines.

There are different kinds of ships that are designed to carry specific kinds of cargo. Depending on the kinds of materials flowing through your supply chain, you may rely on several kinds of cargo ships. The most common freighters these days are container ships; bulk carriers; tankers; and roll-on, roll-off vessels.

Cargo that isn't liquid is called dry goods cargo, and dry goods can be shipped in bulk or placed in shipping containers. Container ships are designed to carry break bulk dry goods that are loaded in standardized sea containers. Bulk carriers, called bulkers, haul bulk dry goods that don't need to be placed in containers, such as ores. Tanker ships haul liquids, especially petroleum and liquefied natural gas. Roll-on, roll-off vessels, called *ROROs*, are used to transport cars and other large items that need to be driven or dragged on and off the ship.

Rail

For big, heavy cargo that needs to travel long distances over land, railroads are often the way to go. The type of railroad car you use depends on the type of cargo you're shipping. Boxcars are enclosed, providing the greatest flexibility and protection for cargo (see Figure 9-1). Refrigerated boxcars are used for food products that need to be temperature-controlled. Hopper cars are used for bulk cargo such as grain and coal. Tankers haul liquids and compressed gases. Flatcars haul just about everything else.

FIGURE 9-1:
A boxcar.

BREAK BULK CONTAINER SHIPPING

There are two kinds of dry goods cargo: bulk and break bulk. Bulk dry goods are commodities like coal and iron ore that can be poured into the ship's storage area, called the *hold*. Break bulk dry goods are placed into containers. In the old days, shippers put break bulk cargo in barrels, buckets, bags, and just about every other kind of custom-made packaging that you can imagine. This meant there was a huge amount of manual labor involved in loading a ship with these individual packages, and that created many jobs for longshoremen and stevedores. Since the 1950s, a growing amount of this break bulk freight has been transported by specialized container ships in standardized 20- and 40-foot sea containers (see the figure). The sea containers can be quickly loaded and unloaded from a ship using gantry cranes, which has greatly increased the speed and efficiency of global supply chains.

The size of a container ship is measured by the number of 20-foot containers that it can carry. The unit of measure for container ships is 20-foot equivalent units (TEUs). One 40-foot container takes the same amount of room as two 20-foot containers, of course. The largest container ships can carry almost 20,000 TEUs, but these ships are too large for many ports and canals.

If you ship an entire container from one destination to another, the transportation mode is called full container load (FCL). Sometimes, several smaller shipments are combined in a single container; this mode is called less than container load (LCL). Because it's complicated to combine multiple shipments in one container, LCL tends to be more expensive than FCL.

When you send shipments by rail, you're at the mercy of the railroad's schedule and the locations of the railroad tracks. Your car will get tied with other cars that are heading in the same general direction, and they will need to stop along the way to drop off some cars and pick up others. Your car may get dropped off and end up sitting somewhere for quite a while, waiting for another train to pick it up and take it on the next leg of its journey. The result is that rail cargo is often slow, and transit times can be unpredictable.

For a train to pick up and deliver cars, it needs railroad tracks. Many factories and distribution centers that ship a lot of cargo on trains have their own set of tracks installed, called *rail spurs.* If no rail spur exists, the cargo may have to be loaded on trucks to be delivered to a railroad ramp — a facility that railroads use to move cargo between trucks and trains.

Truck

One of the most common ways to ship cargo overland is to use big trucks. Some people call these trucks 18-wheelers, but the professionals refer to them as tractor-trailers. The companies that operate these big rigs are called carriers. The truck itself is a tractor or a power unit, and the trailer is called . . . well, a trailer.

The amount of cargo that a single truck can carry is limited by two things: size and weight. Trailers have to be small enough to fit under bridges and short enough to turn corners. Also, trailers can't be so heavy that they damage the roads that they run on, and weather conditions such as freezing and thawing can change the strength of a road. So there are regulations that limit the amount of weight you can load onto a trailer, and these might change depending on your location and the time of year. Regulations also govern how long truck drivers can spend behind the wheel and how often they need to stop for breaks.

Two trucking modes are common in the United States: full truckload (FTL) and less than truckload (LTL). Even though the trucks and trailers look virtually identical, the process and the pricing for FTL and LTL are different.

With FTL, you can choose any origin and destination, and generally pay a flat rate per mile. It doesn't matter whether you're shipping a single shoebox or enough shoeboxes to fill the trailer to the top; you pay the same price either way. Therefore, it's in your best interest to fill your trailers as full as possible. In other words, you should maximize the utilization of your trailer capacity.

TIP

Because FTL shipments travel directly from the origin to the destination, without stopping in between, they generally are the fastest and most reliable way to ship a load.

With LTL, however, your cargo is combined with other shippers' cargo in the same trailer. You're only charged for the amount of capacity you're using in the trailer. Depending on the carrier, you'll be charged for some combination of the weight and the dimensions of your shipment, as well as the distance over which it's being sent.

FTL is more economical for large shipments, and LTL is better for small shipments. It is common to set a threshold weight to decide which mode you should use for a shipment. Many shippers use 15,000 pounds as their threshold. Any shipment that is lighter than 15,000 pounds should be LTL, and any shipment heavier than this should be FTL.

Trucking prices are a function of supply and demand, and they change all the time. Trucking prices are also different depending on origin and destination. A shipment from Spokane to Savannah could cost more than a shipment from Savannah to Spokane.

TIP

Trucking prices can change over time. When prices go up because demand for trucks is outpacing carriers' supply, you don't have much choice but to pay the higher price. Otherwise, your freight will get left behind while your carriers go where they can make more money. When prices are going down, your carriers may still try to collect the highest amount they can from you. The price that you would pay to hire a truck today is called the *spot market rate*. If you ship frequently you can negotiate lower rates, called *contracted rates*, with a carrier. Negotiating rate contracts with trucking carriers provides some protection against price swings, but those contracted rates might not be honored if the market price for trucking goes too high, too quickly. If you do a lot of shipping by truck, it's a good idea to regularly compare the rates you're paying with the amounts that other shippers are paying. Two companies that provide this benchmark data are Cass Information Systems, Inc. and Chainalytics. This can help to ensure that you aren't paying more than you should, and can also show if your rates are too far below the market.

Parcel

If you're sending a relatively small load, such as a couple of boxes, you'll probably choose a parcel carrier. In the United States, the parcel market is dominated by four companies: United Parcel Service (UPS), FedEx, DHL, and the U.S. Postal Service (USPS). The price you pay for a parcel shipment is determined by four things: weight, dimension, O–D pair (refer to "Understanding Modes of Transportation" earlier in this chapter), and speed. If you're sending a big, heavy box far away and need it to arrive tomorrow, that shipment will be expensive. If you're shipping a small, light box across town and don't care when it arrives, that shipment will be relatively cheap.

TYPES OF TRAILERS

The three types of trailers that are most common in the United States are dry vans, flatbeds, and refrigerated trailers.

Dry vans are basically big aluminum boxes with wheels on the bottom. You can ship virtually anything in a dry van as long the cargo fits inside and isn't too heavy. Because the doors are in the back of the trailer, you have to load from front to back; you can't get to the cargo in the front of the trailer until you unload everything behind it.

Flatbeds are good alternatives for cargo that doesn't need protection from the elements and that's easier to load and unload from the side. For example, it's a lot easier to load long pipes from the side of a flatbed than it is to push them into the back of a dry van.

For perishable foods, you need *refrigerated trailers* (or, as we say in the biz, reefers). Reefers are similar to dry vans, except that they are insulated and have a refrigeration unit mounted in the front that cools the air inside.

TIP

With the rise of e-commerce, parcel shipping has become much more important for many retail supply chains. As more customers order products online and have them delivered to their homes, retailers are spending more money on parcel shipping. If you're in the retail business, review your parcel rates on a regular basis to understand how much you're spending and where you have opportunities to lower costs.

Air

For cargo that needs to travel long distances quickly, the best option usually is an airplane. (See Figure 9-2.) Generally speaking, heavy items cost more to ship by air than light items do, which means that it's easier to justify the cost of air freight for small, light items such as cellphones than it is for heavy products such as tractor parts. Nonetheless, you may need an item so urgently that you're willing to pay the high cost of air freight. Air cargo is often loaded into special containers called *igloos* that are designed to protect both the cargo and the airplane.

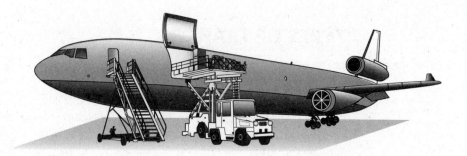

FIGURE 9-2:
Air cargo.

Selecting Modes of Transportation

Managing logistics includes selecting your modes of transportation. Your choice of transportation mode for your freight shipments depends on three factors:

» **Product characteristics:** You need to think about what modes make sense for the product that you are shipping, and you also should consider the type of container that you need to ship it in. For example, small, light, and valuable products can be shipped cheaply by air. But air freight is usually not a practical choice for big, heavy, and low value products. LTL may be cheaper than FTL, but your freight is more likely to be damaged because it will be loaded and unloaded several times during its journey. Some food products can be shipped in a dry van, and others require a reefer. Some products, such as lumber and pipes, are easier to load and unload from a flatbed than from a dry van trailer.

» **Facility characteristics:** You need to consider the design and capabilities of the facilities that the product will flow through. This includes the origin and destination facilities, and the distribution centers, ports, and cross-docks in between. Some facilities have rail spurs, but many don't. There are different designs and heights for loading docks in facilities. And every distribution center has different material handling equipment. You might find a situation where you could save money shipping a 10,000 pound load by LTL, but because the dock at the destination is the wrong height you need to ship the load FTL instead.

» **Time constraints:** You also need to factor in issues related to time. Naturally, speed is an important consideration in transportation; faster modes usually cost more money. But spending more money on transportation can have other benefits, too. For example, it is relatively cheap to ship computers in sea containers that take 30 days to cross the ocean. But this means that customers have to wait a long time for their computers to arrive, and they may decide to buy from a competitor, instead. Meanwhile the shipper's working capital is tied in this inventory that is out on the ocean. Shipping those same computers by air, while more expensive, could increase revenues and decrease inventory costs.

By evaluating these factors, you can look at the costs for each transportation mode to determine which one makes the most sense for a particular shipment — in other words, which lane provides the most value for the lowest price. You can create a document called a *routing guide* that specifies rules about which modes to use and which carriers to select based on factors such as the type of cargo, the size of the load, and the O–D pair.

If you don't ship much cargo, you're going to have to pay market rates for your freight. If you ship often, you may be able to negotiate a better price from your carriers. These negotiations lead to contracts, and contracted rates can save you a lot of money on transportation.

If you're a large shipper, you may be able to get carriers to bid against one another to give you the lowest price. Carriers base their bids on the location of the O–D pairs and the amount of freight you expect to ship. In other words, bids are based on the expected freight volume for each lane. The process of picking up a load at Point A and dropping it off at Point B seems to be pretty straightforward, but carriers also need to find a customer that will pay them to pick up a load at Point B and bring it back to Point A. This arrangement is called a *backhaul.* If your carriers think that they can find backhauls to match to your loads, they'll offer to move your freight for a lower cost. If the carrier can't find a backhaul, and their truck has to return empty, the carrier charges you for mileage in both directions.

Although one mode or another may look best on paper, two practical challenges can catch you by surprise and create problems for your supply chain:

>> Whether the mode you want to use is available for your origin and destination. (You can't ship something by railroad if no railroad tracks are nearby.)

>> Whether capacity in your chosen mode is available. (You can't ship something by truck if no trucks or drivers are available.)

Managing Warehousing and Inventory

In virtually every supply chain, gaps exist between when something is made and when a customer is ready to buy or receive it. Those gaps mean that products end up sitting around. The problem is that someone owns those products and has money tied up in them. In addition, someone needs to keep track of where those products are and protect them from damage (and perhaps even theft). In other words, even when products are sitting around in a warehouse or distribution center, they still cost a lot of money. That's why inventory management is so important.

The goal of inventory management is to balance the needs of your customers with the cost of meeting their needs. The higher your customers' expectations are, the more you'll need to spend on inventory to meet their needs, and the more they'll need to pay you to have those needs met.

Suppose that you run a fast-food restaurant. You know that it's very important to never, ever run out of French fries. You have to decide how many French fries you need to keep in inventory: enough for an average week, perhaps, or enough for the busiest week you've ever had. The only real way to guarantee that you'll never run out of French fries would be to have an infinite amount of inventory, which would be silly, so you have to determine some reasonable target for inventory. That amount depends on demand (how much your customers are going to buy) and supply. If you know that your suppliers can ship a load of French fries in 24 hours, you don't need to keep much inventory in your restaurant. But if it takes your supplier a week to send you a new shipment, you probably need to have more inventory on hand as a buffer against an upward spike in demand.

You can think about inventory in terms of the chart in Figure 9-3. Every time a new shipment of French fries arrives, the amount of inventory goes up. As you sell French fries to customers, inventory gradually goes down. You need to make sure that a new shipment shows up before your inventory level reaches zero; otherwise, you'll have customers who don't get their French fries. This situation is called a *stockout*, and it creates two problems:

>> It's a lost sale. (You've lost out on money that you could have earned.)

>> It makes your customers unhappy. (Unhappy customers stop buying from you and also tell their friends about their lousy experience.)

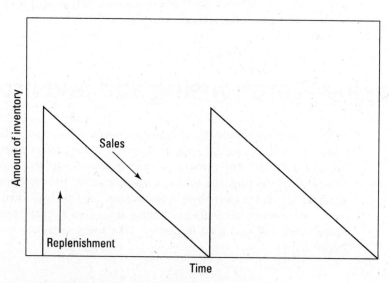

TIP

Stockouts are major challenges that often go unrecognized. Analyzing the sales that a company makes is easy, but discovering the sales that the company missed because of stockouts is hard.

Any store, factory, or distribution center employs eight high-level processes for physical inventory:

» Receiving

» Put-away

» Inventory counts

» Picking

» Packing

» Shipping

» Yard management

» Over, short, and damage

Receiving

When products arrive at a facility, someone needs to let them in. The process for accepting inventory when it arrives is called *receiving*. Receiving often involves scheduling appointments for deliveries to occur, along with unloading the goods and performing a quality inspection.

Receiving is often done at a loading dock — a part of the facility that's designed to make loading and unloading freight on trucks or railcars easy. In addition to unloading physical goods, receiving includes doing the paperwork and making computer entries to add the inventory to your records.

Put-away

After products have been received and passed a quality inspection, they need to be stored so that you can find them when you need them. This process is called *put-away*. The spot where you store a particular product is called a *location*. Distribution centers often have thousands of locations, all managed by a warehouse management system (WMS). (There's more information about WMS systems in Chapter 12.) Because products have different characteristics (dimensions, weights, and so on), dividing your locations often makes sense. One section of a warehouse might have small locations for light items; another area may have large locations on the floor for heavy items. This type of division is called *slotting*. In order to minimize the distance that people will travel, you should lay out a distribution center so that the products you ship most frequently are easiest to get to and the products you ship less often are farther away.

Inventory counts

Inventory is money, so anyone who's looking at your business from a financial perspective wants to make sure that she knows how much money you have and where it's located. Periodically, you need to perform physical inventory counts to make sure that your records are accurate.

There are two common approaches to physical inventory counts. The traditional approach is to shut down a facility during a slow time of year to count everything, one item at a time. This process is slow, expensive, and (unfortunately) not very accurate. The people who count the inventory may make mistakes along the way, so instead of fixing the inventory records, you may actually create some new inaccuracies. Therefore, many companies have switched to cycle counting, in which they divide the facility and count a little bit of it at a time throughout the year. By the end of the year, the company has done at least one physical inventory count in each section of the facility and corrected any errors that it found. Generally, cycle counting is more efficient and accurate than traditional physical inventory counting.

Inventory counts can be important for accountants, who want to make sure that the numbers they see on the books line up with what's happening in the store. Inventory counts are also useful for logistics personnel to confirm that inventory isn't being lost, damaged, or stolen. When inventory disappears for unexplained reasons, that disappearance is called *shrinkage*. Shrinkage is part of the game of inventory management, but it's important to measure shrinkage and keep it as low as possible.

Picking

When a customer wants a product that you've been storing in your distribution center, you need to pick that item off the shelf (or off the floor) and get it ready for shipping. Depending on how big your distribution center is, picking can take a while. (Many distribution centers cover more than 1 million square feet.) If two customers order the same product, you want to pick both items at the same time. And if a single customer orders two products, you want to pick both products during the same trip. When you think about how much time it takes to travel between where items are stored and where they're packaged for shipment, you see how important — and inefficient — picking can be.

The good news is that technologies introduced in the past few years make picking more efficient. A warehouse execution warehouse execution system (WES) uses sophisticated routing algorithms to translate customer orders into pick paths that minimize time and distance for the people or robots that will pick the orders. Pick-to-light systems and other displays give pickers visual cues that help them work faster and more accurately. Pick-to-voice systems have conversations with pickers, telling them where to go and what to pick, and confirming that they've done the work correctly. Picking is a great example of how people and technology work side by side in a supply chain to improve efficiency. There's more information about WES systems in Chapter 12.

Packing

When you're going to send something to a customer, you need to make sure that it will arrive in good condition, and packaging is the key. Packaging is a form of protection; it's like an insurance policy against all the handling and environmental threats that your product will face from the time it leaves your facility until the time your customer is ready to use it.

Choosing the right packaging for a shipment depends on the products, the shipping method, and the destination. The right packaging method is the one that ensures that your product arrives in good condition for the lowest cost.

By far the most common form of packaging is cardboard, also known as corrugated fiberboard or just corrugate. Corrugate is cheap, strong, and light, so it's a perfect material for packaging all kinds of products. Some products can still get damaged if they move around inside a cardboard box, however. One solution is to add filler materials such as packing paper, packing peanuts, or bubble wrap.

If the products you're shipping are sensitive to moisture, you may also need to use an anticorrosion coating, special wrapping, or moisture-absorbing packets. Electronic products are sensitive to static electricity, so these products require special protection against electrostatic discharge.

Shipping

You have lots of ways to ship a product from one place to another. The mode of transportation you choose determines how you need to prepare the freight for shipment, including getting the paperwork and labeling correct. The paperwork for shipping a domestic package via a parcel carrier is very different from the paperwork for shipping internationally on a container ship.

When you arrange to ship products to someone else, you need to agree on details, such as where it will be picked up, where it will be dropped off, who will pay duties, who will pay for insurance, and who will pay the shipping costs. The contract between a shipper and a carrier which specifies the terms of their agreement is called a *bill of lading* (BoL). The BoL is issued by the carrier to the shipper and serves as a receipt to prove that the carrier has picked up the material and agreed to deliver it.

To avoid confusion, the 11 most common combinations of these options are defined by a shorthand called International Commercial Terms (Incoterms). Each Incoterm is a three-letter code that represents a particular shipping arrangement, so when you specify the Incoterm it immediately becomes clear who will pay for each part of the shipping process. For example, the DDP (short for Delivered Duty Paid) Incoterm means that everything — including shipping costs and all duties — will be paid by the shipper, whereas the DAP (short for Delivered at Place) Incoterm means that shipping will be paid by the seller, but duties will be paid by the recipient.

Incoterms are used around the world and are periodically updated by the International Chamber of Commerce. The latest update to Incoterms was published in 2010 and is available at `https://iccwbo.org/resources-for-business/incoterms-rules/incoterms-rules-2010/`.

Some products, such as alcohol and tobacco, require special licenses or permits. Other products are subject to trade restrictions when they're shipped to another country. Also, some products are hazardous and may not be accepted by a particular carrier. Getting all these shipping details right requires communication between the seller, the buyer, and each carrier that handles the freight while it is in transit. In the best cases, mistakes and miscommunications can cause delays which prevent products from reaching customers quickly and safely. In the worst cases, poor management of shipping processes could lead to lawsuits and fines.

Yard management

An important, often-overlooked aspect of managing a distribution facility is *yard management*, which is the process of tracking the trailers in your parking lot. To understand why yard management is such an important part of inventory management, you first have to realize that carriers have two ways to deliver and pick up your freight:

>> **Live load and unload:** A carrier shows up, unloads your freight from its trailer, and then leaves. Another carrier backs up to your loading dock, puts your cargo on its trailer, and carries it away.

The good part of live loading and unloading is that it keeps your freight moving. The bad part is that the truck has to sit and wait while it's being loaded.

>> **Drop and hook:** With drop and hook, when a truck arrives at the destination, it drops off the trailer and leaves. You can load a trailer and have it ready for the truck to hook up and haul away when it arrives.

Drop and hook is much faster for the truck than live load and unload, and it can be a better choice for making the supply chain run smoothly. The main problem is that when you're using a drop-and-hook system, you have inventory sitting in trailers in your yard.

Managing inventory in the yard is just as important as managing the inventory inside your distribution center.

Over, short, and damaged

When you have lots of inventory, either in a store or in a warehouse, lots of things can go wrong. Shipments may not have the right number of units in them, for example, or they could get damaged somewhere along the supply chain.

To deal with these issues, you should have an over, short, and damage (OS&D) process. A good OS&D process plays two important roles:

>> It allows you to spend the time you need to deal with exceptions without interfering with the normal flow of products and information.

>> It allows you to fix problems efficiently and maintain accurate records of how they've been resolved.

You may discover an OS&D issue when you receive products in a store or distribution center, or when you're selling or shipping a product. Also, while that material is in your facility, it may be dropped or otherwise abused.

Establishing Inventory Ordering Policies

Trying to keep the right amount of inventory on hand is a tricky business. Keep too much inventory, and you're wasting money by tying up working capital. Keep too little inventory, and you'll miss out on revenue because you won't have anything to sell to your customers. Two of the most important decisions you can make are when to order more inventory and how much to order. The approach you use to make that decision is called your inventory policy.

Start with the question of when to order more inventory from your suppliers. You may need to place an order when your current inventory levels drop below a certain level, in which case the current inventory level is the trigger for your inventory policy. Or you may want to order inventory on a set schedule, such as once a week, in which case your inventory policy is built on periodic orders. Triggering orders based on inventory levels is usually more efficient than periodic orders. But suppliers often schedule deliveries periodically because it is more convenient. So you need to understand the dynamics of a particular supply chain to make the best decision about which inventory trigger to use.

The next question is how much to order. A mathematically precise approach to choosing the perfect order quantity, or lot size, is called the economic order quantity (EOQ). The EOQ formula balances the cost of placing an order against the cost of holding inventory. This works well on paper but usually needs to be tweaked to work in the real world. For example, you may calculate that your EOQ is 15 widgets, but discover that widgets actually come in packages of 20. You also need to consider other factors when deciding how much to order, such as when a big promotion is coming up and whether you expect to have increases or decreases in demand for a product.

The items that are managed by an inventory policy are called stock-keeping units, or SKUs (rhymes with *clues*). Suppose that your distribution center handles the same type of toothpaste in three sizes. Each size is a separate SKU.

Establishing and implementing inventory policies can become complicated. Imagine what it might be like to optimize the inventory policies for 10,000 SKUs at the same time! For that reason, inventory policies usually are managed automatically by a WMS.

TECHNICAL
STUFF

One of the important innovations in the Lean philosophy (which is covered in more detail in Chapter 4) is an approach to inventory ordering called *kanban*. In a kanban system, you pick a lot size for each SKU, and the lot size never changes. When you use all the items in a lot, another full lot is waiting behind it. When you start pulling from that second lot, the system automatically places an order for another lot. A kanban system is the same thing as a policy that's triggered at a certain inventory level and has a fixed order quantity (lot size). The kanban system is simple, and it prevents many expensive mistakes (such as overordering and stockouts) that can occur with more sophisticated inventory policies. kanban systems help to ensure that inventory arrives when it is needed, and not before, so it is a form of just In time (JIT) replenishment.

Selecting Material Handling Equipment

Many tools and technologies are available to help increase the safety and efficiency of moving and storing products. Industrial engineering expert Dr. Michael Kay of North Carolina State University created a material handling equipment taxonomy that classifies these tools in five categories:

>> **Transport equipment:** Transport equipment includes anything that's used to move a product from one place to another. Forklifts are common types of transport equipment. Conveyors and cranes are also common, especially in automated facilities.

>> **Positioning equipment:** Positioning equipment moves products over small distances, such as within a particular work area. This type of equipment might be used to elevate a product so that the person who's packaging it can stand in a more comfortable position.

>> **Unit load formation equipment:** Combining several items into a single container or unit load can make it easier to move them, but when you combine several products on a pallet, you need ways to hold them together. Clear shrink wrap and packing straps are two common examples of unit load formation equipment.

TECHNICAL STUFF

When you're shipping freight, combining smaller units into bigger ones reduces the number of steps required to move them. When products are bundled together into a single unit, like when they are placed on a pallet, they are called a *unit load*.

>> **Storage equipment:** Storage equipment enables you to increase the amount of material that you keep in a particular area: your storage capacity. Real estate is expensive, so businesses often increase the amount of storage capacity in a distribution center by building racks and mezzanines like the ones shown in Figure 9-4. Adding a rack with three levels quadruples the amount of material you can store in the same floor space, but to access the higher levels of the rack, you need transport equipment that can reach it. A mezzanine provides a whole other floor for storing materials. Mezzanines are generally used to store small, light items that people walk around to pick.

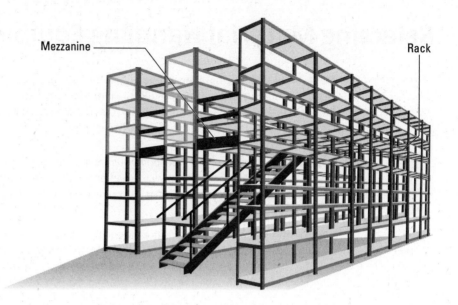

Mezzanine ———

Rack

FIGURE 9-4:
Storage racks and mezzanine.

TECHNICAL STUFF

In automated facilities, the storage equipment may also handle transport, picking, and put-away. These systems are called automated storage and retrieval systems (AS/RS). AS/RS systems can work around the clock and tend to be much faster than their human counterparts. These systems are expensive, however, and they generally aren't very flexible. If your volumes go up significantly in a few years, your AS/RS may become a bottleneck.

>> **Identification and control equipment:** Identification and control equipment helps you keep track of inventory. This area of inventory management has advanced rapidly in the past few years. Bar codes are common, and reading them requires bar code printers and readers. Other common methods are radio frequency identification (RFID) and drones.

TECHNICAL STUFF

RFID tags are small electronic chips that store identification data (like a serial number) and then communicate wirelessly with devices called RFID readers. RFID tags are now common in everyday things like credit cards, passports, and car keys, but they are also used to track products in the supply chain. Retail stores and distribution centers can use RFID to track the location of products and to improve the accuracy of their inventory counts. Some companies are planning to attach RFID readers to drones, which would fly around inside of a distribution center or a trailer yard performing fully automated physical inventory counts.

TIP

You can read more about Kay's material handling equipment taxonomy at www.mhi.org/cicmhe/resources/taxonomy.

Managing and Filling Orders

An important part of logistics is understanding how your customers order products or services from you. Some methods include

>> Ordering via your website

>> Calling an account manager

>> Using an inventory system to automatically trigger an electronic order

Even if you're communicating electronically, it helps to think about an order as if you were preparing a written sales order (like the one in Figure 9-5) to send your customer that lists the things they have purchased. Each item that a customer orders goes on a separate line of the sales order. Ordering multiples of the same item just changes the quantity shown on that line. But if they order two or more SKUs, each one of these items goes on a separate line. When you're measuring your success rate in filling customer orders, you can use lines (the percentage of lines you were able to ship) or orders (the percentage of complete orders you were able to fill). Since you need to fill every line in order to fill a complete order, achieving a high fill rate for orders is much more difficult than getting a high fill rate for lines.

Item Number (SKU)	Description	Quantity	Price	Amount
1A1	Lightbulbs	5	$1.00	$5.00
2B2	Batteries	10	$2.25	$22.50
3C3	Flashlights	3	$10.00	$30.00

FIGURE 9-5: Sample sales order.

In many cases, orders can be filled with products that are held in inventory. When not enough products are available to fill an order, that item is back-ordered. In a back-order situation, you can't send a shipment to your customer until you make more products or get a replenishment from your supplier.

Manufacturers, retail distribution centers, and e-commerce fulfillment centers all receive orders from customers, but there are differences in the way that these orders are placed and filled:

>> **Manufacturing and wholesale:** In manufacturing and wholesale supply chains, customer orders often come in the form of purchase orders (POs). A PO is a contract in which a buyer agrees to pay its supplier for delivering a product or service. A PO can be a paper document, or it can be transmitted electronically.

DISTRIBUTION CENTERS VERSUS FULFILLMENT CENTERS

Traditional distribution centers are often designed around pallets because unit loads are an efficient way to move products. A distribution center might receive a unit load containing 100 widgets and then use a forklift to move that pallet to a storage location on the floor or in a rack. When a customer places an order, the pallet is retrieved by a forklift, loaded onto a truck, and shipped to the customer. This is a simple and efficient process: Costs are minimized because the entire pallet of widgets is one line on a customer order and very little labor is required.

But for an e-commerce fulfillment center there is a lot more work involved. Rather than shipping the entire pallet, a fulfillment center ships widgets out one at a time to 100 different customers. In other words, there are 100 different customer orders to fill. That means workers make 100 trips to the location where the pallet is stored, picking one widget each time. Obviously, a lot more labor is required in a fulfillment center than in a traditional distribution center, which makes the fulfillment center much more expensive to operate. It also means that you need to slot your storage locations so that people can reach the products easily. Because you have more people walking around, you need to design traffic patterns in the facility that protect pedestrians from forklifts.

E-commerce is growing quickly, many companies have introduced software and robots that automate much of the work of picking, packing, and shipping individual items to customers. Finding new ways to improve the efficiency of e-commerce fulfillment is one of the hot topics among supply chain management professionals.

>> **Retail:** For distribution centers that serve retail stores and restaurants, orders can be triggered in a variety of ways. You might receive a PO from a store, but if the store and the distribution center are part of the same company, the ordering process may be informal. The distribution center may be able to monitor the store's sales and send replenishments automatically. This approach is an example of vendor-managed inventory, which is discussed in Chapter 15. In some cases, the central distribution center may even push new products and promotions out to a store without the store asking for them.

>> **E-commerce:** One interesting supply chain challenge that has emerged in the past few years is managing e-commerce orders. Of course, e-commerce orders are placed online by customers around the world, and the orders are usually for a small quantity of products. Most traditional distribution environments were built to increase efficiency by using unit loads to ship products to

a limited number of sites. But for e-commerce order fulfillment you need the flexibility to pick, pack, and ship single items efficiently, which requires a different approach to facility layout and slotting.

Leveraging Third-Party Logistics

Logistics can be complicated and expensive. You probably couldn't find a single company anywhere that handles all the logistics for its supply chain. Instead, many companies hire other companies that specialize in logistics. Using a third-party logistics provider (3PL) is a strategy that can lower costs and improve service for you and your customers.

Following are some common types of 3PLs:

>> **Asset-based 3PL:** A company that handles trucking

>> **Non-asset-based 3PL:** A company that handles warehousing

>> **Value-added service:** A company that handles kitting, packaging, or returns processing

>> **Freight forwarding service:** A company that helps navigate the movement of freight between carriers

>> **Customs brokerage service:** A company that works with foreign governments to move freight across borders

>> **Flexible workforce or workforce augmentation service:** A company that provides temporary workers to reduce the need for full-time employees

TIP

Any company can call itself a 3PL. The term is just a buzzword; it means that the company can help with some part of your logistics process.

Chapter **10**

Managing Product Returns and Reverse Supply Chains

S upply chains don't always flow in one direction, and they don't have to end at your customer. There are many supply chains that operate in reverse, with products flowing upstream from a customer back to a supplier, but reverse supply chains often don't get as much attention as manufacturing and retail supply chains.

Companies can even use reverse supply chains as a way of increasing sales, growing market share, and lowering their manufacturing costs. Reverse supply chains also play an important role in reducing the environmental impacts of a product. This chapter covers reverse supply chains and explains how managing them effectively can provide benefits to businesses and their customers.

Growing Revenues with Easy Returns

A well-managed reverse supply chain can increase customer loyalty and grow sales revenues. Some online retailers have built their business strategy on offering their customers free returns. Zappos.com, the online shoe store, is an example. If you order a pair of shoes on the company's website and decide not to keep it you can send the shoes back at no additional cost. Free returns are a great deal for customers for customers, eliminating the risk of getting stuck with a pair of shoes that don't fit properly or that look better in a picture than they do in real life. As a result, the free return policy has played a key role in the Zappos.com strategy to grow sales revenues and increase market share.

But the return service isn't actually free. Zappos.com still has to pay for the return shipping, of course, and it needs to process the returned shoes to make sure that they're in like-new condition. After that, the company needs to get the returned shoes ready for another customer and restock them in inventory.

Think about some of the costs involved in this "free" return transaction:

>> Shipping to customer

>> Return shipping from customer

>> Inventory carrying costs from the time the product is shipped until it's restocked

>> Receiving processing

>> Performing quality inspection

>> Processing customer refunds

>> Repackaging

>> Restocking

All these costs must be absorbed in the price that the company charges for the percentage of shoes that don't get returned. In other words, these costs are overhead expenses. In order for the Zappos.com strategy to be successful, they need to ensure their reverse supply chain is extremely efficient.

If your company handles returns for your customers — and almost every company does — you need to think about how returns fit into your overall business strategy. Every dollar that your company can save by reducing overhead expenses is pure profit, so ensuring that you have an efficient process for managing your reverse supply chain and handling returns should be a high priority. The next few sections cover different reverse supply chain scenarios and the issues you should consider in each one.

TECHNICAL STUFF

Many businesses insist on giving their customers permission to return a product by issuing a return material authorization (RMA) — an agreement from the company that it will accept the product when it's returned. The RMA number makes it easier for the company to process returns when they are received.

Processing Returns of New or Excess Products

When you are a customer, especially in a retail environment, you usually expect that you can return an unused product for a full refund. A store that has a liberal refund policy encourages customers to buy more and makes them loyal to a brand; a strict refund policy has the opposite effect, making customers reluctant to commit to a purchase.

Retail returns may come from a customer who received an unwanted gift; perhaps they didn't like the color or it was the wrong size. These returns increase dramatically around holiday shopping periods.

There are other return scenarios that occur in both retail and wholesale supply chains, such as when the customer changes her mind or when she overorders. Overordering occurs when a customer isn't sure how much she'll need, so she buys a lot and returns whatever was left over. You can summarize these scenarios as

>> Changed mind

>> Gift return

>> Excess return

Before accepting the return of an used product, you need to consider issues that can occur including minor wear and tear, tampering, and substitution. You need to have a plan in place to handle any of these situations.

Minor wear and tear

Just handling a product sometimes leaves scratches or other light damage on the packaging or the product. In that case, another customer may not be willing to pay full price for the product. You have a couple of choices. You could have a process for cleaning, polishing, and repackaging the product so that it looks like new, or you might reduce the price and sell the product at a discount. The key is to decide how much a customer would be willing to pay for the product in its current condition, how much it would cost to repackage the product, and how much more the product would be worth once it has been repackaged. If the increase in value is greater than the cost of repackaging then repackaging is a good investment. Otherwise, you are better off selling it as-is with a discount.

Damage or tampering

Some products lose all their value after their packaging is opened. Medicine is a great example. Would you buy a bottle of pills that someone else opened and then returned to the store?

Damage or tampering can occur with any product, including electronics and computers. Before restocking an item and selling it to another customer, you need to have a process that checks for tampering and ensures that the products truly are in working, like-new condition.

Substitution

Once in a while, a customer returns the wrong product, either by accident or on purpose. A customer who is remodeling her house, for example, might buy similar accessories from several home improvement stores, get the products mixed up, and return one of them to the wrong store. If your store accepts returns you need to have a process in place to handle that kind of accidental substitution.

Or you may have a customer who replaces an old fixture with a new one and then tries to return the old one to you in the new packaging. That kind of substitution — when it's intentional rather than accidental — can be trickier to handle. For details, see "Handling Unauthorized Returns and Fraudulent Products" later in this chapter.

Processing Returns of Used or Defective Products

Sometimes, customers return products after using them, either because they don't want the products anymore or because the products didn't work as expected. How you handle returns of used and defective products can greatly affect your relationship with customers.

Accepting returns of used products is usually considered to be a courtesy. Retailers sometimes allow customers to return used products as a way to build brand loyalty. In most cases, used products can't easily be sold, so these returns are commonly resold at a deep discount, without warranty; auctioned off as salvage; or thrown away.

Because they want to build customer loyalty, retailers must handle their salvage or disposal process quickly, recovering as much value as they can without running the risk of compromising their brand by selling substandard used products to other customers.

Managing Closed-Loop Supply Chains

Over the past several years, companies, consumers, and governments have become more concerned about what happens to products at the end of their life. For supply chain managers, this concern means thinking about products in terms of their entire life cycle: beginning to end, birth to death, dirt to dirt. Supply chains begin with raw materials from the Earth and end with used products being returned to the Earth — ideally, in a way that doesn't harm the planet. Supply chains that circle back on themselves in this way are called *closed-loop supply chains.* In a closed-loop supply chain, you recycle all the components when the product reaches the end of its usable life.

A great example of a closed-loop supply chain involves batteries for electric cars. These batteries are made of expensive materials but are designed in such a way that more than 90 percent of the components can be recycled. When one of these batteries reaches the end of its life, most of it can be reused in a new battery, which reduces the amount of material that ends up in a landfill.

The closed-loop supply chain for these batteries has another interesting effect: It dramatically reduces the cost of raw materials for the next battery, which benefits consumers, the planet, and the manufacturer. It's a win-win-win situation!

A closely related strategy is called remanufacturing. In *remanufacturing,* a part is designed in such a way that it can be rebuilt and reused over and over. A used part that's being returned for remanufacturing is called a *core.* Remanufacturing is a common strategy for the parts used in cars, airplanes, and heavy equipment; remanufacturing these parts typically costs much less than making new parts from scratch, which saves the manufacturer money. These savings can be passed along to consumers. Everyone benefits from remanufacturing because it reduces the amount of energy that is used to make a product and it reduces the amount of material that's sent to landfills.

WARNING

In managing a closed-loop supply chain, inspection and sorting of incoming components is critical. Poor-quality cores result in poor-quality remanufactured parts.

Handling Unauthorized Returns and Fraudulent Products

In any supply chain, products are sometimes returned in mysterious ways. Customers may send back products that they never bought from you in the first place, or you may not be able to identify what the product is, where it came from, or where it belongs. This situation involves a delicate balance. You don't want to waste time and money doing an investigation that costs more than the product is worth, but it may be worthwhile to do some investigation to find out how much the product is worth and how best to recover that value. Odds are that you'll end up throwing away some items that were valuable, but you'll never get back the time and money you spend chasing down the identity of a part that turns out to be worthless.

Unfortunately, reverse supply chains have become targets for criminals. One common trick is to buy a product legitimately and return a different product for a refund. Someone could buy an expensive piece of clothing and return a cheap counterfeit, or he could buy an expensive computer and return a different computer with low-end components. Your refunds-processing department needs to authenticate the products coming back from your customers to make sure that the products are what they're supposed to be.

Fraudulent returns don't necessarily come from criminals, however. Unsuspecting customers sometimes end up purchasing counterfeit products by accident, especially online, and then try to return them to a local store when the products don't work properly. These returns can be useful for helping your business understand the market for counterfeit products.

TIP

Counterfeiting is a major problem for some products; it costs your company money because fake products take revenue away, and the counterfeit goods are often low-quality, which damages your brand. Counterfeit products have a social cost as well, because the profits often go to support organized crime. One way to know whether your products are being counterfeited is to look for fakes among your customer returns.

Obviously, you need to prevent counterfeit parts from entering your supply chain as returns. Handling the customers who return fraudulent products can be trickier. You need to know when to ignore the problem and when to press legal charges. Many large companies have teams within their legal department — often made up of experienced law enforcement professionals — that investigate these incidents and offer recommendations about how to handle them.

Managing Trade-Ins

Many businesses offer their customers credit for trading in an existing product when they buy a new one. Cars and cell phones are two common examples. You probably see ten television commercials each day in which a dealer promises to give you "top dollar" for your trade-in. Trade-ins are also becoming common for other products, such as appliances, books, and batteries. Once, while traveling overseas, I discovered that I couldn't buy beer at the grocery store unless I had a used bottle that I could trade in. Amazon.com now encourages customers to trade in items that they have purchased.

Trade-ins often make sense for products that have a long life. They can be great ways to make more money and to make customers' lives simpler. Trade-in credits reduce the purchase price of your product, so they can increase your sales. If you can sell the traded-in products for a profit, you get to make money on those transactions too. Meanwhile, your customer gets a shiny new product and doesn't have to worry about disposing of the old one.

For a trade-in program to be effective at increasing sales, it must be easy for customers to use, and customers must feel that they're getting a good deal. For a trade-in program to be profitable, you need to have a good process for appraising the true value of the trade-in and a good system for selling the product after you get it.

IN THIS CHAPTER

» Aligning business rules and performance goals

» Tracking and protecting your assets and products

» Using information technology effectively

» Building your supply chain team

» Improving your project management capabilities

Chapter **11**

Enabling Your Supply Chain

The SCOR Model (see Chapter 5) helps you organize the supply chain processes within a business so that you can manage them more effectively. Most of the processes that drive supply chains can be categorized as planning, sourcing, making, delivering, or returning. This chapter discusses other critical processes that don't fit neatly into any of these SCOR categories. These are called enabling processes because they are foundational to making the other processes work. Examples of enabling processes include your approach to the management of business rules, performance objectives, assets, physical security, information technology, human resources, and projects.

Managing Your Business Rules

Whether you realize it or not, your business is run by a set of rules. You may have rules that define what happens when a shipment is two days late, how much credit to extend to a new customer, and where you store finished goods before you ship them. Rules provide consistency in a supply chain, and tell your employees know how to handle specific situations. Many of these rules may be written in a policy manual, captured in standard operating procedures, or programmed into a computer application. Other rules may be filed in memos, or they may only exist in people's heads and get passed around by word of mouth. Although the results of these rules — the outcomes — are often obvious, finding the rules may require some detective work.

TIP

Conflicts between employees, suppliers, and customers are often an indication of a problem with business rules. The Five Why's technique can be used to identify contradictions or gaps in your rules. Start by asking "Why do we do this?" After you answer that question, ask "why" again. And continue asking "why" until you uncover the business rules that are causing the conflict.

Business rules create problems when they fail to address an important factor, or when they contradict one another. Here's a good example of how business rules can create conflicts in a supply chain. Suppose that a company's transportation department develops a routing guide with instructions on shipping material from a supplier to its manufacturing plant. The routing guide provides the following business rule, designed to minimize transportation costs:

> For shipments of less than 10,000 pounds, use a less-than-truckload (LTL) carrier, which requires a two-day transit time. For shipments greater than 10,000 pounds, use a full-truckload (FTL) carrier, which requires only a one-day transit time.

Meanwhile, to increase their supply chain flexibility, the manufacturing plant implements its own business rule:

> Suppliers need to fill all orders within one day.

Each of these rules seems like a good idea, but complying with both could be impossible. Any time the supplier is given an order that weighs less than 10,000 pounds they need to choose which of the two business rules they should violate. In this case, you may need to change one of the existing rules, decide which one takes priority, or create a new rule that covers shipments that weigh less than 10,000 pounds.

Managing Supply Chain Performance

What really matters is how the whole supply chain performs and how your business is doing. As the saying goes, what gets measured gets done. You need to ask yourself what you want to get done (performance goals) and how you can measure it (metrics). You can then develop metrics that can be shared with your customers and your suppliers, which helps to create supply chain alignment.

Setting performance goals

Almost every performance goal in supply chain management involves trade-offs related to asset utilization — in other words, to how efficiently and effectively a company uses the money it has to create value for its customers and generate profits. You might track, for example, the amount of working capital that is tied up in inventory. If the inventory is too low, you could lose sales due to stockouts or you could waste manufacturing capacity due to shutdowns; if the inventory is too high you could be tying up working capital unnecessarily. You need to set a performance goal for inventory that strikes a balance between these conflicting business priorities. Then you need define metrics that will show whether you have achieved these goals, and whether they had the desired outcomes.

To identify what your performance goals should be, start with your company's business plan. If the business plan says that your company is trying to grow market share, then your supply chain performance goals should focus on availability and customer service. If your business plan is focused on cutting costs, then the performance goals could target inventory reductions, capacity utilization, and supplier price reductions. Aligning your supply chain performance metrics with the business plan makes it easier to see the value that supply chain management is adding to the bottom line.

Align your metrics with your customers

People and companies both have a natural tendency to focus on their own needs and wants, but supply chain management is a team effort. All of the companies in a supply chain are ultimately working together to provide a product or service to an end customer at a price that the customer is willing to pay. By aligning their metrics, these supply chain partners can do a better job of managing the flow of money, material, and information from raw materials all the way to their end customers.

A simple way to align supply chain metrics is for each company in a supply chain to ask its customers, "How do you measure the performance of your suppliers?" When the suppliers have that information, they can adopt those metrics as their own. This can lead to a shift from internal metrics to external metrics for each company; rather than focusing on internal metrics such as profitability, they may start to look more closely at external metrics, such as on-time delivery.

Just as important as knowing your customers' metrics is understanding precisely what those metrics mean. For example, some customers measure delivery performance based on when a product is shipped from a supplier, and others measure it based on when the shipment arrives. Some customers include transportation costs and taxes when they compare the cost of one product to another, and other customers don't. Understanding what factors are included in a customer's metric reduces confusion and makes it easier for customers to do business with you.

Share Your Metrics with Your Suppliers

To meet your needs, your suppliers have to understand how you measure their performance. If you have a scorecard for your suppliers (see Chapter 18) consider sharing the scores with them. You should also explain what the measurements are based on and why those performance goals are important to you. When you and your suppliers look at the same metrics, it becomes much easier to collaborate on improvements that will benefit all of you.

Suppose that your customers are beginning to make procurement decisions based on the sustainability of the products they buy. To meet your customers' needs, you will need to have your suppliers report their own sustainability. Collaborating with your suppliers on ways to improve sustainability may allow you to come up with solutions that benefit your entire supply chain such as packaging changes, methods of streamlining transportation, and reductions in inventory.

TIP

For more detailed information on supply chain metrics, see Chapter 16.

Managing Your Assets

The word *asset* means slightly different things in different contexts. For an accountant, an asset is anything that has value — including money. In this section, assets refer to the tools and equipment that are used to manufacture and distribute products. Supply chains tend to be asset-intensive, meaning there is a lot of money tied up in tools and equipment.

Assets fall into two main categories that are based on whether they can be easily moved. Permanent assets are also called fixtures because they are attached to a building and difficult to move. Most manufacturing machinery, as well as material handling equipment such as racks and conveyors, are permanent assets. Movable or mobile assets can be moved around, and include containers, vehicles, and tools.

One common goal of supply chain managers is to increase asset efficiency, which can be done in two ways:

>> Reduce your assets.

>> Use your assets more.

The efficiency of supply chain assets is measured by your capacity utilization (see Chapter 8). As your capacity utilization increases, you are using your assets more efficiently.

Movable assets tend to get less attention than fixed assets because they are usually less expensive. But when you use a large number of them in your business, managing moveable assets properly can have a big impact on your profitability. Many manufacturing facilities, for example, move parts around in containers called totes, tubs, or bins. These containers are mobile assets. Managing containers effectively involves making sure that you spend as little money as necessary to buy them, buy no more than you really need, and use the ones you buy as much as possible. Asset management for these containers may also involve cleaning, performing routine maintenance, and disposing of the containers when they're no longer serviceable. If the containers are not managed efficiently, then the company will need to buy more containers, and this will reduce the company's profits.

In order to manage the efficiency of mobile assets in supply chains, you need to know where the assets are located. In the past few years, many companies have begun to use tracking technology to improve their asset management. Radio-frequency identification (RFID) tags and global positioning system (GPS) units, for example, can make it much easier to track mobile assets in real time. As a result, there is less time spent looking for these assets, and less money spent replacing assets that were lost.

Labeling Your Products

Keeping track of products as they flow through your supply chain can be a big challenge. With few exceptions, you need to label each product so that you know what it is. When you think about your labeling processes, you should consider five things:

>> What will the label be applied to? In some situations, you need to apply labels directly onto a product or package. In other situations, you may want to label a larger unit, such as a case, a pallet, or shipping container. If you know which items are in a shipping container, for example, then you don't need to look at each item individually — you can just look at the label for the shipping container.

>> What information does the label need to contain? For many products it is important to track the lot number, the stock keeping unit (SKU), and the expiration date. The label may also include a serial number, so that you can look all of the information about that item up in a database. If the product will

be sold in a retail supply chain, you may want to include the price on the label; this will save retailers time and money because they won't need to affix their own price tag.

» Who needs to read the label? Sometimes you want it to be easy for a person to read a label without any special equipment; in that case, the text needs to be clear and large enough to read. It also needs to be written in a language that the person reading it will understand. (Remember, many supply chains are global.) In other cases, you may want the label to be read by a computer; it is much more efficient for a computer to read bar codes or quick response (QR) codes than it is for them to read text characters. Finally, you may want to add security features to a label, such as magnetic inks or invisible markings that can be read only by using special equipment.

TECHNICAL
STUFF

Many products benefit from having a bar code as a label. Bar codes use lines to represent numbers, which makes it easier for computers to read the label. If bar codes are to be shared across partners in a supply chain, a central authority must issue the numbers. This service is usually provided by a global standards organization called GS1 (https://www.gs1.org). Using standardized bar codes and product identification numbers allows manufacturers, distributors, and retailers to use the same label to identify and manage a product.

» How will you apply the label? Sometimes you can apply information directly to a product by stamping, printing, or engraving it onto the surface. In this case the label actually becomes part of the product. However, it is often easier to print information on a label made out of paper, plastic, or metal and then attach the label to the product.

» How durable does the label need to be? You should think about how the information on a label will be used, and what environments the label will be exposed to, when deciding how durable the label needs to be. Some labels are designed to be temporary, and some need to be permanent. Temporary labels may include information that is irrelevant once the item has been purchased (such as the price and SKU) or instructions for getting a new product setup properly (such as the website to use for registering the product for a manufacturer's warranty). Temporary labels should be durable enough to last until the product has been purchased, and it should be easy for your customer to remove the label without causing damage to the product. There are other situations where you want the label to be a permanent feature of the product. With computers, for example, the serial number label can help users troubleshoot problems. With service parts such as oil filters, having the model number printed on the product reduces the chances for a mix up.

A well-thought-out, well-executed labeling process is easy to take for granted, but when labels lack information, contain errors, or don't hold up to the wear and tear of a supply chain, you can run into some expensive problems. In extreme cases, improper labeling can lead companies to scrap entire production runs of valuable products. More commonly, improper labeling leads to bottlenecks and delays while people try to find the information they need to process a transaction. Think about the last time you were at the grocery store and heard someone announce "Price check on aisle 10!" The cashier had to stop the checkout process because of a question about labeling.

Addressing Supply Chain Security Issues

There are a number of safety and security issues that supply chains need to address. These includes threats such as theft and counterfeiting, as well as special precautions that ensure delicate or perishable products are kept in the proper conditions throughout the supply chain.

Ensuring physical security

Supply chains have a physical presence — a physicality — that is easy to overlook. People, facilities, computers, and equipment are critical to making supply chains work properly. All these factors are subject to a variety of threats, which is why you need to secure your supply chain physically.

In distribution centers, for example, physical security includes systems that protect your people. Sadly, in some cases disgruntled workers have become violent with their colleagues or attempted to sabotage a facility. Burglars could break in to steal equipment or inventory. At the same time, plenty of workers have stolen products from the facilities where they work or run crime rings inside legitimate distribution operations. Nobody wants to think about these situations, but they do happen. You need to protect your supply chain from these risks by having security processes and systems in place.

Dealing with counterfeiting

Counterfeit products have been a major problem for supply chains for a long time. Trends such as globalization and e-commerce make it easier for counterfeiters to penetrate legitimate markets and sell their goods to unsuspecting customers.

Counterfeit products deprive legitimate companies of revenue, cheat governments out of taxes, and, in some cases, endanger consumers. Investigating counterfeiting operations and persuading law enforcement agencies to prosecute the perpetrators can be difficult, however. It doesn't help that some customers are willing to purchase fake items for a bargain.

When it comes to high-value products such as pharmaceuticals, customers expect — and need — to receive high-quality, authentic goods. For the companies that make the authentic products and own the brands, it's critically important that customers recognize the difference between genuine articles and counterfeits.

Fortunately, you can use a variety of technologies to tag authentic products. These technologies include RFID, holograms, and special inks that have unique textures or react to ultraviolet and infrared light. You may have no way to keep criminals from copying your products, but using anti-counterfeiting technologies can make it easier to differentiate between your authentic products and the fakes.

Having an anti-counterfeiting strategy could protect your company from product liability. If someone gets hurt by a low-quality counterfeit, you want to be able to prove that the product wasn't yours. In a growing number of industries, government regulations require manufacturers and distributors to ensure that the products they sell can be traced to legitimate sources.

Tackling regulatory compliance

Every country, state, county, and city where you do business has its own set of laws and regulations, which may change frequently. These rules can have effects up and down your supply chain, so you must maintain regulatory compliance. I don't have space to list all the ways that regulations could affect your supply chain, but here are some examples:

>> In the United States, federal regulations dictate how much time a truck driver can spend behind the wheel before taking a break.

>> Many countries have regulations about what kinds of wood can be used to manufacture pallets.

>> Some countries impose tariffs and quotas on products that are imported from other countries.

>> The United States and the European Union have laws regulating which suppliers can sell tungsten, tantalum, tin, or gold — often called *conflict minerals* — because many of the mines that produce these minerals support criminal, inhumane, and terrorist activities.

Failing to observe these rules and regulations can lead to major disruptions in your supply chain such as having shipments impounded by customs inspectors. In extreme cases, violations can result in fines and even jail sentences. Ensuring regulatory compliance needs to be a priority for your supply chain.

Addressing unique product requirements

Some products require special considerations at every step in a supply chain. To ensure that these products are handled properly, you may need to provide special signs or labels. You may also need to use special sensors that monitor your products throughout the supply chain. For example, you might place a thermometer inside a refrigerated shipping container so that you can tell if the contents have gotten too warm during their journey. Following are some examples of products that require special handling:

>> Fresh food needs to be kept cold, which is why products that need to be refrigerated at all times are sometimes described as *cold chain*.

>> Some chemicals need to be kept warm. Bulk rubber, for example, can become unusable if it gets too cold.

>> Products such as batteries, tires, gasoline, and explosives are hazardous materials; they need to be stored and transported in ways that reduce the risk that they could catch fire or hurt someone.

>> Radioactive materials require special supply chains that include regular monitoring and testing for radiation exposure.

Protecting supply chain information

As companies rely more heavily on information technology they also become more vulnerable to attacks from computer viruses and hackers. Since customers and suppliers often provide each other access to their information systems, they can become targets through which attackers gain access to sensitive information. So information security processes need to be included when you think about managing your entire supply chain.

Some aspects of your information security process are technology related, such as password policies, encryption methods, and antivirus tools. But many information vulnerabilities rely on exploiting human behavior, such as phishing emails that trick users into exposing their usernames and passwords. In addition to having strong information security processes for your own systems and staff, you should ensure that customers and suppliers who have access to your systems have robust safeguards in place.

Leveraging Information Technology

Information technology (IT) has a profound effect on just about every business, so staying current with IT capabilities has become an important part of supply chain management. Since the 1970s, the speed of business information processing has been driven by Moore's Law, which says that computers double their processing power every 18 months. Faster processing means that supply chains can use computers to process and share more information more quickly.

Figure 11-1 shows a chart that I call the *information value chain,* which illustrates the relationship between people and IT in the supply chain. Like people, computers are able to process data, make decisions, and take actions. If you put this on a scale from simple to complex, you progress from data (on the left) into information, knowledge, and (eventually) wisdom (on the right).

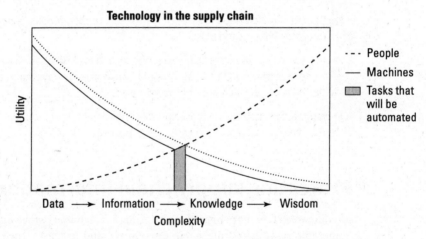

FIGURE 11-1:
The information value chain.

Computers efficiently process huge amounts of data but become less efficient as ideas become more complex. People are not as efficient at processing simple ideas but are very efficient at dealing with complex ideas that involve knowledge and wisdom. Computers can already do many of the same tasks as people, and as the processing power of computers continues to grow, computers are taking on more of these tasks better, faster, and cheaper than their human counterparts. The key to optimizing the role of IT in supply chains is striking the right balance on the information value chain: Use computers to process data and information so that people can focus on tasks that require knowledge and wisdom.

HOW IT HAS CHANGED SUPPLY CHAINS

I once sat in a meeting about some IT challenges that the project team faced while starting up a new distribution facility. Frustrated and unwilling to accept a delay, the senior executive said, "We used to fill this paperwork out by hand, and it worked just fine. We're not going to hold this whole building up because of one of the computers."

A few months later, the facility opened without the IT issues having been resolved. The manual receiving process was inefficient, and the company soon had a long line of trailers waiting to be received. The executive learned that getting the IT challenges resolved had to become a top priority because their old manual processes couldn't keep up with the new speed of their business.

Chapter 12 covers specific types of software that you can use to improve supply chain processes; the information value chain applies to all of them. Your goal is to automate the data and information tasks throughout your supply chain where computers can do this work better, faster, and cheaper than humans can. As technology becomes more powerful, the range of tasks that should be automated grows.

Leveraging Human Resources

A supply chain is made of people, processes, and technologies. Supply chain managers tend to focus on the processes and the technology and often underestimate the importance of the people. A supply chain with great products, perfect processes, and cutting-edge technology can still grind to a halt if you don't have the right people in the right places using the right skills to do their jobs properly.

People up and down the supply chain decide who to do business with, which processes and technologies are implemented, and how to resolve problems. Getting the right people on board, giving them the skills they need to be successful, and keeping them around to do their jobs are incredibly important parts of enabling any supply chain.

Most of the human resources problems that supply chain managers need to think about can be broken down into three processes: recruit, develop, and retain. Following are some things that you need to consider to ensure that your human resources capabilities support your supply chain:

>> **Recruit:** You need to decide how many people are needed to do the work at each step in your supply chain, and what skills they need to have in order to be qualified for a job. You also need to figure out where you can find these

people, how much will it cost to hire them, and which are the best ways to connect with them and attract them to your company. Partnering with high schools, technical schools, and universities can make it easier to recruit students. Active engagement in the local community and with professional associations can help you recruit experienced talent.

TIP

It is often difficult to provide a business case for the cost of recruiting. However, it helps to look at the problem differently. Rather than asking, "How much should we pay for recruiting?" ask "How much will it cost us if this position is unfilled, or if it is filled by someone who doesn't have the necessary skills and experience to do it well?" The true cost might involve lost sales opportunities, dissatisfied customers, or overtime and burnout for other employees. Helping people to see the cost of leaving a position open can make it easier to justify the investment required to recruit qualified candidates.

>> **Develop:** There may be a difference between the skills required to get a job and the skills required to perform that job. For example, even if you require candidates to have an engineering degree before you hire them, you may still need to train them on the characteristics of your product and the tools available in your company. Your development efforts should identify the knowledge, skills, and abilities (KSAs) that each person needs to be successful in their job. Focusing on KSAs can help you and your team members agree on the training that they need, and make it easier to demonstrate the tangible benefits of your investment in developing them.

TIP

People are all different, and we learn in different ways. Rather than developing a one-size-fits-all approach to talent development, it is usually more effective to provide people with options and encourage them to choose the method that works best for them.

>> **Retain:** Your employees ultimately create the value for your company, and talent goes where it is treated the best. Part of treating people well is making sure that they are paid fairly for the work they are doing. One way to do this is by performing a compensation study that compares the salaries of your employees to those of similar firms. While pay and benefits are important incentives, they may not be enough to keep your employees happy. Helping people see that their work is important, and giving them a voice in how decisions are made, can keep them more engaged. Other retention techniques that are popular in some industries include flexible work arrangements, tuition assistance programs, and office perks, such as free snacks. The cost of these initiatives can often be offset by a reduction in turnover and an improved ability to attract top talent.

TIP

Treating workers with respect and soliciting input from everyone are key parts of the Lean philosophy (see Chapter 4).

LINKING TALENT DEVELOPMENT TO CORPORATE PERFORMANCE

The executives in a global manufacturing company realized that many of their supply chain problems were the result of communications gaps between managers. The cost of this problem was hard to calculate, but it probably led to millions of dollars' worth of lost profits due to unnecessary inventory. Furthermore, supply chain managers throughout the company were spending time arguing about supply chain terminology rather than aligning their performance goals. In order to get everyone on the same page, the executives decided that all of their supply chain managers throughout the company would be required to earn an advanced supply chain certification. To pass the certification test, all these people would need to study the same material and learn the same method for describing supply chain processes.

The managers all had the same development goal — to complete the certification — but could meet it in different ways. Many of them chose to take instructor-led classes or online courses, while others studied on their own. The company would support them no matter which option they chose, but if they didn't successfully complete the certification within two years, they would no longer be allowed to work as supply chain managers.

Shortly after the managers began to get trained, it was clear to the executives that the nature of their discussions had changed. The supply chain managers now spoke the same language and were able to communicate more effectively about the challenges and opportunities they were facing.

Mastering Project Management

Businesses change through projects, so project management is an important enabling process in your supply chain. That's also why project management is the final step in the New Supply Chain Agenda (see Chapter 1). Many companies find it difficult to implement supply chain projects successfully, so there has been a growing demand for supply chain project managers.

One of the best resources for project management training is the Project Management Institute (PMI), which has created the *Project Management Body of Knowledge* (PMBOK). The PMBOK looks at projects in terms of five main phases, and within each of these phases, there are specific tasks for which the project manager is accountable.

>> **Initiating:** Broadly outline the goals of the project.

>> **Planning:** Create a detailed plan including a budget and timeline.

>> **Executing:** Complete the activities in the plan.

>> **Monitoring:** Track key performance indicators to ensure that goals are met.

>> **Closing:** Complete all of the final steps such as performing a lessons-learned analysis and assigning team members to new roles.

PMI offers several certifications, including Project Management Professional, that are built upon the PMBOK. Visit `www.pmi.org/` for more information.

A common challenge with supply chain projects is that they involve cross-functional teams. The DIRECT project leadership model (see Chapter 4) is a useful way to remember the six things that leaders need to help cross-functional teams focus on:

>> **Define the objective:** The project leader needs to ensure that the project goals are clearly laid out for the entire team, often in a document called a project charter.

>> **Investigate the options:** The project team needs to cast a wide net and think about all the ways in which they could meet the objectives.

>> **Resolve to a course of action:** After reviewing the options, the team needs to decide what to do and create a plan.

>> **Execute the plan:** Project teams need to follow the plan and report their progress regularly. Plans commonly change, so executing any plan includes managing changes in the scope, schedule, and budget.

>> **Change the systems and processes:** Projects usually lead to the implementation of new processes and technologies, often involving complicated decisions and complex choreography. If you're starting a new distribution center, for example, you need to plan the time when you're going to start accepting orders. Preparing for that change involves a lot of precise planning, such as how the first orders will be redirected to the new facility. Changeover issues are often separate projects within a larger supply chain project.

>> **Transition the people:** Supply chain projects affect people as well as technology and processes, and you have to consider what adjustments people need to make. Learning a new set of routines takes time, and people often resist changes if they don't understand the reasons for them. Managing the transition for all the stakeholders affected by a change can make the difference between success and failure.

Recruiting, developing, and retaining effective supply chain project managers can be challenging for two reasons. First, you want someone who understands two disciplines — supply chain management and project management — and people with these skills can be hard to find. Second, project management jobs are often temporary; when the project is finished, the project manager is out of a job. So supply chain professionals often view project management as a stepping stone into a more stable, permanent role. Once they find that new position, there will be one less supply chain project manager for you to hire.

One of the most effective ways to resolve this issue is to create a project management office (PMO). A benefit of a PMO is that it allows project managers to develop and share best practices across all your supply chain projects. For this reason it may also be called a center of excellence (CoE). If all of your supply chain projects are managed through a PMO it is also easier see and address conflicts between projects, such as when two projects are competing to solve the same problem. Because there are ongoing projects from different areas of the supply chain, the PMO provides a greater level of job security for your project managers so they are less likely to be concerned about working themselves out of their jobs.

A PMO can also be a great training ground for supply chain professionals. People who are rotated into and out of the PMO learn about many parts of the business and develop a better understanding of how the parts fit together. This broad knowledge is hard to develop when people are stuck in functional and professional silos.

3
Using Technology to Manage Supply Chains

Chapter **12**

Managing Supply Chain Software

nformation technology has become an essential part of supply chain management because virtually every process in a supply chain involves entering, processing, sharing, and retrieving data. Automating the tasks for a process can increase your efficiency, but choosing the best way to automate a task can be complicated. Because there are so many processes in a supply chain, there also are many different categories of software that you need to manage. Within each category of software you'll find several companies that sell software packages with different features, capabilities, and price tags.

For some reason, almost every category of supply chain software is described by a three word name, and supply chain managers use the software category initials as a sort of shorthand. For example, it would be quite reasonable for a supply chain manager to ask her colleagues whether the WMS and the TMS are sharing BI data with the ERP. (You'll read about each of these later in this chapter.) Unfortunately, these abbreviations can also lead to confusion and make supply chain software seem more difficult to understand than it should be.

The good news is that if you start by understanding what needs to happen in a supply chain — the processes — it's much easier to understand what the various software tools are intended to do and how they work together. This chapter explains how supply chain processes evolve into software platforms, how these platforms integrate with one another, and how to get help in choosing the right combination of software for your supply chain.

Understanding How Processes Evolve

These days, it's hard to find a supply chain process that isn't tied to a piece of software. You can't place an order, make a phone call, or move a box without logging a transaction in one or more systems. But processes don't become automated instantly — they need to evolve.

An approach that tracks the evolution of a process or the software that supports that process is the *capability maturity model* (CMM). CMMs usually take four or five steps to describe a journey from "immature" to "mature." Figure 12-1 shows a four-step CMM.

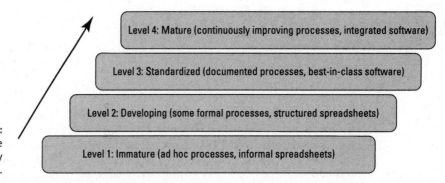

FIGURE 12-1: An example capability maturity model.

Level 4: Mature (continuously improving processes, integrated software)

Level 3: Standardized (documented processes, best-in-class software)

Level 2: Developing (some formal processes, structured spreadsheets)

Level 1: Immature (ad hoc processes, informal spreadsheets)

People naturally want to jump from having an immature process to having a mature one, but virtually every process and every piece of software has to make the journey from immature to mature in gradual steps. Understanding where you are on a CMM can help you focus on where you are headed and what you need to do next to get there.

TIP

A process needs to be stable and repeatable before it can be automated effectively. Automating an immature process often leads to extra work, such as correcting inaccurate data and overriding rules in the system.

Supply chain software is a business investment. When evaluating any business investment, it is a good idea to compare the financial consequences of making something versus buying or renting it. You can apply this approach to evaluating an investment in automating a supply chain process by comparing four options:

>> Run the process manually, without software (do nothing).

>> Buy software off the shelf from a vendor (buy).

>> Subscribe to a cloud-based solution (rent).

>> Create a program from scratch (make).

The buy option is straightforward. You talk with a sales representative, spend some time negotiating price, install the software on your computers, and train your team.

The rent option is newer but rapidly becoming the norm. Instead of buying and installing software on your own computers, you can get a subscription to software that runs in the cloud. You have nothing to install; you just access the software through a web browser or an app and pay for it as you use it. In other words, you rent the software. (See Chapter 12 for more information about cloud-based solutions.)

Making supply chain software involves writing your own software code. For companies that have unique requirements, writing their own software may be a worthwhile investment. However, many companies end up making their own software without realizing it is happening and then realize it was a mistake. Here's an example of how companies can accidentally create problems by making their own software:

1. Someone decides that he has a lot of information to keep track of and that things are slipping through the cracks, so he creates a spreadsheet to start organizing his data. The spreadsheet becomes a critical part of managing that process.

2. The spreadsheet takes on a life of its own, with more fields being added, and it's shared with other people who also start to rely on it and make improvements.

3. As the spreadsheet gets bigger and is used more often, people start writing macros and creating complex formulas that automate process steps. At this point, the spreadsheet has actually become a simple software application, but no one realizes that fact yet.

4. The spreadsheet file gets so big that it starts to run slowly, and eventually the data gets messed up when someone makes a data-entry mistake. To improve the performance of the now-critical spreadsheet, someone creates a database, using a tool such as Microsoft Access.

5. Access is too limiting, so soon the database is rewritten in Structured Query Language (SQL). Now the database is really, truly storing critical data and it is essential for operating the business, but no documentation or training materials exist. Then the system crashes unexpectedly and no one knows how to fix it.

6. A vendor shows up with a piece of software that does something very similar to the database, but does it better and has more bells and whistles. The cost of buying (or renting) this software is cheaper than the cost of maintaining your homegrown system. You need to decide whether to discard all your old data and start fresh or spend a bunch of time and money to import your old data into the new system.

The lesson is to be careful about storing important data in spreadsheets. Although using a spreadsheet may be a low-cost option in the short term, it could lead to an expensive migration in the future. If you see this scenario starting to play out in your supply chain, it's probably a good idea to stop and ask whether a better commercial solution is available. Recognizing that there are software solutions available for most supply chain processes, and starting with them early in your process maturity, can save you time and money.

REMEMBER

An important rule applies to every supply chain software system: The usefulness of the system depends on the accuracy of the data it has to work with. In other words, garbage in, garbage out. Providing quality data to the system in the first place is very important; so is maintaining the integrity of that data over time.

Using Transportation Management Systems

A *transportation management system* (TMS) keeps track of shipments and carriers. It may contain features such as a routing guide that tells you which mode of transportation and which carrier you should use for a shipment. A routing guide may have weight breaks, specifying (for example) that any domestic shipment less than 100 pounds should go by parcel, a shipment between 100 pounds and 10,000 pounds should go by less-than-truckload (LTL) transport, and any shipment over 10,000 pounds should be sent via full-truckload (FTL) transport.

A TMS may help you analyze your freight history, tracking how many loads you ship in each lane. You can use this history as the basis of a freight forecast — an estimate of how much you expect to ship on each lane in the future. The freight forecast helps you collect bids from carriers that are interested in hauling your freight. When the transportation bidding is complete and the contracts are in place for each lane, this information is loaded into the routing guide of the TMS.

Many TMSes monitor the handoffs as a product moves through the supply chain, and this can help you — and your customers — keep track of your shipments. When you schedule the shipment for a product, you notify the TMS. (This notification is sometimes called an advance ship notice [ASN].) When the carrier comes to pick up the shipment, the TMS is notified, and the status for that product is updated. Each time the carrier hands the product off in the supply chain, your TMS can be notified. (These messages are often called shipment status messages.) After the product is received, the TMS can trigger additional actions, such as invoicing the customer and authorizing payment to the carrier.

Some TMSes can do route planning by analyzing the freight that needs to be shipped. These systems figure out the best combinations of loads to maximize the use of transportation capacity while minimizing costs. They can even make changes to routes as new shipments get entered into the system. This sort of transportation planning and execution is a good example of how technology can solve problems and come up with solutions that even an experienced human would find extremely difficult to create. The systems that perform these advanced functions are also called transportation planning systems, transportation execution systems, or freight routing systems.

Following are some TMS vendors:

>> **BluJay**

www.blujaysolutions.com/solutions/transportation-gtn/transportation-management/

>> **C.H. Robinson**

www.chrobinson.com/en-us/logistics/managed-tms/

>> **GT Nexus**

www.gtnexus.com/solutions/transportation-management

>> **JDA**

https://jda.com/solutions/adaptable-manufacturing-distribution-solutions/intelligent-fulfillment/transportation-management

>> **MercuryGate**

http://mercurygate.com/

- » **Oracle**

  www.oracle.com/applications/supply-chain-management/solutions/logistics/transportation-management.html

- » **SAP**

  https://www.sap.com/products/transportation-logistics.html

- » **TMS First**

  www.tmsfirst.com/

- » **Transplace**

  www.transplace.com/transportation-management/

Using Warehouse Management and Execution Systems

Keeping track of all the stuff that's stored in a warehouse or distribution center is a big, complicated job. The tool that does that job is called a *warehouse management system* (WMS). Figuring out how to pick each order and combine the individual order lines into shipments is an even bigger job. The system that makes these decisions is called a *warehouse execution system* (WES). Really, though, the line between WMS and WES is blurry.

You can think of a WMS as being like the system that manages the passenger manifest for an airplane. Each passenger is assigned a seat and given a boarding pass before he or she gets to the airport. In other words, the WMS knows what material is coming in and knows where it's supposed to be stored. As passengers board the plane, their boarding passes are scanned. For a WMS, this process is the receiving process. When you're dealing with warehoused items instead of flight passengers, the WMS receives items in inventory as shipments arrive from suppliers, and the WMS keeps track of where those items are stored in the warehouse.

A WES works in reverse. The gate agent might say, "Hey, Flight Attendant 3, bring me passenger Cassandra Jones from seat 12B." The flight attendant would find the passenger and then escort that person off of the airplane and back to the gate. A WES receives orders for items that need to be shipped to a customer and determines who should pick each of those items from inventory. In other words, the WES decides what has to happen — what warehouse processes to execute — and issues those instructions.

The main functions of a WMS mirror the functions of a warehouse: receiving, putting away, picking, and shipping. The WMS also provides tools that help with doing inventory counts and making adjustments in inventory levels. The WMS may help with more complicated processes, such as combining individual products into kits, or *kitting*. An example of kitting is combining all the parts needed to do an engine tuneup, so that a customer can order them all at the same time. The WMS may be able to track the process of breaking bulk shipments into smaller units, a process called *break bulk*. Break bulk is common in warehouses that handle replenishments to small stores or that do direct-to-customer e-commerce fulfillment.

TIP

The real differences between a WMS and a WES often have more to do with marketing than they do with technology. The important point is that you need software to manage the movement and storage of materials in a warehouse. Call the system something that makes it easy for people to understand what you mean and makes you feel better about the amount of money that it costs.

Following are some WMS vendors:

>> **HighJump**

www.highjump.com/supply-chain-management-solutions/warehouse-management-solutions-wms/warehouse-management-distributors

>> **Infor**

www.infor.com/product-summary/scm/supply-chain-execution/

>> **JDA**

https://jda.com/solutions/profitable-omni-channel-retail-solutions/intelligent-fulfillment/warehouse-management

>> **Manhattan Associates**

www.manh.com/products/warehouse-management

>> **Oracle**

www.oracle.com/applications/supply-chain-management/solutions/logistics/warehouse-management.html

>> **SAP**

www.sap.com/products/extended-warehouse-management.html

>> **Softeon**

www.softeon.com/our-solutions/product-solutions/warehouse-management

>> **Tecsys**

www.tecsys.com/supply-chain/solutions/warehouse-management/

Using Demand Planning Systems

Determining how much of your stuff customers are likely to buy is one of the biggest challenges in any supply chain. This process is called forecasting or (if you want to sound fancy) demand planning. This guess about the future can be based on many inputs, such as how much you've sold in the past, how strong you think the economy will be in the future, or how effective you expect your marketing to be. You have many ways to forecast demand, but doing so often requires a combination of math and judgment. Preparing these forecasts over and over across a range of products requires a special kind of software called a *demand planning system* (DPS).

A DPS typically provides many methods for forecasting demand and enables you to add information or adjust the forecast. It helps you look at the forecasts at different levels, from the individual stock-keeping unit (SKU) level forecast to your master demand schedule. You can configure the DPS to use different forecasting methods for products based on whether their demand is steady or volatile. If you have products that sell more during the winter and less in the summer, you may need your forecast to account for seasonality.

A DPS commonly interfaces with a customer order history so that it can incorporate information about past sales into the forecast. The DPS may also tie into a material requirements planning (MRP) system (see the next section) because that system provides a starting point for creating a master production schedule.

Following are some DPS vendors:

>> **Demand Solutions**

www.demandsolutions.com/forecast-management-demand-planning-inventory-forecasting-software.html

>> **Infor**

www.infor.com/solutions/scm/planning/

>> **John Galt**

http://johngalt.com/

>> **Kinaxis**

www.kinaxis.com/en/solution/supply-chain-planning-solution/demand-planning/

>> **Logility**

www.logility.com/solutions/demand-planning-solution

>> **Oracle**

www.oracle.com/applications/supply-chain-management/solutions/supply-chain-planning/demand-management.html

>> **SAP**

www.sap.com/products/advanced-planning-optimization.html

>> **ToolsGroup**

https://knowledge.toolsgroup.com/demand-planning

Using Material Requirements Planning Systems

Before you can assemble a product, you need to have all the necessary pieces, parts, or components. Sometimes, the assembly process has multiple steps that need to occur in different places and in a particular sequence. The purpose of a *material requirements planning* (MRP) system is to figure out what parts you need, and when and where you need them, so that you can manufacture your products.

To start with, the MRP system needs to know what you plan to make and when you plan to make it. That is, it begins with your production forecast, also called the master production schedule. Based on that schedule, the MRP system looks at the bill of materials for each product you want to make. This document lists all the components that are needed to make a product. After looking at each bill of materials, the MRP system checks the inventory level for each component to see whether you have the parts you need when you need them. If inventory falls short, the MRP system calculates how much you should order and when you should order it so that the material arrives in time for you to make your product.

In some cases, the MRP system goes beyond planning to executing tasks. The system can issue purchase orders for components, for example, and monitor the performance of your manufacturing process to adjust the plan as needed.

Suppose that you run a factory that makes two bicycle models: one for boys and another for girls. The frames for these models are different, but everything else about the bikes is identical, including the wheels, pedals, chains, and other parts. How do you decide how many units of each part you need and when you should order those units from your suppliers to make your bikes?

The simplest approach is to decide how many units of each type of bike you plan to make in a certain period of time, called your *planning horizon*. Suppose that your planning horizon is one year, and you decide to make 100,000 units of each bike model during that time. This figure is your production target: 100,000 of each bike model, or 200,000 bikes total.

During the year, your factory is open for 50 weeks (closing for two weeks for maintenance and holidays). To hit your production target, you need to make an average 2,000 units of each type of bike every week, or 4,000 total bikes per week.

The bill of materials for each bike includes two wheels, a frame, a sprocket, a chain, two pedals, and a set of handlebars. Each component comes from a different supplier, with different lead times and different lot sizes.

You could order all order all the parts you need at the beginning of the period — enough parts to make 200,000 bikes. But this approach would be a mess for everyone! Your suppliers would be scrambling to fill your order, and you'd need to have all the parts delivered before you could start working. All that inventory would cost you money. You'd need to pay your suppliers for all the parts that they made, and you'd need to store and protect all those parts in a warehouse. Some parts are likely to get lost, damaged, or stolen, resulting in shrinkage costs.

An MRP system tries to improve this situation by comparing the master production schedule with the expected inventory levels and then ordering the parts you need so that they arrive just in time.

TECHNICAL STUFF

Some people use the term *manufacturing resource planning* to describe software that performs these tasks. You may even see material requirements planning called MRP and manufacturing resource planning called MRP II. Unless you're truly interested in a career managing supply chain software systems, it's unlikely that you'll ever need to describe the differences between MRP and MRP II.

Following are some MRP vendors:

>> **IFS**

www.ifsworld.com/us/solutions/enterprise-resource-planning/

>> **Infor**

www.infor.com/solutions/erp/

>> **Microsoft**

www.microsoft.com/en-us/dynamics365/nav-overview

>> **Oracle** (also called JD Edwards)

www.jdedwardserp.com/functional-modules/manufacturing/

>> **SAP**

www.sap.com/products/supply-chain-iot/manufacturing.html

Using Distribution Requirements Planning Systems

Sometimes, businesses need to forecast inventory and plan replenishment orders across several tiers of distribution centers. A master facility might receive FTL shipments from suppliers and break these shipments into pallets that are shipped to local distribution centers. The software system that works through this process is called a *distribution requirements planning* (DRP) system. A DRP system is similar to an MRP system (refer to "Using Material Requirements Planning Systems" earlier in this chapter). Whereas an MRP system focuses on ensuring that material is available to support a manufacturing process, a DRP system focuses on managing the availability of products in warehouses and distribution centers.

The forecasting elements of a DRP system resemble the functions of a DPS system (refer to "Using Demand Planning Systems" earlier in this chapter), allowing the system to use a variety of inputs to prepare the most accurate forecast.

In addition to forecasting demand at each distribution point, the DRP system has to account for order quantities (called lot sizes). The system also has to factor in order lead times for each product to decide when each order should be placed, thereby minimizing inventory costs and ensuring that inventory stays at the desired level.

Following are some DRP vendors:

>> **Infor**

www.infor.com/solutions/scm/planning/

>> **Microsoft**

www.microsoft.com/en-us/dynamics365/ax-overview

>> **Oracle**

www.oracle.com/applications/jd-edwards-enterpriseone/manufacturing-management/requirements-planning/index.html

>> **SAP**

www.sap.com/products/extended-warehouse-management.html

Using Labor Management Systems

Supply chains aren't just about inventory items; people are involved too. You have to decide how many people you need on each shift to meet the demands on your warehouse. You also have to track the performance of your workers and identify those who deserve rewards and those who need more training. You perform these tasks with a piece of software called a *labor management system* (LMS).

LMSes can help with scheduling to make sure that you have enough people to do the work on each shift. This system reduces the risk of not getting the work done because you're short-staffed, which can translate into overtime for the next shift. It also reduces the risk of having people sitting idle because there isn't enough work for all the people on a shift. LMSes can track performance in ways that help you understand how efficient your associates are, as well as how and where you can improve efficiency.

In many warehousing and distribution centers, labor is a huge part of operating costs, so having an LMS that does a good job of planning requirements and monitoring performance can have a huge effect on the efficiency of a facility.

Following are some LMS vendors:

» **enVista**

www.envistacorp.com/labor-management-systems.html

» **HighJump**

www.highjump.com/resources/product-literature/
wms-highjump-labor-management-solution

» **Intelligrated**

www.intelligrated.com/software/labor-management-software

» **JDA**

https://jda.com/solutions/adaptable-manufacturing-
distribution-solutions/intelligent-fulfillment/
warehouse-labor-management

» **Manhattan Associates**

www.manh.com/products/labor-management

Using Customer Relationship Management Systems

Keeping track of your customers is essential for every business, and the software applications that perform this tracking are called *customer relationship management* (CRM) systems. A CRM system can track who your customers are, who their employees in various divisions are, and what they've bought from you in the past. A CRM system can help you understand what deals you have in the pipeline so that you can do a better job of forecasting future sales. It can manage accounts receivable by tracking contracts, payments, and credits for each customer account. It can help you increase revenue by looking for customers who may be interested in new products and services. It can target offers and messages to customers based on their unique characteristics.

A CRM system can tell you a lot about your sales organization, providing reports on how often each sales representative engages with his or her accounts, for example. The CRM system can tie into other systems to improve the flow of information along the supply chain. If a CRM system is integrated with a TMS system (refer to "Using Transportation Management Systems" earlier in this chapter), for example, your customers may be able to track their own shipments.

Fundamentally, a CRM system connects your organization to your customers and ties your customers to you, which makes it a critical link in your supply chain.

Following are some CRM vendors:

>> **Infor**

www.infor.com/product-summary/cx/infor-crm/

>> **Microsoft**

https://dynamics.microsoft.com/en-us/

>> **Oracle**

www.oracle.com/applications/customer-experience/crm/index.html

>> **Salesforce**

www.salesforce.com/

>> **SAP**

www.sap.com/products/crm-commerce.html

Using Supplier Relationship Management Systems

Managing relationships with your suppliers is an important part of supply chain management. The computer program that keeps track of supplier information is called a *supplier relationship management* (SRM) system.

At minimum, an SRM system tells you who your suppliers are, what products you buy from them, what payment terms you've agreed to, and what contracts you have in place. The system should help you keep track of communications among various members of the supplier's team and the people in your company who interact with them. The system should help you analyze and report on supplier performance.

SRM systems are especially useful for making strategic supply chain plans. The system can identify the suppliers and products that are most likely to create bottlenecks if you try to increase your production targets. It can identify the suppliers that are most likely to benefit from additional investments, such as training or new equipment. Finally, it can help you spot suppliers that are at risk or should be replaced.

An SRM system plays the critical role of linking your company with your suppliers, which makes it an essential tool for managing your supply chain.

Following are some SRM vendors:

>> **Ariba**

www.ariba.com/about

>> **BravoSolution**

http://srm.bravosolution.com/

>> **SAP**

www.sap.com/products/supplier-relationship-management.html

Using Enterprise Resources Planning Systems

Many stand-alone systems support individual supply chain functions, which may lead you to ask, "Why all the different systems?" These systems largely evolved from simple spreadsheets to support individual functions, as shown in Figure 12-2. Now the systems have started to converge into massive, integrated programs called *enterprise resource planning* (ERP) systems. Depending on the brand and the configuration, an ERP system can contain modules that perform all the functions of the systems discussed earlier in this chapter, as well as many more.

An ERP system can automate many of the functions and processes in a supply chain, from scheduling production to ordering replenishments to responding to customer orders, and ensure that the information moves smoothly from one step in the process to the next. That's the good news. The bad news is that ERP systems are extremely complex, and configuring them often involves massive effort and changes in existing manufacturing processes that can be difficult to implement.

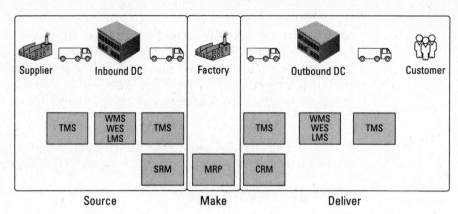

FIGURE 12-2:
Basic ERP system
modules.

Following are some ERP vendors:

>> **Infor**

www.infor.com/solutions/erp/

>> **Microsoft**

https://dynamics.microsoft.com/en-us/

>> **Oracle**

www.oracle.com/applications/erp/index.html

>> **SAP**

www.sap.com/products/enterprise-management-erp.html

Using Supply Chain Modeling Software

Figuring out what your supply chain looks like can be a huge challenge. With suppliers, customers, distribution centers, and factories spread around the world, it can be difficult to choose the best supply chain configuration.

Supply chain modeling software can help by taking two approaches to analyzing your supply chain network:

>> **Simulation:** You create a computer model of the supply chain that you have — or that you want — and then simulate how that supply chain would perform. You simulate what happens as customers buy products so that you see what actions the purchase triggers through the rest of the supply chain.

The simulation shows you whether you can meet expected demand, as well as what happens to inventory levels and transportation costs. You can run simulations of different supply chain configurations to determine how each configuration performs. This process usually is much faster and cheaper than building a real supply chain and waiting to see what happens.

>> **Optimization:** You tell the software what your supply chain needs to do, and the software tells you how to configure your factories and distribution centers. Optimization software eliminates bottlenecks and extra capacity throughout your supply chain. It calculates safety stock levels and reorder points for products in each area of your distribution network.

Most supply chain software — the stuff that goes into an ERP system (refer to "Using Enterprise Resources Planning Systems" earlier in this chapter) — is really just a big database, storing transactions and tracking relationships among different types of data. But supply chain modeling software uses sophisticated math and performs complex calculations to predict the behavior of actual supply chains.

Supply chain modeling can be based on either of two mathematical approaches:

>> **Deterministic:** In this type of model, you're precise in your guess about how something will work. You might make the deterministic estimate that the demand will be for 500 units, for example.

>> **Stochastic:** In this type of model, you model probabilities. Your stochastic model might estimate demand to be between 400 and 600 units, for example.

The stochastic models are a bit more complicated than deterministic models, but they often do a better job of representing how a supply chain will operate under real-world conditions.

You use supply chain modeling software to save time and money when making improvements in your supply chain. The software helps you achieve a larger goal. The model needs to be only good enough to provide the right answer. When you have confidence in the results of a model, spending more time and money to make the model better may not provide any benefit to your business or to your supply chain.

Following are some vendors of supply chain modeling software:

>> **anyLogistix**

www.anylogistix.com/

>> **Arena**

www.arenasimulation.com/industry-solutions/industry/
supply-chain-simulation-software

>> **Flexsim**

www.flexsim.com/flexsim/

>> **Llamasoft**

www.llamasoft.com/

>> **Simio**

www.simio.com/index.php

>> **simul8**

www.simul8.com/

Using Business Intelligence Software

Understanding what's happening across a supply chain involves tapping many data sources for analysis and reporting. The software that enables people to perform these tasks is called *business intelligence* (BI) software.

BI software needs to do three things well:

>> **Connect with data:** The software needs to be able to connect with your data, no matter where it's stored. A BI system may need to talk with your other supply chain systems. Alternatively, you may need to combine the data from all these systems into a single data warehouse so that your BI system can access that data easily.

>> **Combine and analyze data:** A BI system needs to combine and analyze data from other systems, even though it's often difficult to link data from different systems. Fortunately, BI systems have sophisticated techniques that make this task relatively easy.

>> **Provide insights:** A BI system needs to provide answers to questions about your supply chain in ways that are easy for people to understand, sometimes illustrating the data in graphs, charts, and pictures.

BI features are sometimes built into other supply chain software, such as ERP systems (refer to "Using Enterprise Resources Planning Systems" earlier in this chapter). Because these systems already contain much of the data that you need, including a BI tool in them makes sense.

Another trend in BI systems is to create dashboards that allow managers to see what's happening in their business. These dashboards can be automated, which makes it easy to track what's happening in real time so managers know where to focus their attention right now.

Following are some BI vendors:

>> **IBM**

www.ibm.com/business-intelligence

>> **Microsoft**

https://powerbi.microsoft.com/en-us/

>> **Oracle**

www.oracle.com/solutions/business-analytics/business-intelligence/index.html

>> **Qlik**

www.qlik.com/us/

>> **SAP**

www.sap.com/products/analytics/business-intelligence-bi.html

>> **SAS**

www.sas.com/en_us/solutions/business-intelligence.html

>> **Tableau**

www.tableau.com/

Leveraging Software Analysts

So many categories of supply chain software are available, with so many competing applications in each category, that keeping track of them is a full-time job. Professional software analysts study supply chain software so that they can make recommendations to the rest of us about which tools are the most useful.

Some analysts work for supply chain software vendors. These analysts focus on defining capabilities and demonstrating the benefits of their company's software compared with competitors' software.

GARTNER'S MAGIC QUADRANT

Analysts often develop models to compare the strengths and weaknesses of various supply chain software vendors. Gartner has popularized a concept called the Magic Quadrant (see the figure). Each software vendor in a category is rated based on the completeness of their vision and their ability to execute. The leading software providers should have both a complete vision and ability to execute. There's room for niche players who may not rate well on either dimension, and there are spots for contenders and visionaries. Models like the Magic Quadrant make it easier to tell which vendors will be a good fit for your needs.

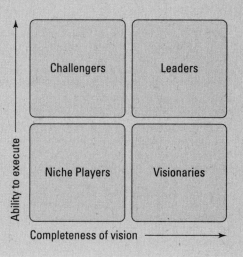

Other analysts are independent, working on their own or with small consulting teams, and they specialize in studying industry trends. Two good examples are Supply Chain Insights (`http://supplychaininsights.com/`) led by Lora Cecere, and Adelante SCM (`http://adelantescm.com/`) led by Adrian Gonzales. Even though these firms are small, their leaders are well-known, and their opinions are valued by many executives in the supply chain industry.

Some supply chain software analysts work for large companies that publish research reports and support major consulting projects for selecting, installing, and integrating these tools into an existing supply chain. Four of the best-known supply chain analyst firms are Gartner (`www.gartner.com/technology/supply-chain-professionals.jsp`), Aberdeen (`www.aberdeen.com/_aberdeen/Supply-Chain-Management/SCMA/practice.aspx`), ARC Advisory Group (`www.arcweb.com/`), and Forrester (`https://go.forrester.com/research/vendor-selection/`).

Software analysts often charge thousands of dollars for access to their research, but that is cheap compared to the time and money it could take for you to research software on your own. More importantly, analysts can help to protect you from the mistake of buying software that isn't a good fit for your business.

Anticipating the Future of Supply Chain Software

Technology is evolving from helping people plan tasks to executing those tasks automatically. In that sense, supply chain software is evolving from a *planning* role to an *execution* role.

Referring to any software platform as a supply chain execution solution implies that it somehow addresses all your supply chain needs, which isn't the case — yet. The day may come when all these software platforms are truly integrated, which would eliminate the need for people to be involved in any part of a supply chain. Artificial intelligence may lead to autonomous supply chains someday, and at that point, automated supply chain execution will become reality.

Chapter **13**

Integrating Advanced Manufacturing into Your Supply Chain

With machines getting smarter, stronger, and faster every day, dealing with the rapid pace of innovation has become an important part of supply chain management. Many of the principles of supply chain management are built on assumptions about the capabilities of manufacturing and distribution processes. How much you can make, how far you can move it, and how much it will cost all depend on what technologies you use. New technologies are changing the way supply chains work, and will require supply chain managers to re-evaluate the best ways to plan, source, make, deliver, and return products in the future.

The problem with these new technologies is that it is hard to predict how quickly they will become available and how significantly they will impact a supply chain. In many cases, new technologies provide new ways to perform the same tasks we are already doing, but the technologies enable us to do those things better, faster, and cheaper. In other cases, new technologies disrupt entire industries and could make the tasks we are doing today obsolete.

These new technologies for making products and managing processes are often described as *advanced manufacturing*, but the trend goes beyond manufacturing to include design and distribution. Really, it would be better to use the term *advanced supply chains*.

This chapter discusses many of the important trends and technologies that are likely to change the way that manufacturing and distribution are done in the future. These advanced technologies will lead to changes in the way we design and manage supply chains, too.

Avoiding Obsolescence

Advances in technology can quickly make an entire supply chain obsolete. Obsolescence can occur in two ways: products become obsolete or processes become obsolete.

Examples of products that have been made obsolete by technological innovation are easy to find: the typewriter, the film camera, the video cassette. Companies that made a lot of money manufacturing these products are now extinct. The demand for the products that these companies made went away because customers found that a new type of product worked better.

A good example of a process that became obsolete is the story of the ice industry. Did you know that ice — plain old frozen H2O — was the number-two product exported by the U.S. in 1850? Back then, there was a huge industry built around harvesting, transporting, and storing ice. The ice supply chain crisscrossed the globe, and companies in the United States were the leading suppliers. Later in the 1800s, though, after refrigeration technology was developed, it became possible to manufacture ice on demand, anywhere. In other words, the development of refrigeration technology changed the process and made the old supply chains for the ice industry completely obsolete.

The story of the ice trade is an example of how a new technology can disrupt an established process. The key point from the story is that the demand for the product—ice — did not diminish and the supply didn't go away. In other words, people didn't stop using ice, and refrigeration actually made ice much more widely available. However, the long global supply chains for ice that involved transportation and material handling were more expensive and less reliable than the newly invented refrigerators; therefore those global supply chains went away as they were replaced with the newer technology and processes.

No matter what business you are in, there are new technologies being developed that could disrupt your product or your process. Part of your job as a supply chain manager is to be aware of emerging technologies, and try to anticipate the effect they will have on your business. You may be able to gain a competitive advantage by adopting new technologies early. Or, if a new technology will make your business obsolete, you might need to be proactive in developing a plan to remain profitable in a shrinking market.

Capitalizing on Advanced Manufacturing

There are several new technological capabilities that are changing the way engineers think about designing and manufacturing products. As a group, these technologies are creating a new field called *advanced manufacturing*. Three of the capabilities that are enabling advanced manufacturing are

>> Automated manufacturing

>> Computer-aided design

>> 3D printing

Automated manufacturing

Automated equipment is a critical part of virtually every supply chain. The work of creating, installing, and maintaining this equipment is often called industrial automation. Automation usually starts with machines that are programmed and operated by people, but it can evolve into completely automated manufacturing systems that basically operate autonomously. In the future, you might even see machines in a factory that are able to detect problems and repair themselves!

Automated processes can be controlled in two ways:

>> **Open loop:** In an *open-loop* system, the automated process operates based on a fixed input. The process may operate on a set schedule or produce a specific number of widgets, for example.

>> **Closed loop:** In a *closed-loop* system, the automated process receives feedback that it uses to make decisions. For example, a process might monitor yield and then adjust the production target to ensure enough usable products are manufactured. (See Chapter 8 for more information about yield.)

A good example of the difference between open-loop and closed-loop systems is a security light. If a light turns on and off according to a set schedule, the system is an open loop. If the light is triggered by a motion sensor so that it turns on only when something moves nearby, the system is a closed loop. The evolution of closed-loop systems that can receive inputs and respond appropriately is driving much of the growth of automated manufacturing.

Computer-aided design

Computers have become essential to the process of designing products. In the old days, a draftsman created a blueprint for a product by hand. These days, that entire process is done via computer-aided design (CAD). Rather than send a physical blueprint to a factory, a designer sends a CAD file directly to a computer-aided manufacturing (CAM) system, which decides how to manufacture or assemble the product from the CAD file. The whole process — from design through manufacturing and assembly — can be done with computers, reducing or eliminating the need for printouts and prototypes. When CAD/CAM processes are automated and integrated with one another, they are called *virtual design, virtual manufacturing,* or *virtual assembly* processes.

3D printing

One exciting technology development is 3D printing. In order to decide whether a supply chain is likely to be affected by 3D printing you first need to understand how 3D printing works.

Many — if not most — products have been made by *subtractive manufacturing,* which means removing extra material until you have the shape you need. (Think of Michelangelo chipping away at marble to create a sculpture.) 3D printing is the opposite process. Instead of removing extra material, 3D printing adds material to make a product. That's why the process is called *additive manufacturing.*

3D printing is a broad term that covers many techniques, most of which use one of three types of material *(feedstock)* to make products: solid materials (usually in spools), powders, and liquids.

By far the most common 3D-printing technology uses spools of plastic as feedstock. These printers deposit small amounts of molten material in layers, gradually building a finished part through a process called *fused deposition modeling* (FDM). FDM is similar to a hot-glue gun or a wire-feed welder. The raw material usually comes on a spool and is fed into a nozzle, where it's melted and then squeezed onto a platform. The nozzle is mounted on arms that allow it to move front to back, side to side, and up and down. In other words, the nozzle prints in three dimensions. Figure 13-1 shows an FDM 3D printer.

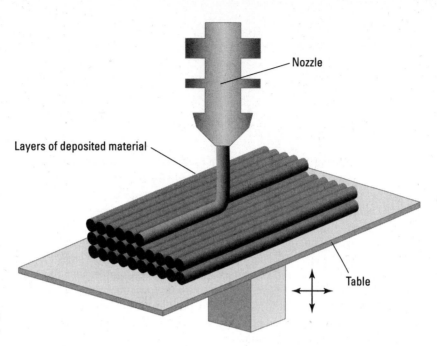

Nozzle

Layers of deposited material

Table

FIGURE 13-1:
FDM 3D printer.

TECHNICAL STUFF

Squeezing a melted material through a small opening is called *extrusion,* which is a common manufacturing method for metals and plastics. FDM printers create extruded products, but because the nozzle moves in three dimensions, FDM is more flexible than traditional extrusion techniques.

Because of the material limitations of FDM, other 3D-printing technologies may be more useful for your supply chain. You can print powdered materials through a process called selective laser sintering, for example, and you can print hardened liquids through a process called stereolithography.

3D printing has potential benefits for manufacturing supply chains:

>> Manufacturers can print shapes that would be difficult to make with other processes.

>> Waste and energy consumption are lower.

>> Inventory and transportation costs are lower because products can be printed when and where they're needed. (See the section on postponement in Chapter 15.)

3D printing also has some limitations:

>> Options for the materials used to make a product are limited.

>> The size and quality of a product are limited by the capabilities of the printer.

>> 3D printing tends to be much slower than traditional manufacturing.

3D printing works well with CAD (refer to "Computer-aided design" earlier in this chapter). When you have a CAD file for the object you want to make, you can send those instructions to a 3D printer just as you'd send a document to a regular printer.

When making a prototype or a small number of items 3D printing also has real advantages. For example, the cost of 3D printing a single prototype is often much lower than the cost of creating the dies, molds, and tooling required for mass production of parts with traditional manufacturing techniques. And 3D printing can be a better alternative for products that have unpredictable demand, for customers who need products quickly, and for customers who are a long way from the factory or distribution center.

When and where 3D printing makes sense in your supply chain are two questions that you'll probably need to ask and answer over and over. As your business, products, and customers change, you may have to adopt 3D printing. As the technology gets better (which it certainly will), the barriers to using 3D printing will fall.

3D PRINTING IN HUMANITARIAN SUPPLY CHAINS

Humanitarian supply chains may reap great benefits from 3D printing. One example is the use of 3D printing to make plumbing fittings in remote parts of the world. A humanitarian organization might ship all the components needed to install a water well in a remote village, but when workers start to assemble the plumbing, they realize that they're missing a part that isn't available locally. The whole project would stall. Rather than shipping the part via a parcel carrier and dealing with logistics and customs issues, the humanitarian organization instead might be able to send a file to a nearby 3D printer.

Another supply chain that could be affected by 3D printing involves parts for industrial equipment such as tractors and electrical generators. This equipment is expensive, and breakdowns can have life-threatening consequences. As a result, companies spend lots of money on inventory for spare parts just to make sure that they're available. If a company could print those parts, it might be able to eliminate that inventory.

AUTOMATION LINGO

Several technical terms come up frequently when people talk about automated manufacturing and distribution. Being familiar with the following terms will make it much easier for you to follow the conversation:

1. **Artificial neural network:** An artificial neural network (ANN) is a type of computer program that uses feedback loops to recognize patterns and learn from its own experience. ANNs are an example of artificial intelligence that enables computers to perform tasks that used to require human intervention. For example, ANNs play a key role in voice recognition systems such as Apple's Siri.

2. **Control limits:** The acceptable upper and lower bounds of a process output are called the control limits. For example, you may say that every widget you manufacture needs to weigh 100 pounds, plus or minus 1 pound. In other words, as long as the widget is between 99 pounds and 101 pounds, it is within the control limits.

3. **Human-machine interface:** A *human–machine interface* (HMI) is a device that allows machines and humans to exchange information. The display of your computer is an HMI, for example. In advanced manufacturing, HMIs can include displays, touchscreens, voice-recognition systems, keyboards, and joysticks.

4. **Interface:** An *interface* is a piece of software that exchanges information between two computer systems.

5. **Interlock:** An *interlock* is a device that connects two systems. Interlocks are often used as safety precautions. The access door for an area that has a robotic arm may have an interlock installed so that if someone opens the door, the robot stops moving.

6. **Operating parameters:** Automated equipment is generally designed to work under a range of conditions called the operating parameters. For example, if it is too hot or too cold, the temperature could fall outside of the operating parameters and the equipment could malfunction.

7. **Programmable logic controller:** A *programmable logic controller* (PLC) is a special kind of computer that controls automated equipment. PLCs are designed to be simple, flexible, and durable.

Automated Mobile Robots

If you've been in a factory or distribution center lately, you've seen how common automated material handling systems are. Long, winding conveyors move and sort packages, and many facilities have tall automated storage and retrieval systems. This equipment can move more material than people can, so it radically increases the capacity of a facility. However the equipment requires a large upfront investment in equipment, and once it has been installed it is difficult to make changes. In other words, the drawbacks to traditional automation equipment are that it is expensive and inflexible.

A different type of automated material handling system is starting to become popular in fulfillment centers: autonomous mobile robots. These robots are relatively inexpensive and extremely versatile. You can increase or decrease your picking capacity by adding or removing robots from the network. These robots can work around the clock, seven days per week, so one robot could replace three or four human pickers. Some robotic systems can change the layout of your facility simply by programming the robots to move your racks to different locations. Companies like Amazon Robotics, Locus Robotics, inVia Robotics, and Swisslog all make robots that can pick inventory in a warehouse and carry it to the area where it will be packed and shipped.

As robots become more common, supply chain managers will need to re-evaluate how their fulfillment centers are designed and operated. These robots could greatly increase the productivity of human workers, but also could eliminate many jobs that are currently done by people.

Unmanned and Autonomous Vehicles

For many years, unmanned vehicles have been important tools in supply chains. Factories use remote control vehicles to move heavy objects; in mines, loaders and other equipment are operated by remote control. The new generation of unmanned vehicles are called *drones*. Drones are different from traditional remote-controlled vehicles because drones are autonomous, meaning that they can travel from one place to another without getting instructions from a person.

Drones fall into four categories:

>> Unmanned aerial vehicles (UAVs) fly through the air, like airplanes or helicopters.

>> Unmanned ground vehicles (UGVs) travel over land, like cars and trucks.

>> Unmanned surface vehicles (USVs) travel over the water, like ships.

>> Unmanned underwater vehicles (UUVs) travel under the water, like submarines.

The line between remote-controlled vehicles and autonomous vehicles can be blurry if a person is providing instructions at the same time that the vehicle is making some of its own decisions. For example, there may be a person directing the drone to travel to a certain location, but the drone is still considered autonomous because it is calculating its own flight path based on wind velocity, hazards, and so on.

It's pretty easy to identify places where drones could make supply chains faster, safer, cheaper, and more reliable. Google Waymo and Uber Freight have both developed autonomous ground vehicles that could carry freight thousands of miles without getting tired. Amazon is one of many companies with an autonomous aerial vehicle that can deliver packages to your doorstep, speeding up delivery while reducing traffic on the roads.

On the one hand, you need to be careful about getting caught up in the hype. For drones to do a lot of things that people are dreaming of, the technology needs to get better, to get better. On the other hand, there are many companies working hard to make the needed improvements. You should pay attention to how drone technology is advancing so that you can incorporate it into your supply chain when and where it makes sense.

One of the factors of using autonomous vehicles that you need to consider is the risks that the vehicles present. For example, there are reasons to doubt whether drones will be reliable enough to support many supply chains. If a drone makes a mistake, such as delivering products to the wrong location, the consequences could be severe.

Some people are skeptical about the business value of using drones. In order to provide a business benefit, you need to have a clear understanding of how drones actually help you increase revenue, reduce costs, or avoid costs in the future.

There are also questions related to the brand impacts of using drones in a supply chain. On one hand, using autonomous vehicles could make your brand more valuable (as in, "Yeah, that brand is awesome because they have drones"), but it could also cause damage to your brand (as in, "Nope, those guys are awful because they employ robots instead of humans").

Chapter **14**

Managing Digital Supply Chains

Virtually every supply chain transaction boils down to a three-step process: A customer gives a supplier some money, the supplier gives the customer a product or service, and the customer and supplier exchange some information. That's why it's common to think of a supply chain as three flows: money, material, and information. (See Chapter 2 for a description of this approach.) Advances in information technology are changing all three of these flows and generating new opportunities to create value with digital supply chains.

Your *digital supply chain* consists of all the information about your products, transactions, and locations that is stored or shared electronically. Warehouse management systems, transportation management systems, and all of the other systems discussed in Chapter 12 are part of your digital supply chain; each of them helps your business operate more efficiently.

But there are three trends that are redefining the role of digital tools in supply chain management:

» The evolution of products from analog to digital to digitalized

» The convergence of planning, execution, and visibility systems

>> The desire by customers to have products and services customized to their specific needs

This chapter looks at each of these trends and why they are making digital supply chains so important. It also discusses some of the technology, tools, and applications that are making these trends possible.

Digitalizing Products and Services

One of the major trends that is occurring around us is digitalization. Digitalization is the process through which the physical products and services people buy become dependent on virtual products and services. As products and services are digitalized, they create new opportunities and challenges for a digital supply chain.

The most extreme examples of digitalization occur when a physical product or service is replaced by an electronic version. For example, digitalization has been apparent in the supply chains for movies for several years. A few years ago most people would buy a movie by purchasing an analog video tape, which had a pretty conventional supply chain. A factory would make the video tapes and then ship them to distribution centers; the distribution centers would ship the tapes to retail stores.

Then movies were converted to a digital format and stored on DVDs. Even though the movies were digital, the DVDs were still physical products, and the supply chains for DVDs were similar to the supply chains for video tapes. Today, movies are becoming digitalized. Instead of buying a DVD, now you download movies from the Internet. The physical supply chain for movies is being replaced by a digital supply chain that allows movie producers to eliminate inventory and transportation costs, and customers can watch those movies on a TV, a computer, or even a phone.

TECHNICAL STUFF

Converting anything from analog to digital involves translating it into a series of 0s and 1s that a computer can understand. Once a product becomes digital, it can often be digitalized — the product can become completely virtual.

Services can also be digitalized. The supply chain for education, for example, is being changed by online learning. In the past, college students had to travel to a university to take classes on complex topics. Today, many of those courses are available anywhere in the world over the Internet. Other service businesses that are being digitalized include travel agencies, taxi dispatch, and even healthcare. Technology is transforming the way that these services are delivered to customers. In this transformation process, digital supply chains are becoming more essential.

Digitalization doesn't always eliminate physical products. Smartphones are an example of a physical product, with a physical supply chain, that is also dependent on a digital supply chain. In order for a smartphone to deliver the value that customers expect, the physical supply chain has to deliver a phone, and the digital supply chain has to deliver apps and data.

The good news about digitalization is that customers often get more options for the same products, which means digitalization tends to make supply chains more customer-centric. The bad news is that offering both physical and digitalized versions of a product costs businesses money. Because not all customers make the switch from physical to digitalized products at the same time, companies have to carry the cost of making both available.

Integrating Planning, Execution, and Visibility

The different categories of supply chain software (see Chapter 12) generally fill one of three roles: planning, execution, or visibility.

>> Planning software uses forecasts to make decisions about how a supply chain should operate. For example, an inventory planning system might decide when to place a replenishment order.

>> Execution software looks at real-time data about orders, inventory, and capacity and makes decisions that determine how a supply chain will operate. For example, a warehouse execution system might receive an order from a customer and then instruct an associate to pick that item from a particular inventory location.

>> Visibility software aggregates real-time data to show supply chain managers what's happening. For example, visibility software could show which replenishments have been placed, which customer orders are being processed, and whether there is a risk of a stockout.

Planning, execution, and visibility are all important capabilities for a digital supply chain. Advances in information technology, such as faster processors and cloud computing (discussed in a later section) are making it possible for the information from all three types of systems to be processed and shared much faster. This may change the way that we think about supply chain management.

In a traditional supply chain, the first step is planning, which is followed by execution, and visibility brings up the rear. You plan what you are going to sell, forecast how much your customers are going to buy, estimate how much inventory you are going to need, and so on. Then you execute by receiving orders, shipping products, and tendering loads. All the while, you try to get visibility so that you can see what has happened.

As digital supply chains mature, the three steps can happen simultaneously. A digital supply chain can have visibility to what customers are buying and how much inventory is available. With this visibility it can make execution decisions while taking into account the current state of the entire supply chain. As these execution decisions are made, planning systems are able to make real-time adjustments to forecasts, production schedules, and replenishment orders.

The result of integrating planning, execution, and visibility is that digital supply chains are becoming more responsive to customer needs.

Creating Customer Centricity

Henry Ford was famous for saying that customers could buy a Model T car in any color they wanted, as long as it was black. Ford Motor Company built its early success on standardizing processes and products, which drove down the costs for its supply chain and allowed Ford to offer low prices to its customers.

One-size-fits-all supply chains are efficient because they create economies of scale, but they often don't satisfy customers very well. Many customers would rather have customized, or *bespoke*, products and services that are tailored to their needs. For example, some customers prefer to have clothing that is made to fit their measurements rather than mass-produced garments. The ability to offer customers bespoke solutions at a reasonable cost can provide a company with a strong competitive advantage and has led to a supply chain strategy called *mass customization*. Companies that operate with a mass customization model wait until a customer places an order and then manufacture a product that meets the customer's exact specifications. Mass customization relies on the make-to-order production system (see Chapter 6).

Dell Computer used mass customization to gain a competitive advantage in the early days of the PC industry. While other computer companies offered standard models with predefined components, Dell allowed each customer to decide exactly which components she wanted to include in the computer when she placed an order. Because Dell couldn't begin assembling the computer until after an order had been received, the company needed to ensure that all of the manufacturing and distribution steps occurred very quickly. Dell's very successful use of a mass customization strategy relied on the ability to capture, store, and share information in its digital supply chain.

Another important aspect of customer-centricity is delivery flexibility. Amazon.com has been a pioneer in providing delivery flexibility, but the trend is now spreading to other retailers and logistics providers. Customers like the convenience of having products delivered to their homes or offices, and they also like to have products delivered quickly, or to have the ability to schedule a delivery time. Many retailers now offer customers the choice of buying products in a store, ordering online and picking the products up in a store, ordering online and having the products shipped to their homes, or ordering in the store and having the products shipped to their homes. Delivery flexibility is only possible if a company has a digital supply chain that can efficiently match customer demand with information about inventory and transportation capacity.

Sharing with Blockchains

Information sharing in digital supply chains is often constrained because of three problems:

>> **Systems mismatch:** Information is stored in different systems, which makes it hard for the parties in a supply chain to share data efficiently.

>> **Data reliability:** Companies need to have complete confidence that their supply chain information is accurate and that no one can change it without their permission.

>> **Trust in partners:** Companies do not know all the people and companies in their supply chain and are reluctant to share information with strangers.

Blockchain is a new technology that tries to solve these problems. A *blockchain* is a ledger that's distributed to many computers, called *nodes*. The ledger is a database made up of blocks of data that are connected in a chain. To make a change in the database, such as adding information, you need to add a new block of data to the chain. Before you can add the block to the chain, all the nodes need to agree to add that block. After a block is added to the chain, it can never be changed — that is, it's immutable. For that reason, blockchains are often called immutable distributed ledgers.

An immutable distributed ledger is useful for supply chains because it allows companies to share information in a way that's very difficult to change or hack. As a result, companies can have a high level of trust in the information in the blockchain. With a blockchain, you create rules for what information is shared and who gets to see it. A blockchain provides a common platform that lets many participants in a supply chain track and share information about the transactions that matter to all of them.

One feature of blockchains that may transform supply chains is the *smart contract:* an agreement between parties to perform some actions. You can digitalize a contract and post it to a blockchain. As each party to the contract does the things that it agreed to do, that information is added to the blockchain, and the contract executes automatically.

Suppose that you sold a widget to a customer you've never met who lives in another country. You and your customer both need to manage the risk of doing business with a stranger. One way to manage this risk is by using a blockchain in a process that might go something like this:

1. You enter into a smart contract with the customer and post the contract to a blockchain. You and the customer can both see and agree to the contract.

2. The customer gives his payment to a third party, such as a bank, on condition that the bank will pay you when the product is delivered.

3. You pay a third-party logistics company to deliver the widget and require that company to log the delivery in the blockchain.

4. When the product is delivered, the bank is notified, and you're paid. In other words, the contract is fully executed.

This approach is likely to change the way that many supply chains are managed in the future. It's also likely to create interesting opportunities for entrepreneurs who can take advantage of the ability to transact business quickly and efficiently with strangers, as well as with their traditional supply chain partners.

Harnessing the Internet of Things, Big Data, and the Cloud

One of the key drivers of improvements in supply chain visibility is the emergence of the Internet of Things (IoT). Today, there are more than twice as many devices connected to the Internet as there are people in the world, and IoT devices are growing at about 20 percent per year.

Many of these devices are sensors that share information about where they are and what's happening around them. In other words, they provide information that improves supply chain visibility. Some of these devices also receive instructions over the Internet, make decisions, and take action based on the data that they collect. In other words, IoT devices can be useful for supply chain execution. For example, a truck driver might carry an IoT device that transmits her location to a transportation management system while also providing instructions about where she will deliver her next package based on the latest traffic conditions.

The growth of supply chain information systems and the emergence of IoT have contributed to another trend that is important for digital supply chains: Big Data. Big Data is great for supply chains because it can help companies find out about their customers, their products, and their infrastructure. The growth of Big Data also means that there's really no limit to how much a company can spend on technology. Companies may seem to be on a treadmill, continually buying bigger servers with more storage and upgrading them with newer software. They also need to keep their hardware, software, and data secure, all of which can be major expenses.

Many companies are replacing on-premise supply chain information systems with virtual computers, called *cloud-based servers*, which can be accessed over the Internet. One of the advantages of cloud-based supply chain solutions is that you can share the data in real time with people anywhere in the world.

Other advantages of cloud-based solutions include

>> Scaling processing and storage up or down based on business needs

>> Instant access to software upgrades

>> Reductions in infrastructure and staff

>> Access to applications on any kind of device anywhere in the world

Cloud-based solutions also have disadvantages:

>> You depend on the service provider to keep your business working.

>> Data and applications are on the Internet, where bad guys could hack or steal them.

>> All users must have access to the Internet.

>> Switching platforms can be difficult.

Employing Artificial Intelligence

Many of the jobs that are critical to making supply chains work properly involve collecting data and making decisions. Advances in artificial intelligence (AI) are making it possible for computers to do many of these jobs as well, or better than, their human counterparts. In other words, AI is taking jobs that used to be part of the physical supply chain and moving them into the digital supply chain. For example, one of the supply chain challenges that computers can address more effectively than people is instantly interpreting inputs from multiple data sources, such as Big Data that's mentioned in the previous section.

What makes AI different from traditional computing is that with AI the computer doesn't need to be told exactly how to do something. Instead, the computer is able to start with a basic set of instructions and then learn how to respond over time. This process is called *machine learning*. A computer program that is designed with AI to perform a certain task is called an intelligent agent. An example of an intelligent agent that uses machine learning to get better over time is Apple's Siri voice recognition system.

AI has the potential to change the role that people play in supply chains. For example, intelligent agents are already replacing people in roles like customer service representatives and dispatchers. With the trend toward planning, execution, and visibility systems converging it is likely that AI will play an important role in managing digital supply chains in the future.

Retooling for Omnichannel

As a consumer, you may take e-commerce for granted. You open a website, find a product to buy, enter your credit card number, and the stuff you ordered is on its way. For the company that needs to fill this order, though, e-commerce creates supply chain challenges.

One of the biggest differences between a traditional supply chain and an e-commerce supply chain is how products are delivered from the company to the customer. The final distribution leg, called the *last mile*, is also one of the most expensive steps in any supply chain. In a traditional retail supply chain, customers do the work and pay the transportation costs to get products from the store to their homes. In the world of e-commerce, the retailer is responsible for picking items from the shelf and delivering products to consumers, including the last mile. Rather than customers picking up the product at a store, retailers need to pay people to pick, pack, and ship that product; they also need to pay a parcel freight carrier to drop it off. This adds a significant cost to the retailer's supply chain.

Although many customers enjoy the convenience of online shopping and home delivery, most of them aren't willing to pay extra to have products delivered to them. So retailers are stuck with a big problem: To remain profitable, they have to increase revenue or lower supply chain costs to offset the effect of last-mile logistics.

The place that a customer goes to buy a product or service is called a channel. Retail stores represent a sales channel for a supply chain. Many people refer to retail stores as a *brick-and-mortar* channel. E-commerce is a different sales channel. Each channel may sell the same products — and might even sell to the same customers — but the supply chains for these channels are different. For example, a retail distribution center may ship out pallets of merchandise on a full truckload carrier, whereas an e-commerce fulfillment center needs to ship out individual items to customers by parcel carrier.

To compete in both the brick-and-mortar and the e-commerce marketplaces retail companies are now focused on developing an *omnichannel distribution* model. With an omnichannel supply chain a customer could buy a product online and return the product to a retail store. A customer could also look at the products in a store but have them shipped directly to their houses, an approach called *showrooming*. The opposite of showrooming is called *click and collect*, when a customer buys a product online and picks it up at a store. In other words, an omnichannel model makes it easier for customers to do business with you, and makes your supply chain more customer-centric.

Omnichannel distribution is a business strategy that is made possible by digital supply chains. An omnichannel approach requires you to have lots of flexibility and excellent information sharing across all the customer-facing parts in your supply chain. For example, your website may need to show whether an item is in stock in each of your retail stores, and your retail stores need to have a process for managing returns from online purchases. This end-to-end integration is different from the way that many traditional supply chains were engineered, so making the shift often requires the integration of multiple information systems (see Chapter 12) into a single digital supply chain.

TIP

The New Supply Chain Agenda (see Chapter 1) is a good starting point for implementing an omnichannel supply chain.

4

Driving Value with Supply Chain Management

IN THIS CHAPTER

» Minimizing inventory by improving
information flow

» Reducing complexity by eliminating
unprofitable products

» Trimming costs and working capital
requirements

» Financing innovation and
improvement with quick wins

Chapter 15

Transforming Your Supply Chain

S upply chain management becomes most valuable when you are able to improve service levels to your customers and increase the profitability of your company. By making strategic choices about how to transform your supply chain, you can drive significant improvements such as increasing product availability for your customers, reducing working capital requirements, and increasing the flexibility of your business. But you probably can't do all of them, and you certainly can't do them all at the same time. In this chapter, you look at 12 strategies that can help you provide significant benefits for your business using supply chain management tools and techniques.

Improve Transparency and Visibility

Effective supply chain managers catch problems when they're small, before they affect the company or its customers. Because supply chains cross so many functions and so many companies, it can be hard to get complete and accurate data. Even if you can get the data, you may not be able to analyze it fast enough to make accurate decisions. A good example is the challenge that companies face when there is a natural disaster, such as a hurricane. In order to understand how their supply chain might be affected they need information from many different sources. To improve your ability to manage a supply chain, you need to have visibility — current and accurate data about what's happening in as close to real time as possible.

A powerful way to increase visibility is to build a supply *chain control tower*. A control tower is a hub that pulls in real-time information from each of your supply chain information systems. (See Chapter 12 for a closer look at the different types of supply chain information systems.) A control tower can also pull in data from systems run by your customers and suppliers, and third-party sources such as news and weather reports. A supply chain control tower can be useful for responding to a disruption, such as a hurricane, or for identifying and fixing problems as they arise throughout your supply chain. In other words, it can increase your supply chain's responsiveness (see the section on SCOR Metrics in Chapter 16). But a control tower can also be useful for tracking how your entire supply chain is performing, and whether process improvement efforts are benefiting your supply chain's metrics, such as order fulfillment cycle time and total cost to serve.

It is sometimes best to have a control tower located in control room with powerful computers, skilled analysts, and a backup power supply. But many companies are also creating virtual supply chain control towers that consolidate supply chain information and make it available to managers throughout a company via the Internet. The benefit of these virtual supply chain control towers is that they ensure everyone in the company has access to the same information, at the same time.

Deploying Demand Shaping

In many ways, supply chain management is really about balancing supply and demand. Companies do their best to control supply — to make sure they have the right product in the right place at the right time. But companies can do a lot of things to control demand, too. As your ability to make and deliver products changes — perhaps as a result of seasonality or the availability of raw materials — you can employ tactics to change the demand for your product. Following are some methods that can influence demand:

>> You can use promotions such as price discounts to increase demand.

>> You can use price increases to reduce demand.

>> You can offer to substitute one product for a different one.

>> You can provide incentives for customers to order products at different times or to accept different delivery dates.

Airlines use demand shaping extensively when selling tickets. If they have unsold seats on a flight from Chicago to Los Angeles, then they will lower the price to increase demand. As those seats get sold, they will begin to increase prices to lower demand. They might offer a substitute for a direct flight from Chicago to Los Angeles, such as taking two flights with a connection in Phoenix. One of the results of demand shaping in this case is that everyone on the airplane is likely to pay a different price for their seat. But in the end, the goal of the airline is to sell the capacity they have available, and to maximize their profits along the way, and demand shaping helps them do this successfully.

Demand shaping gives you more control of the delicate balance between supply and demand. Generating value from demand shaping requires cross-functional communication and alignment throughout the supply chain. For example, if a promotion increases the demand for a product too much, then you need to pay more to expedite a replenishment order and you might even run out of inventory, which would disappoint your customers. You also need to be careful because excessive demand shaping can contribute to the bullwhip effect, which is discussed later in this chapter in the "Control the Bullwhip Effect" section.

Performing Postponement

If your product requires any kind of customization for your customers, you should look for ways to postpone that customization for as long as possible. This is called *postponement* or *delayed differentiation*. By delaying the customization, you preserve the flexibility to change the characteristics of the finished product or even to sell it to a different customer. You also postpone the cost of those customization steps, which means that you are keeping inventory at a lower value for a longer time.

The value of your total inventory is the sum of the values of all of the individual products that you are storing. Every time you touch or change a product, you add value. As you do any kind of work on a product, you are investing money in it. Polishing, painting, and assembling parts will increase their value, and therefore increase the total value of your inventory. Since postponement focuses on keeping products in the lowest value state for as long as possible, it can reduce your inventory cost, even though it doesn't affect inventory levels or turns.

One great example of postponement occurred in Benetton's supply chain for sweaters. The company made the same sweater, using the same materials, in several colors. Originally, the supply chain was designed so that the wool would be dyed before it was knitted into sweaters. The company tried to guess how many sweaters it should make in each color. The guesses were often wrong, however, so the company would run out of sweaters of one color and be overstocked in sweaters of other colors. Then the company changed its supply chain to incorporate postponement: knitting the sweaters first and dyeing them later. That small change made it much easier for the company to provide sweaters in the colors that customers wanted. They could keep undyed sweaters in inventory, and dye them based on which colors their customers were actually buying.

Here's another good example of postponement. Hewlett Packard makes inkjet printers for customers all over the world, but different countries have different electrical power systems, so the printers have to be customized with the right kind of plugs and power supplies. The company implemented postponement by adding the power supply to the printers just before final packaging rather than during manufacturing. This change gave the company more flexibility in deciding where to sell each printer that it manufactured.

Renewing Regional Sourcing

When companies go shopping for suppliers, they don't always do a good job of making apples-to-apples comparisons. Companies sometimes get quotes from suppliers located in other countries thinking that global sourcing will provide huge savings. In many cases, this works well. But in some situations, global sourcing creates big problems and can even end up costing extra. Following are some of the often-overlooked challenges in global sourcing:

>> Long shipping distances result in higher transportation costs; greater lead-time variability; and larger, less-frequent shipments.

>> Long lead times reduce supply chain flexibility.

>> Differences in time zones and languages can make it more difficult to resolve problems and collaborate effectively.

As a result of these types of challenges, many supply chains now focus on local or regional sourcing. This might involve changing from an overseas supplier to a domestic supplier, which is called *reshoring*. A good example of a company that is practicing reshoring is Walmart, which is the leading importer of shipping containers in the U.S. Walmart has launched an initiative to reshore $250 billion of purchases to U.S. suppliers over 10 years. While many of the U.S. suppliers they are working with charge more for their products than overseas competitors, Walmart benefits from lower transportation costs and greater flexibility. By working with suppliers located closer to their facilities, companies like Walmart can simplify their supply chains and, in many cases, reduce their total costs.

Reducing Stock-Keeping Units

One of the things that makes supply chain management challenging is that every version of each product you sell has to be managed separately as a unique stock-keeping unit, or SKU (pronounced "skew"). Even if you only make a single product, you will usually have multiple SKUs. For example, if you were making bottled water — a single, simple product — you could easily have several SKUs to manage:

» 12-ounce bottles sold in a 4-pack

» 12-ounce bottles sold in a 20-pack

» 16-ounce bottles sold in a 4-pack

» 16-ounce bottles sold in a 10-pack

Although the product seems to be the same, each of these SKUs has a slightly different supply chain. You need to have a separate sales forecast for each SKU, as well as a production schedule, inventory policy, and distribution plan. You may buy 12-ounce bottles from one supplier, and 16-ounce bottles from another. You may have one customer that wants only 4-packs, and another that wants only 10-packs. All of the additional work and inventory created by each SKU adds costs to your supply chain.

Companies often try to keep their product image "fresh" by introducing new variations of a product or different packaging options. Although this can be an effective marketing strategy to increase revenues, it also leads to an expensive proliferation of SKUs. Even when adding SKUs does increase revenues, it often reduces profits because of the additional cost.

A common way to balance the revenue that each SKU generates with the cost of maintaining it is to use ABC Analysis. First, group your SKUs into four segments based on total sales. Assign these segments names, A, B, C, and D. Segment A contains your biggest sellers, and segment D is your slowest movers. Because SKUs in the D category cost you money to maintain and don't generate a lot of revenue, you should probably discontinue those items. Here's a very simple ABC Analysis with the bottled water example:

» Segment A: $500,000 total sales (16-ounce bottles sold in a 4-pack)

» Segment B: $150,000 total sales (12-ounce bottles sold in a 4-pack)

» Segment C: $100,000 total sales (16-ounce bottles sold in a 10-pack)

» Segment D: $25,000 total sales (12-ounce bottles sold in a 20-pack)

Segment D contributes very little to the total sales and should probably be eliminated. It is likely that the customers who are buying this SKU are willing to buy one of the other SKUs instead. So ideally, by eliminating your slow moving SKU you reduce your costs and increase the sales of your other SKUs at the same time.

TIP

An alternative way to do ABC Analysis is to segment by profits rather than by revenue. Using the profit approach, you may find that some of your low-volume products are actually very profitable.

Optimizing Inventory

Inventory is a major expense for most manufacturing, wholesale, and retail companies. Without inventory, though, selling products is hard, so it's a necessary evil. Keeping the right amount of inventory in stock is one of the primary goals for supply chain management.

The key to optimizing your investment in inventory is deciding how often you're willing to tell customers that you've run out of the product that they want to buy. Here's why. Inventory management (see Chapter 9 for more details on inventory management) is one part of the supply chain that benefits greatly from statistics and probability. You can look backward at your statistical performance (how much you've sold in the past) and generate forward-looking probabilities (how much you guess you'll sell in the future). Many mathematical models and computer simulations can analyze your sales patterns and tell you how often you're likely to have a stockout (also in Chapter 9) based on how much inventory you keep on hand. If you want to be able to fill eight of every ten orders you get, you'd say that you have an 80 percent service level target. If you want to be able to fill nine of every ten orders, you'd be shooting for a 90 percent service level.

The difference between an 80 percent service level and a 90 percent service level sounds small, but it requires an exponential increase in inventory. Each improvement in service level requires a larger investment in inventory than the last one (see Figure 15-1). To optimize the amount of inventory you carry, you need to choose a service level target, which means deciding how often you're willing to run out of inventory.

Deciding how often it's appropriate to be out of inventory is very difficult, because no one ever wants to lose out on a sale as a result of not having inventory in stock. The math is clear, however: The only way to ensure that you never run out is to have an infinite amount of inventory. Because maintaining that level of inventory probably isn't going to be a smart business decision, you should instead think about how you handle stockouts to minimize the effect on your customers. Perhaps you can substitute a different product or fill an order from a different location. Also look for ways to increase the velocity of your supply chain so that stockouts can be eliminated quickly through replenishment.

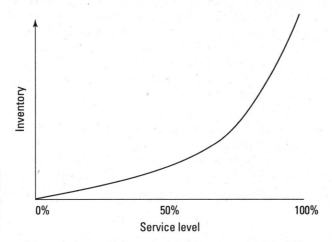

FIGURE 15-1:
Relationship between service level and inventory.

You may discover that it makes sense to have different service level targets for different products or channels. You may decide that you want to have a service level of 80 percent for widgets in your retail stores, for example, and a service level of 98 percent for purchases made through your website. That way, you reduce the amount of inventory in your stores but ensure that customers can almost always get your products by going online.

TIP

ABC Analysis, which was discussed in the previous section, can provide a basis for setting service level targets. For example, you could establish a policy stating that you have a 98 percent service level for your A items, a 95 percent service level for your B items, and a 90 percent service level for your C items.

The risk that you run, of course, is that customers will be disappointed if they can't buy the product that they want when they want it and could end up buying from your competitors. When you look at optimizing your inventory, don't look just at how much money you can save. Also think about how having a high service level (in terms of a high level of product availability) can help you grow your revenue and build your brand.

Incorporating Vendor-Managed Inventory

Sometimes, the best way to manage inventory is to let your vendors do it for you. Allowing your vendors to check your inventory levels, place replenishment orders, and keep you from running out of the products you need can save you time and money. This has become common, for instance, with companies who supply packaging materials and chemicals. It is also common for distributors who sell sodas and snacks to convenience stores. Using a vendor-managed inventory (VMI) strategy is great for the supplier because it gives them the power to order their products for you. VMI can be good for their customers, too, because it reduces the effort required to manage their inventory.

A similar approach that goes a step further is consignment inventory. In consignment inventory, vendors keep their inventory in your facility. As soon as you pull the inventory, it becomes yours, and then the vendors charge you for it. Consignment inventory is becoming popular for safety equipment in factories, where employees can purchase items like safety goggles and gloves from vending machines.

Many companies are experimenting with innovative ways to use VMI and consignment inventory to make their supply chains more efficient. For example, automotive manufacturers often require suppliers to provide their parts using a VMI arrangement. And some electronics manufacturers now ask their component suppliers to maintain consignment inventory in the manufacturer's facility so that they can access it immediately rather than needing to order it and wait for delivery.

But VMI and consignment inventory have their drawbacks. Both methods require a huge amount of trust between the parties, and nothing is really free. In VMI, your suppliers absorb the cost of managing your inventory, which will either push their profits lower or push the cost of your materials higher. In consignment inventory, suppliers keep the inventory on their books until you pull it and they can charge you, so this will also reduce their profits or increase your prices.

VMI and consignment inventory strategies can solve problems and reduce costs throughout your supply chain. Look at each option closely, however, to make sure that you aren't giving up too much control of your supply chain and increasing your costs in the long run.

Adjusting Payment Terms

In supply chains, timing is everything, especially when it comes to the payment terms that you offer to customers and negotiate with your suppliers. Two dates are particularly important in the financial cycle of any product:

» The date when you spend the money to buy the components

» The date when you collect payment for your product from a customer

The time between these dates is called the *cash-to-cash cycle time.* The shorter your cash-to-cash cycle time, the less working capital you need and the more efficient your supply chain is.

The dates on which you pay suppliers, and get paid by customers, are determined by the payment terms that you agree to. Cash-to-cash cycle time is calculated as receivable days + inventory days − payable days. The following examples show how payment terms affect the amount of working capital that you need to run your business:

» You extend 30 days of credit to your customers; this is your receivables. Your suppliers give you 30 days of credit; this is your payables. You also maintain enough inventory to cover 15 days of demand. Your cash-to-cash cycle time is 30 + 15 − 30 = 15 days. Because your payable days and your receivable days are the same, you only need enough working capital to pay for your average inventory level.

» You extend 30 days of credit to your customers, but your suppliers require you to pay for products immediately when you place an order. You also need to keep 15 days of inventory on hand. Your cash-to-cash cycle time is 30 + 15 − 0 = 45 days. In this case, you need enough working capital to cover your average inventory plus working capital to cover your sales for 30 days.

» You require customers to pay you when you take their orders, but your suppliers give you 30 days to pay them for the products that you buy. You don't maintain any inventory at all, because you wait to buy materials until you receive an order from your customer. So your cash-to-cash cycle time is 0 + 0 − 30 = −30. In this case, your cash-to-cash cycle time is actually negative. You do not need any working capital at all because you're getting paid before you have to give any money to your suppliers. In fact, if you get really good at this process, you can stockpile cash from your customers in the bank and earn interest on it for 30 days before paying your suppliers.

Payment terms and inventory requirements vary from one supply chain relationship to the next, and this will affect your cash-to-cash cycle time. Suppliers may extend longer payment terms in exchange for charging a higher price for their products. Customers may be willing to pay more quickly in exchange for a discount on the price you charge them. Cash-to-cash cycle time is a useful metric, and there are actions you can take to improve it. Although reducing your working capital requirement is useful, remember that the more important goal for your supply chain should always be to maximize profits.

Using Supply Chain Finance

Managing cash flow can be a challenge for any business. If you run out of money, it's game over.

When a big company places an order with a smaller company, the smaller company often has to make a relatively major investment in equipment, labor, and raw materials, which can create cash-flow challenges. After the small company fills the order, months may pass before their big customer pays for the work. In the meantime, the small company may have trouble paying its own bills if it doesn't have adequate cash reserves.

Supply chain finance strategies give small companies options for managing their cash flow based on orders that they receive. Following are four common supply chain finance strategies:

>> A bank extends credit to a small company while the company is waiting to get paid by its customers. This strategy is a pretty traditional approach to supply chain finance, but it's expensive, because the bank may see the small company as being a high-risk creditor, which means they charge a high rate of interest.

>> A small company sells the right to collect payment from the big company to a third party for a percentage of the order's actual value. This is called purchase order factoring. The small company can use the money it receives to fill the big company's order. But when the big company finally pays the invoice, the check goes to the third party rather than to the small company.

>> A big company cuts out the middleman and extends short-term credit directly to its suppliers. This strategy benefits the big company, because it probably can borrow money more cheaply than its smaller suppliers can. If their suppliers borrowed the money from a bank, they'd likely pay higher interest rates and pass those costs along to the big company. So by lending suppliers money at favorable rates, the big company keeps its own supply costs down.

>> A bank works with a big company to lend money to the company's suppliers. Because the big company is acting as a cosigner on loans to its suppliers, the bank is willing to lend the money at a lower rate than it would otherwise offer.

Control the Bullwhip Effect

The business roller coaster known as the bullwhip effect is one of the most common problems for supply chains. Here's how it works:

1. A big customer order makes you think that demand for your widgets is rising, so you increase production and stock up on inventory to meet the demand.

   Lo and behold, demand drops. But you need cash to pay your expenses.

2. You stop production and sell off your inventory at fire-sale prices.

3. When you're out of inventory, you get a bunch of new orders.

   The cycle repeats.

But this isn't just happening to your company; it is happening to your customers and suppliers, too. The bullwhip effect occurs in all kinds of supply chains and can have devastating effects. Variations in demand get amplified as they move up a supply chain. A small variation in demand for a retailer gets more extreme for the wholesaler and even more extreme for the factory.

TECHNICAL STUFF

The bullwhip effect has been studied and analyzed with mathematical models and system dynamics since the 1960s. One of the best articles, "Bullwhip Effect in Supply Chains," was written by Padmanabhan, Whang, and Lee (*MIT Sloan Management Review*, April 15, 1997; http://sloanreview.mit.edu/article/the-bullwhip-effect-in-supply-chains/.

TIP

An easy way to experience the bullwhip effect is to play The Beer Game (see Chapter 20).

The following sections describe three things that you can do to reduce or even eliminate the bullwhip effect in your supply chain.

Share information with your partners

Many of the behaviors that lead to the bullwhip effect are actually rational responses to uncertainty and come from a desire to avoid stockouts. If you can provide everyone in the supply chain with accurate data about demand, inventory, and lead times, then they are less likely to make decisions that lead to erratic swings in inventory. If suppliers can see actual demand downstream in the supply chain, they're less likely to overreact to small variations. And if customers can see the upstream inventory levels, they're less likely to over-order when their own inventory gets low.

Reduce and align lot sizes

Differences in the amount of product that gets ordered at each step of a supply chain can contribute to the bullwhip effect. Consider a carton of eggs that you buy from a local store. You probably use only one or two eggs per day, but you need to buy them in a lot size of 12. So you end up buying one carton per week. Then you decide to make egg salad to take to a family reunion, so you buy a couple of cartons of eggs for that event. That one-time increase in demand gets amplified because of the lot size. The store sees a spike in demand, so they order an extra case of eggs from their supplier. The demand signal becomes more distorted the further it gets passed up the supply chain.

By making batches or lot sizes smaller and ordering more frequently, you can reduce the amplification of the bullwhip effect. The ideal situation is one in which the lot size is the same throughout the supply chain, from the customer to the beginning of the supply chain. In many cases, however, establishing uniform lot sizes is difficult because sending smaller batches more often leads to higher costs for transportation and material handling. Nonetheless, focusing on making lot sizes smaller and uniform can go a long way toward reducing the bullwhip effect.

Manage promotions

Promotions and incentives can increase sales, but they can also create huge variations in demand and initiate a bullwhip effect in the entire supply chain. It's hard to predict how effective promotions will be. A promotion that does well could lead to stockouts for your product, thereby triggering unrealistic forecasts and overordering, which in turn leads to excess inventory and the need for additional promotion.

A few companies have experimented with eliminating promotions, which can reduce the bullwhip effect. In many industries, however, promotions are a critical tool for marketing and sales. From the standpoint of supply chain management, they may be necessary evils. If your company uses promotions, or if your customers do, factor the bullwhip effect into your supply chain planning and inventory management to ensure that you can meet the demand that promotions create without getting stuck with extra inventory when the promotions are over.

Starting with Small Improvements

Cost is often an obstacle to implementing supply chain improvements. Even supply chain projects that are expected to save money in the future generally require an upfront investment and involve some risk.

To overcome this challenge, start with small projects that are likely to provide tangible savings. The savings that are easiest to get are often called "quick wins" or "low-hanging fruit." As you demonstrate that small supply chain improvements can increase revenue and lower costs, you should have an easier time justifying investment in larger projects. You can even use the value created by smaller projects to fund future improvements.

Suppose that your company hasn't been doing a good job of managing transportation costs. You could launch a project to rebid your freight lanes and track the savings to demonstrate how much value you created for the company. That wouldn't cost very much, but it would generate savings right away. Then you could ask to use part of those savings to invest in a transportation management system that will improve your transportation routing, increase the speed of your supply chain, and save even more money. This strategy of using the savings from one project to fund the next project is a great way to build momentum for supply chain improvements, and demonstrate the benefits that effective supply chain management can deliver to the business.

Creating Sandboxes

It can be hard for a business to make investments in supply chain initiatives when they don't have data and experience to guarantee a positive return on those investments. In many cases, supply chain projects suffer *analysis paralysis*, which is when a desire for more information prevents leaders from making a clear decision.

Supply chain innovations can be risky. Until you try something new, you have no way of knowing whether it's going to save as much money as your team expects, or as a vendor promised.

A good way to minimize risk in innovation and to get past analysis paralysis is to create sandboxes. *Sandboxes* are small experiments inside of working supply chains that allow you to try new processes and technologies on a small scale to collect data about how they perform. This data makes it easier to decide whether, when, and how those processes and technologies should be scaled up and deployed across the rest of your supply chain. For example, you might select a small number of stores or distribution centers as a sandbox and allow them to implement new supply chain processes and technologies on a trial basis. Or you might choose a new product as the sandbox to test a new inventory planning system.

TIP

You may want your experimental projects to be high-profile because they show that your company is innovative, and that may encourage other employees to look for ways to improve your supply chain. In other cases, you may want to keep experiments low-key until you know how well they're going to work. Secret projects (sometimes called skunkworks projects) may be the better choice if a project has a high probability of failure or involves patents or trade secrets.

Chapter **16**

Adopting Supply Chain Metrics

There's a common saying in supply chain management circles: "What gets measured, gets done." Almost everything about a supply chain can be measured, either directly or indirectly. Metrics give you data and allow you to make decisions based on facts rather than on hunches. But measurement costs money because you need to invest in ways to capture the data and because you have to store that data so that you can access it when you need it.

It pays to be smart about what you measure, how you measure it, and what you do with the information that you collect. This chapter examines different ways to measure the performance of your supply chain and how to select metrics that will help you manage trade-offs and drive improvements.

Understanding Metrics

Supply chain measurements are usually called *metrics*. They're reference points that help you monitor whether your people, processes, and technology are performing the way that you want and expect them to.

Metrics fall into two broad categories:

- » **Quantitative:** Quantitative metrics are based on an objective number or property, such as the number of units produced or the amount of revenue you've received. Many software systems in a supply chain track quantitative metrics automatically. For example, a warehouse management system tracks the volume of material that is received, and a transportation management system tracks the number of shipments that you tender to carriers. (See Chapter 12.)

- » **Qualitative:** Many important attributes of a supply chain are difficult or impossible to measure quantitatively, but you may be able to measure them qualitatively. A qualitative metric is based on someone's judgment or perception, and is therefore subjective. Customer satisfaction is a good example of a qualitative metric that can be important for supply chains.

TIP

You can make a qualitative metric look and act like a quantitative metric by using a scoring system or scale. You might rate customer satisfaction on a scale of 1 to 10, for example. Even though you end up with a number, customer satisfaction is still a qualitative metric because it's based on an opinion rather than an objective, independent measurement.

The accuracy of a metric depends how it's measured. If you have a broken gauge, for example, or if the people counting make a mistake, the metric will be wrong. Consequently, the validity of a metric depends on the accuracy, precision, and reliability of the measurement process.

TECHNICAL
STUFF

Any problem that leads to an incorrect measurement is called a *gauge error* because the process you use to measure is a kind of gauge.

It's hard to argue with facts, so quantitative metrics are often perceived as being superior to qualitative ones. However, in many situations qualitative metrics can actually be more practical and more useful than quantitative metrics. A great way to illustrate the role of quantitative and qualitative metrics is with the "Goldilocks and the Three Bears" story. When Goldilocks tried the porridge, the first bowl was too hot, the second was too cold, and the third was just right. Those metrics were qualitative metrics. Instead, if Goldilocks had said, "Porridge 1 was 250 degrees, Porridge 2 was 20 degrees, and Porridge 3 was 125 degrees," she would have been using quantitative metrics.

It's possible to link quantitative and qualitative metrics, but qualitative metrics are based on a subjective standard, whereas quantitative metrics are measurable facts. In this case, Goldilocks's opinion mattered more than the precise quantitative metric. Why waste time and money with a thermometer when you could just ask Goldilocks whether she liked the porridge?

Metrics can also be classified as internal or external. Internal metrics measure things that are important to your company. For example, inventory turns and capacity utilization are internal metrics. External metrics measure things that are important to people outside your company — people such as your customers and suppliers. Some examples of external metrics are perfect order fulfillment (see the "Understanding SCOR Metrics" section later in this chapter) and customer satisfaction.

TIP

Whenever possible, align all of your customer-facing metrics with the things that your customers measure. For example, if your customer is measuring Your on-time delivery rate, you want to make sure that you also are measuring on-time deliveries and that you are measuring them in exactly the same way. Otherwise you'll spend time trying to reconcile the differences in your metrics and the customer's metrics rather than using that time to correct problems with the delivery process.

Identifying Performance Attributes

Before you can define a useful metric, you have to decide what attribute or characteristic of your supply chain you're trying to measure. Choosing which attributes to measure may sound obvious, but it can be quite challenging, especially when you think about how supply chain processes interact and affect one another.

Take the example of a factory that's trying to choose metrics as it implements Lean. From an inventory perspective, the company wants to receive the parts it needs for production no more than one day in advance. If parts are received sooner, the company has more inventory. To measure whether this policy was being followed, it would be natural to measure on-time deliveries. From a transportation perspective, however, the company wants to maximize the amount of freight that's carried on each truck. The company could save money by sending one full truck every other day rather than shipping half-full trucks each day. Tracking this policy would involve using a transportation capacity utilization as a metric.

Each goal in the example — reducing inventory and reducing transportation cost — is tied to an attribute of the supply chain. It's relatively easy to create a metric for each of these attributes. If the transportation planners focus only on the capacity utilization metric, however, and the production planners focus only on the inventory metric, the supply chain is going to suffer. The two groups need to create a combined metric that allows them to work together toward a common goal. In this case, they could create a metric for the total cost of inventory and transportation. Or, they could choose to focus on whichever metric will produce the most benefits.

TIP

If you need to look at several metrics at the same time, you can combine them in a scorecard that provides a more holistic view of how your supply chain is performing. You can find information on creating scorecards in Chapter 18.

Understanding SCOR Metrics

According to APICS, the association for supply chain management, five attributes of the Supply Chain Operations Reference (SCOR) model (see Chapter 5) are most important to success:

>> **Reliability:** The ability to perform tasks as expected. Reliability focuses on the predictability of the outcome of a process.

>> **Responsiveness:** The speed at which tasks are performed and at which a supply chain provides products to the customer.

>> **Agility:** The ability to respond to external influences and respond to marketplace changes to gain or maintain competitive advantage.

>> **Cost:** The cost of operating the supply chain processes.

>> **Assets:** The ability to use assets efficiently.

Within these five attributes, the SCOR model defines ten metrics that can be tracked in every supply chain. Together, these top-level SCOR metrics can give you a good sense of how efficiently your supply chain is working. More important, these metrics make it easier to objectively measure the value of any improvements you make in your supply chain and help you measure the costs of a supply chain disruption.

Reliability

Reliability is measured with a single metric: perfect-order fulfillment (POF). A *perfect order* is one that is . . . well, perfect: the right product, delivered to the right place, in the right quantity, in the right condition, for the right cost. In other words, a perfect order is one in which the supply chain worked flawlessly. When your POF is increasing, it means your supply chain process improvement efforts are working. A drop in your POF metric is a sign that something isn't performing the way it's supposed to.

While the concept of a POF metric makes loads of sense, it can be challenging to collect and connect the data that needs to be included. For example, the customer order data may be in your Customer Relationship Management (CRM) system, whereas the delivery information is in your Transportation Management System

(TMS; see Chapter 12 for more information on these systems). To calculate an accurate POF score, you need to track orders through each step in your supply chain and through each of your supply chain information systems. An alternative approach is to multiply the metrics from each step in your supply chain and use the final number as your POF metric. For example, if you had an order fill rate of 98 percent and an on-time delivery rate of 97 percent you could decide to use the product of these two numbers as your POF metric. In this case, your POF would be 98% x 97% = 95%.

TIP

Information from customer complaints and product returns often provide an indication of issues that need to be addressed to improve your POF metric.

Responsiveness

Responsiveness is measured with a single metric: order-fulfillment cycle time (OFCT). OFCT is the period between when a customer places an order and when he receives a product. In a grocery store, OFCT is 0; customers pay for their products and walk out the door. In the world of e-commerce, though, OFCT can vary wildly from one company to another. Since a short OFCT can drive more sales, higher customer satisfaction, and greater customer loyalty, this metric can be a leading indicator of revenues for your company.

Agility

Agility is measured with four metrics:

>> **Upside supply chain flexibility:** The number of days it would take to respond to an unexpected 20 percent increase in demand

>> **Upside supply chain adaptability:** The amount of capacity you could add in 30 days

>> **Downside supply chain adaptability:** The amount of a drop in orders you could absorb without significant financial effect

>> **Overall value at risk:** The amount of money you would lose if a major disruption occurred in your supply chain

Agility metrics are often based on estimates rather than hard data, and you should validate them periodically. For example, to measure upside supply chain flexibility and adaptability, you need information about your internal manufacturing and logistics capacity as well as information about each of your suppliers' available capacity. A supplier might tell you that it has plenty of capacity today, but as soon as that company gets a big order from another customer, that capacity will no longer be available. So a good practice is to define the data that you need to calculate each of your agility metrics and then have a process for updating them regularly.

TIP

A good way to keep supplier capacity data current is to have your buyers collect it during their routine meetings with each supplier's account manager.

Cost

Cost is measured with a single metric: total cost to serve (TCS). TCS brings together all the costs of running a supply chain, including purchasing, logistics, and operations. It can also include essential functions such as sales and customer support. TCS provides an understanding of how much it costs to operate your entire supply chain, and how this cost is changing over time.

The data for your TCS metric is available directly from your accounting system. It is often useful to track TCS in relation to sales to determine whether your costs are increasing or decreasing in proportion to your revenues. When TCS is growing more slowly than sales, your company is becoming more profitable. TCS can grow faster than sales when your company is making investments, such as building up inventory to prepare for a holiday sales cycle.

Asset management efficiency

Asset management efficiency is measured with three metrics:

>> **Cash-to-cash cycle time (C2C):** The number of days between when you purchase inventory and when you collect accounts receivable. The longer this cycle is, the more working capital you need to run your business. See Chapter 15 for more information about cash-to-cash cycle time.

>> **Return on supply chain fixed assets:** Return on investment from the assets you used in your supply chain. Return on supply chain fixed assets can help you decide whether the money you've invested into your supply chain infrastructure provides an acceptable financial benefit.

>> **Return on working capital (ROWC):** Return on working capital shows how efficiently your end-to-end supply chain is running. ROWC can help you decide whether the money you have invested in inventory is providing an acceptable financial benefit.

Optimizing Operational Metrics

Each function of a supply chain has unique attributes that are key to understanding performance. By selecting the right metrics, you can make better decisions and manage your supply chain operations more successfully. This section introduces some of the operational metrics that can provide insights into the efficiency and effectiveness of specific supply chain functions. Many of these metrics are useful for measuring cross-functional and interorganizational performance as well.

Supplier metrics

Many supplier attributes are useful to track. Tracking the number of suppliers is a good place to start, because every supplier relationship you need to manage has a cost. Supplier performance can also be tracked with metrics such as on-time shipping, on-time receipt, and product quality. A common way to measure quality for a supplier is the number of parts per million that have some kind of problem or defect.

Procure to pay metrics

The process of purchasing products from a supplier and then paying for them is called the *procure to pay cycle*. Measuring the time it takes for each order that you place to be completed provides insight into the combined efficiency of your sourcing functions and your suppliers' delivery functions.

Customer service metrics

Since the whole point of a supply chain is to deliver value to your customer, measuring how your supply chain is performing from your customers' point of view is very important. One common customer metric is *order fill rate,* which is the percentage of customer orders that you are able to ship within your desired response window. For example, if you tell customers that you'll ship a product within 48 hours after they place an order, then your order fill rate measures the percentage of orders that achieve the goal. Other customer metrics include on-time shipment, on-time delivery, and product returns.

On-time shipment and on-time delivery are self-explanatory. Product returns can have a big effect on customer satisfaction but may not be as straightforward as other metrics. For example, one way to measure quality is to study the products that customers have returned, but you also need to identify the reason for the return. If a product is returned because it's defective, you have a quality problem and a dissatisfied customer. But if a product is returned because your customer ordered three units and kept the one she liked best, the return is unrelated to quality. To simplify this analysis, many companies create *reason codes* to categorize returns in their tracking system. For example, items that are returned because they are defective might have a reason code of 10, and items that are returned unopened might get a reason code of 11. Analyzing returns by reason code can help you identify patterns such as products that have frequent quality issues.

Another way to measure customer satisfaction is through customer surveys, and one of the most popular survey approaches is to use a Net Promoter Score (NPS). All NPS questions follow a similar format: "On a scale of 1 to 10, how likely is it that you would recommend our product to one of your friends." If a customer chooses either 9 or 10 — they are very likely to recommend your product — then they are considered a *promoter* of your product. A customer who chooses 7 or 8 is neutral about your product, and a customer who chooses 6 or less is a *detractor*. An NPS can range from −100 to 100, with 100 being the best. The higher your NPS, the more likely it is that your customers are satisfied and will recommend your product to their friends. You calculate an NPS using this formula:

(Number of 9s and 10s) / (Total Number of Responses) − (Number of 6s or less) / (Total Number of Responses) = NPS

Capacity, throughput, and yield metrics

The amount of product you can process is measured as your capacity. Capacity can change over time, so this metric can be useful because it helps you see how your supply chain is evolving. If you are investing in new equipment or process improvements then you would expect to see your capacity increasing. If you are closing down old facilities, you would expect to see capacity decreasing.

While capacity measures how much material you could be processing, throughput measures how much you actually are processing. For example, an applesauce factory might have the capacity to process 100 tons of apples per day, but due to a shortage of apples or a low number of orders the supply chain manager might decide to run at a throughput of only 50 tons per day.

Some of the materials that you process will turn into valuable products, and others will be left over as waste. The amount that becomes a valuable product is called the *yield*. You can measure yield in terms of the amount of product that is produced, or as the percentage of throughput that is usable. In the case of the applesauce factory, the seeds and the skins might need to be discarded. Also, some material is likely to be wasted because of issues with quality. So even though the throughput for the factory is 50 tons per day of apples, the yield might only be 40 tons of applesauce, or 80 percent of the throughput. The higher your yield is, the more efficient your process.

Formalizing Financial Metrics

Managing the flow of money in your supply chain is an essential part of running your business. This section explains some critical financial attributes and metrics you can use to measure your financial performance.

Accounts payable metrics

Accounts payable basically represents money that your suppliers are lending to you. Measuring the amount of money that you owe to your suppliers can provide insight into your relationships with those suppliers. If your accounts payables are high, it may mean that your suppliers aren't getting paid quickly. If you're late paying your bills, you can create cash-flow problems for your suppliers, who might respond by freezing your account or holding shipments. Keeping accounts payable low can reduce many problems and risks that suppliers can pose to your supply chain, but it also increases your working capital requirements.

For example, to pay your suppliers you may need to borrow money, which increases the amount of working capital that your supply chain is consuming. You pay interest on this money, so it increases your costs. If you don't pay your suppliers, then they'll need to borrow money and increase their working capital. That'll increase their costs, and eventually they'll need to charge you more to make up the difference.

Total spend metrics

Tracking the amount of money your company spends is important for several reasons. In terms of your supply chain, a metric that shows how the amount you spend is changing can be critical for understanding how your supply chain is performing.

An increase in spending can be good if it's accompanied by an increase in sales. When spending stays steady while sales are dropping, though, you may have a supply chain problem.

You should divide your spend metrics into direct costs (for the parts that go into your products, for example) and indirect costs (for other things you need to run the business, such as cleaning supplies and safety equipment). Generally, direct costs should rise and fall at about the same rate as sales. Controlling indirect costs can be a simple way to reduce expenses and generate significant savings in a supply chain.

Savings metrics

Tracking the amount of money you save through supply chain improvement projects demonstrates the value of supply chain management. If you can show that your last project saved $1 million, it's much easier to ask for the process changes and investments you need to support your next project.

There are three common ways to demonstrate savings from a supply chain improvement:

» **Cost reduction:** For example, you could show that it used to cost $100 to make each product, and now it only costs $95. Your savings are $5 per product, multiplied by the total number of products you make.

» **Yield improvement:** For example, you could show that your process used to convert 80 percent of your inputs into usable products, and now your improvements have increased that to 90 percent. The value of the additional 10 percent yield is your savings.

» **Cost avoidance:** For example, you could show that if a change had not been made you would have had to pay a penalty of $10,000 per month. By making the change, you have avoided that cost and saved your company money.

Perfecting People Metrics

You have several ways to measure important issues relating to the people who are such a critical part of your supply chain:

» **Engagement:** How engaged people are with their jobs

» **Productivity and efficiency:** How productive and efficient people are in their roles

» **Turnover:** How often people leave their jobs

» **Safety:** How often people are hurt while doing their jobs

These metrics can indicate whether you're effectively balancing the needs of your business and the needs of your employees.

Engagement metrics

Employee engagement measures how satisfied, or engaged, people are with their jobs. Employee engagement is usually measured qualitatively through anonymous surveys. For example, you could ask employees whether they feel like their work is valuable and whether they look forward to coming to their jobs in the morning. There are also quantitative metrics that can provide insights into engagement, such as the number of complaints that employees file against their supervisors. The benefits of maintaining high engagement are that it can help increase productivity and reduce turnover.

TIP

If you're going to measure employee engagement, you need to be transparent about the results and to take action on them. Otherwise, people will feel that their input isn't valued and their level of engagement will decline.

Productivity and efficiency metrics

The productivity and efficiency of many employees can be measured directly. Here are some examples:

>> For customer service representatives, productivity can be measured by the number of calls they answer or the number of issues they resolve.

>> For buyers in your purchasing department, productivity can be measured by the number of suppliers they manage or the value of the materials they purchase.

>> For manufacturing technicians, productivity can be measured by the number of products that they make during a shift.

>> For associates in a distribution center, productivity can be measured by the number of order lines picked or put away per hour, as well as order picking accuracy.

TIP

Many productivity metrics can be tracked automatically in computer systems such as a warehouse management system or labor management system (see Chapter 12). These systems can track the tasks that are assigned to each worker and measure how long it takes for each task to be completed.

Turnover metrics

Measuring the number of employees you lose — your employee turnover — can provide great insights into how your employees feel about your company. People leave jobs voluntarily for many reasons. They may not like their boss, they may not like the work environment, or they may be able to make more money someplace else, for example. People also leave jobs involuntarily for many reasons.

Losing and replacing employees is expensive. There are costs associated with separation, because you often need to fill out paperwork and pay for things like accumulated time off. There are also costs for recruiting and training replacements. Last but not least, there is a cost for the work that doesn't get done while a position is vacant or work that gets done poorly because the people who have to do the work haven't been trained properly.

When turnover is high, you spend more money on recruiting and training. You may also find that high turnover creates challenges for your customers and suppliers because they aren't able to build long-term relationships with contacts in your company.

When turnover metrics are low, it is a good indication that your people are being treated and managed well. As a result, you are avoiding turnover costs and probably building stronger relationships throughout your supply chain.

Safety metrics

Safety metrics may be the most important metrics in your entire supply chain. Making sure that everyone has a chance to go home healthy at the end of the day is one of the basic responsibilities of a business. The most common safety metrics are lagging indicators, meaning that they measure problems after they occur. Some examples of lagging safety metrics include the following:

>> **Lost time incident rate:** Measures how often someone gets injured badly enough that they have to leave work.

>> **Days without injury:** Measures how many days it has been since the last time someone was injured at work.

>> **Cost of claims:** Measures the amount of money spent as a result of an injury.

There is a growing trend toward using safety metrics that are leading indicators to indicate whether you are taking proactive steps to avoid injuries before they occur. Some examples of safety metrics that are leading indicators include

>> **Audits and inspections completed on time:** Measures whether you are looking for issues that could be unsafe.

>> **Number of audits with compliance issues:** Measures whether your audits are finding issues that need to be corrected.

>> **Corrective and preventative action items overdue:** Measures whether you are addressing issues that could cause injuries in a timely fashion.

Solidifying Sustainability Metrics

Sustainability, in a broad sense, means doing things in a way that can go on for a long time. In business, the idea of sustainability is to achieve balance among the needs of a company, the people connected to the company, and the environment around the company. But when people talk about sustainability metrics, they're usually talking about environmental metrics.

Environmental sustainability metrics fall into two categories:

>> **Consumption:** Things that a company consumes. Companies use energy and raw materials in their manufacturing and distribution processes, for example.

>> **Waste:** Things that a company emits, throws away, or gets rid of in some fashion.

Consumption metrics

It helps to break consumption metrics into renewable and nonrenewable resources. *Renewable resources* are materials and energy sources that can be easily regenerated by the environment. Any product that comes from a plant (such as wood or ethanol) is a renewable material. Wind and solar power are examples of renewable energy sources. *Nonrenewable resources* are materials that cannot be easily regenerated by the environment. Metals, minerals, coal, and petroleum are nonrenewable resources.

There are three common ways to gather consumption metrics:

>> **Collect data during a process:** For example, you could place a gauge in your manufacturing facility to measure the amount of water you are using.

>> **Estimate based on other metrics:** For example, if you hired a truck to deliver freight to a customer 1,000 miles away, you can estimate how much fuel the truck consumed.

>> **Ask your suppliers:** Many companies ask their suppliers to provide sustainability reports indicating the resources that were required to produce their products.

One way to improve consumption metrics is to reduce the amount of resources that you use. You could redesign your product or processes so that they require less material. Or you could change the materials you use or change the way you source them. Sometimes, it's possible to switch from nonrenewable to renewable resources. Even if the level of consumption doesn't change, you would improve the sustainability of your supply chain by using renewable energy.

If you must use nonrenewable materials for your supply chain, you can improve sustainability by recycling. Switching to a recycled source for your inputs reduces consumption of nonrenewable resources. Also, it frequently takes less energy to recycle materials than it does to grow or mine them in the first place. Recycling is common for nonrenewable resources such as metals, glass, oils, and batteries. Recycling is also common for some renewable resources, such as cardboard.

Another important consumption metric is water. Water is plentiful and renewable, in that it's renewed by rainfall. However, when water becomes salty or polluted, it's no longer usable for many purposes. Minimizing the amount of water you use and limiting the amount of pollution you create help to make your supply chain more sustainable.

Waste metrics

Waste metrics include things like the carbon that your supply chain emits and the amount of material that you send to landfills. Most of the carbon that's being emitted into the atmosphere comes from burning fossil fuels to create energy. Much of this fuel is used to power ships, trucks, and trains. In other words, supply chains have a huge effect on the amount of carbon that's emitted. As a result, companies are beginning to focus on carbon emissions. Even if your company isn't concerned about the amount of carbon it emits, there's a good chance that its customers are, and so is the government. Minimizing your carbon footprint is a good idea in principle, and it may also be a requirement for some businesses.

Another important waste metric is the amount of material sent to landfills. Many companies have undertaken initiatives to eliminate landfill waste, which requires them to redesign many of their supply chain processes, such as switching to reusable or recyclable packaging materials. These initiatives may require some investment, but they can generate savings by reducing the cost of waste disposal, as well as build brand value and increase customer loyalty.

There are three common ways to gather waste metrics:

>> **Collect data during a process:** You can measure the amount of scrap that is left over after a production run or measure how frequently your trash containers need to be emptied.

>> **Estimate based on other metrics:** If you know that it takes about two gallons of water to make a widget, you can estimate the total amount of water used based on the number of widgets you make.

>> **Ask your suppliers:** You can ask your suppliers to provide data that they collect during their processes, for example, asking your waste management supplier to track the number of tons of garbage they collected from your facility.

Chapter **17**

Managing Supply Chain Risks

You may have heard the saying, "The best laid plans of mice and men often go awry." You can build a great plan for how you want your supply chain to work, but you also need to prepare for the inevitable surprises. This chapter explains risk management, a process that you can use to guide your strategy and deal with the problems that your supply chain might encounter. It includes techniques that you can use to identify, prioritize, and manage supply chain risks. You'll never be able to eliminate all of the uncertainties facing your supply chain, but risk management can give you more control and better options when unexpected events occur.

Challenging Assumptions About the Future

Supply chain plans are built on assumptions about what will happen in the future, and these assumptions are usually based on past experience. For example, if the transit time between one of your suppliers and one of your factories has always been 15 days in the past then you would assume that the transit time will be

15 days for future orders, too. This 15-day transit time will be used to determine when to send an order to that supplier so that it will arrive at the factory on time. But past performance is not a guarantee of future results.

Although we have to make assumptions in order to plan how a supply chain should perform, we need to deal with reality when it comes to managing the day-to-day operations. Think about the potential effects that any of the following events could have on your supply chain:

>> A shipping container filled with raw materials for your product gets stuck in a port for 30 days during a labor strike.

>> One of your factories is struck by a tornado.

>> A key supplier files for bankruptcy protection.

>> A major customer unexpectedly cancels a huge order for your products.

>> A new customer unexpectedly places a huge order for your products.

Each situation represents a scenario that supply chains around the world face every day, and your supply chain needs to be able to respond.

You need to understand a few basic principles to implement a risk management process that spans your supply chain:

>> **Risk = Uncertainty:** Every plan you make is based on assumptions about how the future is going to play out. You can't ignore the future, so it's important to analyze your supply chain and plan the way you want things to work. You also need to be flexible enough — in your planning and in your thinking — to adapt to what's happening around you. Risk management is fundamentally about reducing uncertainty as much as you can and then adapting and responding to the uncertainty that remains.

>> **Statistics ≠ Probabilities:** This principle can save you from a lot of trouble. Analysts commonly look at how often something has happened in the past (statistics) and use that data to predict how often the thing is likely to happen again (probabilities). This approach can be useful in some cases, but it can lead to poor decision-making in supply chains.

Statistics say that only a tiny percentage of shipments sink in the ocean, for example, so worrying about that situation isn't worthwhile. But the probability that a particular ship will sink because of a serious structural flaw may be 100 percent. The problem is that you don't have enough information about the vessel on which your cargo will be shipped to know the true probability of whether the ship will sink. In other words, general statistics about how often ships sink will lead you to underestimate the probability of the risk for this particular ship.

>> **Flexibility = Insurance:** In many cases, the best way to manage a supply chain risk is to have a Plan B. If your risk is that a supplier could go bankrupt, your Plan B could be to have at least two suppliers. If your risk is that a cargo vessel could sink, your Plan B could be to have extra inventory on hand.

In many cases, the flexibility needed to protect your supply chain from a risk comes with a cost, so it may be tempting to eliminate this flexibility to save money. The key is to recognize how valuable that flexibility could be in the event of a supply chain disruption and then decide whether it's worth the cost. In other words, think of the cost of supply chain flexibility as though it were the premium on an insurance policy. Maybe the premium is too expensive, and you're better off paying the price if you have a problem. In many cases, the flexibility is cheap compared to the cost of a supply chain disruption.

TECHNICAL STUFF

The Supply Chain Risk Leadership Council offers a free handbook called "Supply Chain Risk Management: A Compilation of Best Practices" that includes a list of all the different things that can go wrong in a supply chain. You can download this handbook at www.scrlc.com.

Building Supply Chain Resilience

You may find people using the words risk, threat, and disruption interchangeably, but in the context of supply chain management each of them means something slightly different. A *risk* is an event that may or may not occur; a hurricane, for example. A *threat* is impact the risk would have on your supply chain; in the case of a hurricane, one threat could be that your factory would be flooded. A *disruption* is how the threat would impact your supply chain; if there were a hurricane that flooded your factory, your supply chain would be disrupted because you could not manufacture products.

Strictly speaking, risks can be either good or bad; there is a risk you might receive a big order, but there is also a risk that you could lose a customer. Good risks, such as a big order, are called *upside risks* because they are related to growing your business; bad risks are called *downside risks*. Either type of risk can lead to supply chain disruptions. For example, a rapid increase in customer orders can trigger a buildup of inventory and overwhelm a distribution center. The result would be a disruption in the ability of the distribution center to process shipments efficiently. The disruption caused by an upside risk can be just as expensive as the disruption from a downside risk. Even so, it is typical for supply chain risk management processes to focus mostly on the downside risks.

A supply chain's vulnerability to disruptions can have serious consequences for all the businesses involved. Reducing this vulnerability requires collaboration among the firms in a supply chain so that they can help one another deal with threats as they emerge. The goal, of course, is to engineer and manage your supply chain so that it can function during and after a disruption — in other words, to be resilient.

You can think about supply chain resilience in terms of a shipment of bananas bound from South America to a grocery store in the United States. A lot of uncertainty is involved in that supply chain, from weather to commodity prices to the reliability of the cargo ship. From these risks and others, you see that the supply chain has many threats — many things that could go wrong. If a threat occurs, it can cause a disruption. If the ship breaks down, for example, it could delay the delivery of bananas and disrupt the store's supply chain. But if the grocery store has extra inventory or another source of supply then it can continue selling bananas to its customers in spite of the supply chain disruption, so its supply chain is resilient.

Supply chain risk management is very similar to business continuity management. Business continuity plans are often focused on making a particular facility or company more resilient; supply chain risk management looks more broadly at how all of the companies working together contribute to the resilience of a supply chain.

Identifying Risks

The first step in managing risks is identifying them. You probably have a good idea of some of the things that could go wrong with your supply chain. To really understand the scope of risks, however, you need to get input from other people who see, understand, and manage different parts of the supply chain.

Following are some of the groups you should include in your process to identify supply chain risks:

>> Transportation

>> Distribution/warehousing

>> Purchasing

- » Information technology
- » Accounting and finance
- » Legal
- » Sales and marketing
- » Key customers
- » Key suppliers

It might be easiest for you to reach out to each of these groups separately, but you could also invite all of them to join a supply chain risk management committee. However you choose to engage this team, use their input to make a list of the risks that could affect your supply chain. You can create this list by brainstorming, and you may need to give people some ideas to prompt their thinking. Here are some risk categories that you can ask your team members to think about:

1. Accidents
2. Crime, terrorism, and war
3. Financial problems
4. Government regulations and politics
5. Management problems
6. Manufacturing problems
7. Market trends
8. Natural disasters
9. Supplier problems
10. Surge in customer demand
11. Technology trends
12. Transportation and distribution problems
13. Workforce and training issues

Getting people to think about these risks in concrete terms and write them down tends to be an eye-opening experience. The odds that any one of these risks will materialize may be low, but the odds that at least one of them will materialize is high. It's a good bet that something will surprise you, but you have no way to know which thing it will be.

Classifying Risks

Once you have identified your supply chain risks, you need to decide which risks are most important. You may be most concerned about the risk of a fire at your supplier's distribution center, for example, or with the risk of disease outbreak that would shut down travel between countries.

One approach is to classify risks according to their scope. Classifying risks according to their scope is useful when you want to decide how — or whether — to mitigate them. Risks fall into three general scope categories:

>> **Global:** Risks that affect everybody in the world. Managing global risks is the responsibility of senior management, but your risk management planning can ensure that your leaders are aware of the global risks and their potential effects on your supply chain.

>> **Systemic:** Risks that affect more than one facility or company. These risks could disrupt the entire supply chain, not just its parts. Systemic risks are especially important in supply chain risk management because you are looking at how all of the companies in a supply chain contribute to delivering value to a customer. Many times, people don't realize how severe a systemic risk can be because they think about it in terms of how it affects them locally rather than how it affects the rest of the supply chain. The responsibility for managing systemic risks is often shared between leaders in several different companies, so these companies need to collaborate in order to manage the risks effectively.

THE $400 MILLION DOLLAR LIGHTNING STRIKE

A good example of a systemic risk comes from a book called the *Resilient Enterprise* (The MIT Press, 2007), by Yossi Sheffi, Elisha Gray II professor of engineering systems at the Massachusetts Institute of Technology. According to the book, two cellphone companies bought their processor chips from the same manufacturing plant in New Mexico. One day, the manufacturing plant was struck by lightning, which started a small fire in the facility. One of the phone companies realized how serious this problem was and immediately started sourcing chips from other suppliers. The other phone company assumed that the chip facility would be repaired quickly, so it waited. When the repairs took longer than expected, the phone company that chose to wait wasn't able to get the parts it needed and had to shut down its entire supply chain. The lightning strike had a modest financial impact on the supplier, but it cost their unprepared customer $400 million dollars in lost revenue.

>> **Local:** Risks that affect the people in a particular company or facility. Local risks are the responsibility of facility and operations managers and are often addressed in a business continuity plan. Your supply chain risk management process can be useful in ensuring that each of these separate plans are complete and properly aligned.

Scoring Risks

After you identify and classify your risks, the next step is scoring them. Risk scores can help you prioritize which risks you need to be most concerned about.

You score risks based on how likely they are to occur (the probability) and how severe their effects would be (the impact). Then you multiply these scores together to get an overall risk score. There are many different scoring systems for probability and impact ratings, but here's an example to get you started.

On a scale of 1 to 10, assign a value to the likelihood that a risk will occur:

>> **10:** Will occur; 100 percent probability

>> **5:** May occur; 50 percent chance

>> **1:** Very unlikely to occur; 10 percent chance, or less

Use a scale of 1 to 10 to assign a value to the impact of a risk on your supply chain:

>> **10:** Would stop the supply chain or cost someone his or her job

>> **5:** Would be a major problem taking days to fix but wouldn't stop the supply chain from operating

>> **1:** Would create a problem that the supply chain can handle in the normal course of business

Use a scale of 1 to 100 to categorize the risk score after you multiply the probability value by the impact value:

>> **100:** Critical. This risk needs to be resolved immediately.

>> **50:** Major. This risk needs to be monitored closely and mitigated effectively.

>> **25:** Moderate. The company should have a mitigation plan in place for this risk.

A risk can never have a zero score for either probability or impact. If the score is zero in either category, it isn't a risk.

The document that you use to track and score risks is called a *risk register*. Table 17-1 shows a typical risk register.

TABLE 17-1 ## Risk Register

Risk	Probability	Impact	Risk Score
Port strike	9	9	81
Supplier fire	3	9	27
Forklift breakdown	6	1	6
Comet strike	1	10	10
Canceled customer order	8	6	48

If you create your risk register in a spreadsheet program, such as Microsoft Excel, you can sort your risks according to the risk scores. You can also create reports and graphs so that you can communicate the status of your risks more clearly.

A common way to visualize risks is to use a risk plot or a heat map. Figure 17-1 shows an example heat map for supply chain risks.

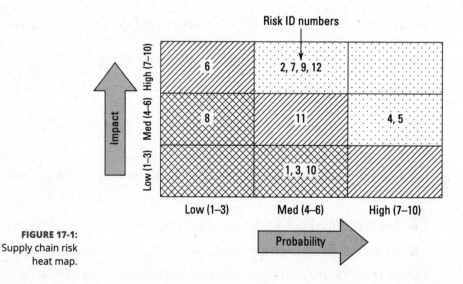

FIGURE 17-1: Supply chain risk heat map.

WARNING

Risk scoring is handy but not perfect. Just because a risk gets a low score doesn't mean that you should ignore it, especially if the potential impact is severe. Any risk that has the potential for someone to get hurt needs to be addressed, even if the probability (and the risk score) are low.

REMEMBER

Risk scoring is like taking a snapshot of risks as they are today. You should keep your risk register up to date as circumstances change, watch for new risks to appear, and monitor changes in the scores of existing risks.

Managing Risks

To make a difference in your supply chain, you need to decide what to do about each risk. The good news is that your options for handling any risk are fairly simple. You have four choices:

>> Accept the risk.

>> Transfer the risk.

>> Avoid the risk.

>> Mitigate the risk.

Accept the risk

Even though you know that a risk exists, you don't always have a good way to resolve it. The risk may be relatively small, for example, or it could be so enormous that it's impossible to avoid. In those cases, you may decide that the risk is part of the business you're in and that you'll deal with the consequences if the risk materializes.

Following are some examples of risks that you may decide to accept:

>> A forklift runs out of fuel in a distribution center.

>> A supply chain manager breaks her leg while skiing.

>> A giant comet collides with Earth.

Could these things happen? Yes. Do you need to devote effort to preparing a special plan for them? Probably not.

Transfer the risk

Sometimes, you can make someone else deal with a risk for you, which is exactly what insurance companies do. You pay them for a policy, and they accept the responsibility to pay for the damages if something goes wrong. You can buy insurance to cover many of the risks that can come up in a supply chain, such as theft, fires, and accidents.

In another scenario, you can write contracts with your customers and suppliers that transfer risk to them in the event that a risk materializes. For example, you could make your suppliers deliver their products to your facility; if a shipment were to be stolen during transit, then your supplier would be responsible. Your supplier will probably charge more for their products in exchange for assuming this additional risk.

Avoid the risk

In some cases, the best way to deal with a risk is to make it go away. If you're concerned that a certain supplier won't be able to meet your requirements, you can switch to a different supplier. If you're afraid that a certain port may have a labor strike, you can ship your freight through a different port. Avoiding a risk can be the cheapest and easiest way to deal with it.

Mitigate the risk

If you can't accept, transfer, or avoid the risk, the only option left is to do something about it — that is, mitigate the risk. The goal of mitigating a risk is to reduce the probability, the impact, or both. In other words, you're trying to lower the risk score. How much you need to lower the score depends on how much the risk could cost you and how much money you can afford to invest in mitigation. Generally, you should mitigate a risk to the point that you're willing to accept it.

If one of your risks is that a customer will cancel a big order, for example, you probably want to mitigate that risk. You could talk with your customer, offer incentives, and make sure that you have a good relationship. You may not be able to eliminate the risk, but you can probably bring it down to an acceptable level and then focus your energy and resources on other parts of the business.

TIP

Commercial agreements can be used to mitigate risks. For example, if your risk register identifies the financial stability of a supplier as a major concern, then you might include in the terms of your commercial agreement that suppliers need to provide periodic financial updates.

The risk register shown in Table 17-2 includes a column for actions. Adding an Action column helps you track how you are planning to manage each risk.

TABLE 17-2

Risk Register with Actions

Risk	Probability	Effect	Risk Score	Action
Port strike	9	9	81	Avoid
Supplier fire	3	9	27	Transfer
Forklift breakdown	6	1	6	Accept
Comet strike	1	10	10	Accept
Canceled customer order	8	6	48	Mitigate

TIP

When you choose to mitigate a risk you should also decide how it will be mitigated and who will be accountable for that work. You may need to create a project to mitigate a risk (see Chapter 4).

IN THIS CHAPTER

» **Understanding the goal of analytics**

» **Preparing for Industry 4.0**

» **Planning analytics projects**

» **Improving visibility with scorecards and control towers**

» **Integrating analytics with scenario planning**

Chapter **18**

Building Supply Chain Analytics

The rapid advances in information and communications technologies over the past 50 years have led to an explosion of data — everything from how much stuff your customers are buying to what the weather will be like in Kokomo, Indiana next week. Analytics is the key to making this data useful for your supply chain.

Supply chain analytics is the process of structuring and filtering data in ways that allow you make better decisions and take action to improve your supply chain. Analytics helps you understand the past so that you can predict more accurately what will happen in the future. In other words, analytics can help you can make better decisions, with more confidence.

In this chapter you examine the technology trends that are making huge amounts of data available, some of the challenges that often arise when working with this data, and some specific ways that you can use analytics to manage your supply chain more effectively.

The Rise of Big Data, Sensors, and the Internet of Things

Data is everywhere in a supply chain. For example, data tells you who your customers are, when your product needs to be delivered, and which carrier is transporting the shipment. The number of new transactions that occur, and the amount of data that we create each day, is actually pretty amazing.

The rapid rate at which new data is being created has led to a trend called *Big Data*. This has an impact on supply chains because it means that supply chain information systems need to store larger and larger amounts of data. To keep up with all that data, you need larger hard drives and faster computers. This often leads to the adoption of cloud-based supply chain information systems. (Read more about Big Data and the cloud in Chapter 14.)

Traditional supply chain data was structured so that it would fit neatly into database tables, and this made it easy for computers to process it. A challenge with Big Data is that much of the data is unstructured. Unstructured data includes things like social media posts, audio recordings of conversations, or digital videos and photos. For example, a social media post about an accident on the freeway could alert you to a supply chain disruption, such as a shipping container falling off of a trailer. A picture of the shipping container could provide useful insights about whether the contents of the container are salvageable. The social media post and the photograph are both examples of the kinds of unstructured data that make managing Big Data a challenge.

Tapping into Big Data can lead to a better understanding of your supply chain. It can give you an advantage over your competitors because it can help you find opportunities that they can't see. On the other hand, if you don't figure out how to use Big Data, you and your supply chain may get left behind.

One of the factors that is feeding the growth of Big Data is the explosion of sensors. A sensor is a device that monitors and reports on something that is happening in the world around it. These sensors provide visibility, which allows you to "see" a supply chain even when you aren't there. Each time one of those sensors takes a measurement, a new piece of data is added to the growing pile of Big Data. Following are some examples of different types of sensors:

>> Optical sensors monitor changes in light.

>> Thermal sensors track changes in temperature.

>> Programmable sensors detect a change and trigger an action or event — for example, activating an optical sensor in a smoke detector triggers the smoke alarm.

LAUNCHING INTO INDUSTRY 4.0

Technology has always been at the heart of industry, and a good way to understand how radically information technology is changing supply chains is to look at how other technologies have revolutionized supply chains in the past. Many experts describe the Industrial Revolution in four stages:

- **Industry 1.0:** Harnessing water and steam to power factories and transportation.
- **Industry 2.0:** Generating electricity to power industrial process.
- **Industry 3.0:** Automating manufacturing and distribution using computers.
- **Industry 4.0:** Connecting complex supply chain processes using IoT and the cloud.

We are entering Industry 4.0 right now, which is why sensors, Big Data, and IoT are becoming so important for supply chain management. During Industry 4.0 supply chains will become more automated, and supply chain analytics will be the tool that people use to design and manage supply chains.

Many sensors are now being connected directly to the Internet. In fact, there are all kinds of devices that are being connected — cars, refrigerators, and thermostats, for example — which has led to another trend called the Internet of Things (IoT). In other words, IoT is a way of describing that the Internet is now being shared by computers, as well as sensors and other devices. Any device that can automatically exchange information over the Internet is an IoT device.

It's not hard to imagine a future in which every part of a supply chain will be connected to the Internet. These supply chains will be IoT-enabled. Some people are even envisioning that virtually every machine around you will be an IoT device. In other words, they expect that in the future there will be an Internet of Everything.

Outline of an Analytics Plan

Analytics is a lot like science because it focuses on discovering new insights. If analytics is to have value to your business, you need to trust the results and be able to take action on the things you learn. There are five steps you should follow to make sure that your supply chain analytics leads to useful insights:

1. Define your theory of the problem or opportunity.
2. Acquire the data.

3. Clean, structure, and filter the data.

4. Query the data and test your theory.

5. Look for correlations and patterns.

The steps don't always go in this order, so use this list as a general guide while staying focused on the goal of finding ways to make better decisions and improve your supply chain.

Define your theory about the problem or opportunity

Analytics projects are focused on using data to answer a question about your supply chain. For example, analytics could be used to understand

» How much it costs to deliver your product to customers in Maine

» How much your freight rates should change when fuel prices decrease

» The main causes of lead time variability for your inbound material

A good place to start an analytics project is to write down your explanation, theory, or hypothesis about how the process you are going to study currently works. Then, throughout your project, you will try to prove or disprove that hypothesis.

For example, imagine that you are interested in reducing lead time variability in your supply chain. You could start your analytics project by writing down your understanding of how the current ordering process works. You would describe the event that triggers an order, and then list each of the steps involved in filling that order. You might include your estimates of how long each step should take, and the amount of variability you expect to occur along the way. Your starting hypothesis could look like this:

1. Purchase order issued to supplier

2. Purchase order received by supplier (1 day)

3. Processing time at supplier (3 days +/– 1 day)

4. Transportation lead time (7 days +/– 3 days)

5. Receiving inspection (1 day)

6. Placed in inventory (1 day +/– 1 day)

7. Total expected lead time = 13 days +/– 5 days

Once your hypothesis is clear, your focus shifts to accumulating evidence to show whether this is an accurate description of the process. In other words, you try to prove or disprove your hypothesis.

This approach provides an easy starting point for defining the scope of your analytics project and identifying the data that you'll need to acquire. Keep in mind that your initial hypothesis may be wrong. As you gain insights throughout your analytics project you should be prepared to refine your hypothesis.

Acquire the data

Analytics is about structuring and filtering data, but figuring out how to get the data you need is often a challenge. For supply chain analytics, you're likely to discover that your data is spread across several information systems. For example, in order study lead time variability you might need data from purchasing systems, transportation systems, and warehousing systems. Depending on the goal of your project you may also need to bring in public data from the Internet, as well as data from your customers and suppliers. If you are looking at transportation variability, for example, you may need to include weather data and the holiday calendar for your supplier's location.

In some cases you may not be able to get all the data that you want, but instead you might be able to find a data set that would work as a substitute or proxy. For example, suppose that you need to know how many associates were employed in a facility, but are unable to get access to human resources data because of privacy rules. In that case, you might try to get financial data and use the amount of money spent on labor as a substitute for the headcount data.

WARNING

When you acquire data from your own information systems or from your partners and suppliers, you need to make sure that you comply with government regulations (such as privacy laws) and with your contractual obligations (such as non-disclosure agreements). Also pay close attention to information security, including viruses. You don't want your supply chain analytics data to get into the hands of a competitor or a malicious hacker!

Clean, structure, and filter the data

When collecting data for an analytics project, you can expect that there will be issues with the data:

>> Some records will have incomplete data, or the data in those records is wrong. For example, in a database of customers, you may be missing some phone numbers, or some of the phone numbers could be out of date.

>> When you are pulling together data from different systems, you need to find ways to link the data together. For example, you might have information about a customer's address in your transportation management system, and information about that customer's order history in your customer relationship management system. In order to analyze both shipments and orders you need to find ways to link these different data sources.

>> Some records will be unnecessary. You will need to filter them out and structure the remaining data in a usable format.

To get around these issues, you need to clean, structure, and filter the data, which can be a laborious process. But business intelligence systems (see Chapter 12) can now do much of this work automatically. Basically, these systems are able to look for patterns in different data sources and automatically suggest ways to structure and filter them.

Query the data and test your theory

After your data is clean and organized, then you get information out of a computer database by running a small program called a query. You can think of queries as questions that are translated into computer language. In other words, you start with the business question that you want to ask, and you translate that into a database query so the computer can understand the question and return an answer to you.

Your goal with queries is to accumulate evidence that supports or refutes your theory. In the lead time example earlier in this section you may start by focusing on products coming from Supplier A. Then you would run a query that asks for all of the purchase orders you issued to that supplier in 2018. You would run another query that asks for all of the shipments received from Supplier A in 2018. You can use the results of these two queries to estimate the total average lead time and test whether your theory seems reasonable.

Look for correlations and patterns

As you run queries and manipulate the data, look for patterns that explain how your supply chain behaves. Correlations and patterns help you translate analytics into insights that can improve supply chain decisions. Here are some examples of the kinds of correlations that might become evident when analyzing supply chain data for a company that makes winter apparel:

>> Demand goes up when the weather gets cold.

>> Shipments cost more when the loads are tendered with short lead times.

>> Suppliers in one region have a lower quality level than suppliers in another region.

Each of these insights could influence decisions about sourcing, making, and delivering the company's products.

When doing analytics projects it is common start with a theory, use that theory to build a query, and then try to find correlations. But unexpected patterns and correlations may lead you to new theories, and deeper insights. When you analyze the data for the apparel manufacturer, for example, you may find that there is always a spike in sales in late March, and you wonder why. Analytics often provides clues that help you investigate what's happening in your supply chain, and you can build on that knowledge to make improvements.

Correlation, Causation, and Interpolation

Three words are the key to almost everything that happens in analytics: correlation, causation, and interpolation. If you understand what they mean and how to use them, the rest of analytics is a breeze.

Correlation and causation are closely related. *Correlation* means that two variables are connected in some way. *Causation* means that one variable causes another to occur. The fact that two variables are correlated doesn't necessarily mean that one causes the other to occur. The correlation could be a coincidence, or some other factor may cause both variables to change. Sales of ice cream and sunblock lotion may be closely correlated, for example, but one variable doesn't cause the other. Both are affected by the season and weather.

Generally, the business questions that you ask should be based on trying to understand causation (such as "Does increasing the amount we spend on marketing lead to an increase in sales?"). You usually answer these questions by looking for correlations. The data can't tell you for certain that advertising was the only reason for the increase in sales, but it can show whether sales tend to go up when you advertise more.

Each piece of data that you collect from your supply chain can be plotted as a point on a graph. For example, the amount of product that you sold on a particular day could be a point on a graph. When you plot several pieces of data, for example the sales on different days, then you obviously end up with multiple points on the graph. To do analysis and look for trends in data, however, you may need to see the data as a line. That is, you collected point data, but you need convert this into continuous data to do some kinds of analysis. Many times, you can create a line that does a good job of averaging or approximating the point data. Converting point data into a line is called *linear interpolation*.

Figure 18-1 shows how linear interpolation can turn points into a line that reveals trends in data. In this example, the upward trend in sales would be hard to see with just the raw point data, but it's clear when you look at the trend of the line.

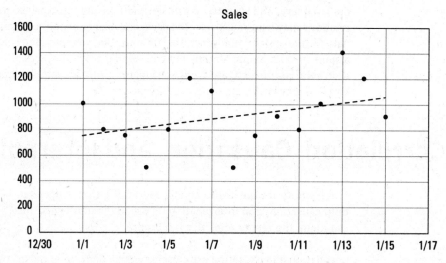

FIGURE 18-1:
Linear
interpolation of
data points.

TIP

Interpolation is commonly used in forecasting. You can create a line based on the data points from the past and then extend that line into the future to create a forecast. Mathematical software such as Microsoft Excel can do interpolations automatically. In Excel, you can add interpolations to a chart by using the trend-line feature. If you want to calculate an interpolation within a cell on an Excel spreadsheet, you can use the =FORECAST() formula.

**TECHNICAL
STUFF**

There are other ways to analyze data using a mathematical process called nonlinear interpolation. Excel graphs includes several trendline options that perform nonlinear interpolation.

Correlations are often easy to see by looking at a graph, but they can be calculated mathematically, as well. Correlations can be positive, negative, or zero.

When two things are perfectly and positively correlated — always happen at the same time — their correlation coefficient is +1.0. Figure 18-2 shows two variables that have a positive correlation. In this example, increasing the amount of money spent on advertising coincides with, or correlates with, an increase in revenue.

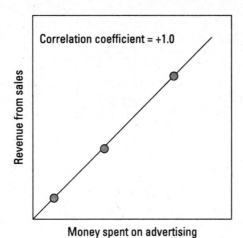

Correlation coefficient = +1.0

Revenue from sales

Money spent on advertising

When one thing goes up while another thing goes down their correlation coefficient is −1.0. For example, Figure 18-3 shows an example of negative correlation in which lowering the price correlates to an increase in the number of units sold.

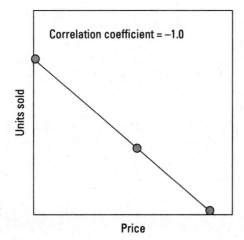

Correlation coefficient = −1.0

Units sold

Price

If is no correlation exists between two things — they're totally independent — their correlation is 0. Figure 18-4 shows two variables that appear to have a correlation of 0. When the correlation between two variables is very low or close to 0, those variables are unrelated.

In real-world analytics problems, you rarely find correlations that are exactly 1.0, 0.0, or −1.0. As a result, it isn't always easy to tell whether the data supports your theory. Deciding what level of correlation is considered significant or meaningful is a common topic of debate among analysts.

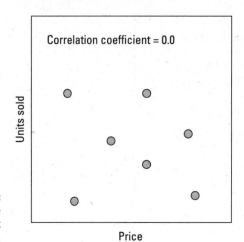

Correlation coefficient = 0.0

Units sold

Price

FIGURE 18-4:
Variables that are
random and not
correlated.

Deciding whether a correlation is significant depends on the question you're asking, the data you're using, and the approach you use to ask the question. You also have to consider confidence (how important is it to be right). There's a big difference in needing to be 80 percent confident and 99 percent confident. Many times, the best approach is simply to ask a team of supply chain analysts or statisticians what they think the level of significance should be.

TIP

Seeing that two things are correlated is often a useful insight that can help you identify ways to improve your supply chain, even if you can't claim a high degree of confidence or prove that one caused the other.

TIP

If you want to learn more about how to perform analytics, check out *Predictive Analytics for Dummies* by Anasse Bari, Mohamed Chaouchi, and Tommy Jung (John Wiley & Sons, Inc., 2016).

Modeling, Simulation, and Optimization

Computer modeling is becoming a popular tool for planning supply chains and predicting how they will perform. Models are generally designed to achieve one of two things:

» To simulate how a supply chain will behave under a certain set of conditions

» To optimize the performance of a supply chain to achieve a particular goal

One argument for models is that it's better to use data than intuition to make supply chain decisions. Supply chain models, however, are only as good as the assumptions on which they are based and on the data they are given. As the saying goes, "All models are wrong, but some models are useful." A good model tries to simplify a problem by capturing the key elements of a supply chain while stripping away the things aren't relevant. To create a useful model, you need to make two decisions:

>> What questions you're trying to answer

>> What factors will have the greatest influence on the outcome

Those decisions will help to ensure that your model is appropriate for the problems you are trying to solve without being unnecessarily complex. A model doesn't have to be an exact copy of the real thing to be useful, and a model that works well in one situation may not be adequate in another.

Simulation

One reason to build a model is to see how the elements of a supply chain interact over time. A model that shows how supply chains behave is called a simulation. Simulation models can illustrate complex dynamics such as swings in inventory that are caused by the bullwhip effect, where demand signals become distorted as they move upstream in a supply chain. (See Chapter 2.) Understanding these dynamics allows you to make supply chain improvements by identifying issues such as bottlenecks and constraints, unused capacity, and unexpected events and relationships.

Optimization

Although simulations can be useful, supply chain managers may want to see more than just how a certain set of variables might change over time. They also want to know how to make improvements, such as:

>> Where to locate a distribution center to minimize shipping times

>> How much inventory is needed to meet the service level target

>> Which transportation modes minimize costs

In other words, supply chain managers want to know the best answer to a supply chain question, and an optimization model can provide this answer. Optimization models try different combinations of variables to find the ones that work best.

BUILDING A MODEL

Building simulation and optimization models can be time-consuming and expensive, and it may make sense to hire a consultant to do this work for you. Whether you build a model yourself, or hire someone to help you, here are some things to consider:

- What questions you're trying to answer
- What factors will influence the decision or outcome
- How stable those factors are (whether they're likely to change over time)
- What other questions you could answer with this model
- How you'll maintain this model

Scenario Planning

Supply chain analytics focuses on using data to provide answers to business questions. Scenario planning complements analytics by identifying the questions which are most important to answer. Combining scenario planning with analytics allows you to use data for long-range planning and making strategic decisions for your supply chain.

Scenario planning is built on the philosophy that the future is filled with uncertainty. In a supply chain, for example, it is hard to predict commodity prices, customer demand, technology adoption rates, and many other variables. You may be able, however, to identify a manageable set of variables that are most likely to shape the future. When you look at these key variables and the ways things could go, you can determine a small number of possible outcomes, called *scenarios*, that represent the most likely versions of the future.

When you understand the potential scenarios that you need to prepare for, focus on what you'd need to do in each scenario. The decisions you need to make and things you could do fall into four categories:

>> **No-brainers:** Some decisions benefit your supply chain in every scenario, involving investments that everyone should agree to make.

>> **No-gainers:** Other decisions don't provide value in any of the scenarios, so there's no point in bothering with them.

>> **No-regrets:** Some options help in one scenario but don't hurt you in the others. In other words, they may turn out to be good investments, or they may be unnecessary but harmless.

>> **Contingent:** Some options help you in one scenario but hurt you in another. You need to know what the future is going to look like — which scenario will emerge — before you can make the right investment.

Identifying the no-brainers, the no-gainers, and the no-regrets options can speed the process of building a strategic plan for your supply chain. The contingent options require constant focus. Because deciding whether to move forward with a contingent option depends on seeing how things change over time, you need to have a process for monitoring the situation and a plan for making the decision. In other words, you might need to set a target or threshold as trigger for a certain scenario.

Here's a scenario involving advertising and e-commerce fulfillment that illustrates how contingent decisions can work Suppose that you're a candy manufacturer that has just begun to sell your products online. Right now, you sell only 100 candy bars per month through your online store. At this low volume it is more cost-effective to outsource your e-commerce fulfillment to a third-party logistics provider than to do this work yourself. However, at a higher sales volume you could do this fulfillment work profitably, so once your e-commerce sales reach 1,000 candy bars per day you want to bring fulfillment back in house.

To boost your sales, you're preparing to invest in advertising, but you don't know how effective the advertising will be. What should you do about your e-commerce fulfillment?

In this case, you're likely to find people on your team with different opinions about what you should do. Some will be optimistic about the effectiveness of the advertising and will want to bring fulfillment in house immediately. Others may be pessimistic about the effectiveness of the advertising, and suggest that you wait to insource fulfillment until you are certain that sales have increased. In reality, this is a contingent decision — selecting the best option depends on how effective the advertising will be.

Making guesses about what is probably going to happen in the future is actually an important part of supply chain management. The beauty of scenario planning is that it helps people with different perspectives and motivations see the things that they agree and disagree on. Where there is disagreement, scenario planning lets you create a process for gathering additional facts and data so that everyone can get onto the same page.

Dashboards and Control Towers

When you drive a car, your primary source of feedback is the dashboard. The dashboard provides data about the car's performance, including its speed, the amount of gas in the tank, and the status of the turn signals (blinking or not). The dashboard also can alert you when something is wrong, such as when it flashes the check-engine light. Like a car, a supply chain is a complex system. If you're responsible for managing a supply chain, you want to have a dashboard for it.

Supply chain dashboards are reports that show the current status of key performance indicators. (See Chapter 16 for more information about supply chain metrics.) Ideally, a dashboard is updated automatically based on live data. But when real-time data isn't available you can manually create dashboards and update them on a regular basis. The goal of a dashboard is to provide a visual representation of data so that people can interpret that data and then make decisions and take action.

Dashboards often use colors and graphical images to show trends and irregularities in data. Figure 18-5 shows a supply chain dashboard that includes graphics.

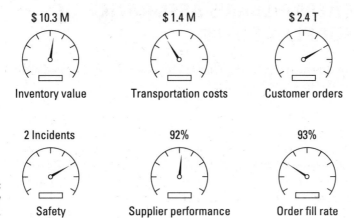

Supply Chain Performance for January

$ 10.3 M	$ 1.4 M	$ 2.4 T
Inventory value	Transportation costs	Customer orders

2 Incidents	92%	93%
Safety	Supplier performance	Order fill rate

FIGURE 18-5:
Sample supply
chain dashboard.

TIP

Many supply chain dashboards use red, yellow, and green to communicate whether a metric is good or bad. A portion of the population is color-blind, however, which means that your colored indicators will be lost on some people. If you choose to use colors in your dashboard, include other features that people with color-blindness can easily spot.

The most common tool for creating supply chain dashboards is Microsoft Excel. (Check out *Excel Dashboards & Reports for Dummies* by Michael Alexander [John Wiley & Sons, Inc., 2016] for step-by-step instructions.) However, business intelligence software tools can make it easier to access data across multiple supply chain information systems, and present that data in scorecards that are attractive and easy to read. (See Chapter 12.)

A dashboard provides a snapshot of key data that gives you insights into what's happening in a supply chain. At times, though, you need to explore data that isn't included in a dashboard. For example, you may need to access additional data to investigate why a process appears to be out of control.

In such cases, you need a supply chain control tower. (See "Improving Transparency and Visibility" in Chapter 15.) Control towers use business intelligence software to provide real-time, flexible access to data so that you can ask complex questions and address business issues. (See Chapter 12 for a list of business intelligence software vendors.) Control towers are useful for strategic management, such as viewing long-term trends, and for managing supply chain disruptions. When a major problem occurs in your supply chain, having easy access to the right information helps you make good decisions and manage trade-offs quickly.

TIP

Over time, the reports that are developed in a control tower can lead to new key performance indicators, which can be added to supply chain scorecards and dashboards.

CATERPILLAR'S ASSURANCE OF SUPPLY CENTER

A good example of a supply chain control tower is the Assurance of Supply Center (ASC) created by Caterpillar, Inc.

In 2012, Caterpillar was struggling to manage its inbound supply chain, which included more than 640,000 stock-keeping units from 7,000 suppliers, which were being shipped to 127 facilities. The company's purchasing division invested in business intelligence software and built a supply chain control tower that could integrate data from many sources, including purchasing systems, transportation management systems, and enterprise resources planning systems.

Once the control was in place it was possible to create scorecards for each supplier and each facility. But the ASC also provided visibility to complex supply chain relationships, such as which plants were receiving parts from each supplier. Having this data available made it much easier for supply chain managers to minimize the impact of supply chain disruptions when a supplier experienced a disaster or when a port was shut down.

For more information, see the "Caterpillar 3000K" video at https://youtu.be/ JeS5SPyvHmA.

5

Building Your Supply Chain Management Career

Chapter **19**

Selecting a Supply Chain Career

Supply chain management can be an extremely rewarding career. Supply chain professionals can work in virtually any sector of the economy; they can be located almost anywhere; and they often collaborate with colleagues, customers, and suppliers all around the world. There are jobs for supply chain professionals to sit at a desk, to work in a factory, and to travel and live on the road. This chapter gives you an overview of jobs in the supply chain so that you can decide on a career path that makes sense for you.

Doing Your Homework

People are the most important part of any supply chain. Lots of jobs contribute to the smooth flow of money, material, and information, and any of these jobs — or a combination of them — can become a career. Finding the right job involves being honest with yourself about what you like and what you're good at, as well as gathering objective information about what jobs are available.

Unfortunately, figuring out how to get started with a career in supply chain management can be hard. Even people who already have supply chain jobs often struggle to find the information they need to understand their options and plan their next steps. Finding the right career in the supply chain industry (or any industry, for that matter) starts with lining up three criteria:

>> The things you're good at doing

>> The things you're qualified to do

>> The things someone will pay you to do

Because all three of these criteria can change over time, you should continually reevaluate your options. The Career Alignment Diagram in Figure 19-1 shows how you can use these criteria to choose a career that makes sense for you today and in the future.

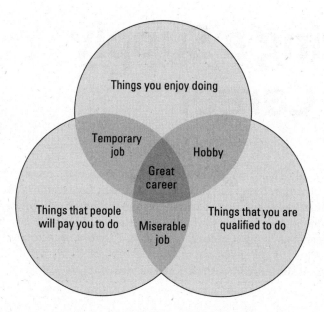

FIGURE 19-1:
Career alignment
diagram.

Examining Supply Chain Career Categories

Supply chain careers and job titles can be confusing, because supply chain management is a relatively new field. (The term *supply chain* has been around only since the 1980s.) Many supply chain jobs are evolving so quickly that the government agencies that track employment data have a hard time keeping up. Staying up-to-date with new job titles is a little bit easier for companies because they can often change job titles fairly easily, without a lot of red tape.

When a new job is created, each company tries to come up with an appropriate title. The result is that different companies may call the same job by different names, and because so many job titles are used for the same job, matching job titles to employment categories can be difficult. For example, drones are rapidly making their way onto the supply chain scene, which means that demand for drone operators is growing. Being a drone operator requires training and licensure, but this job has many titles, such as unmanned aircraft system operator, unmanned vehicle pilot, and commercial drone pilot. So even if you know what kind of job you are looking for, you may still end up researching several different job titles.

TIP

The U.S. Department of Labor collects employment statistics for jobs based on classification codes. These statistics are published on a national website called O*NET. Many researchers, educational institutions, and government agencies structure their programs around these classifications, so the classifications are useful. (This chapter includes information from O*NET OnLine (www.onetonline.org) by the U.S. Department of Labor, Employment and Training Administration (USDOL/ETA). Used under the CC BY 4.0 license. I have modified all or some of this information. USDOL/ETA has not approved, endorsed, or tested these modifications.)

Figure 19-2 shows an example of the information you can find on O*NET.

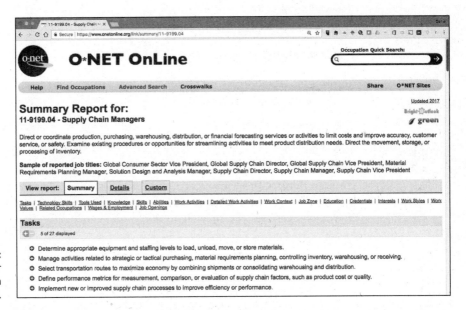

FIGURE 19-2:
Sample career information from O*NET.

To make sense of information about supply chain careers — even from official government sources — you need to understand supply chain processes. A good way to start is to look at job categories, drill down into a category that seems interesting, and find out more about what's involved with the specific jobs in that category. Then you can use this information to tailor your job search (and your résumé) based on the keywords for each job.

The challenge in finding information about supply chain jobs on O*NET is that the jobs are classified in ways that don't make much sense when you think about them in terms of supply chain management. O*NET uses different codes for transportation managers, logistics managers, and logisticians, for example, but in industry, these titles are often used interchangeably.

Ten job categories cover most of the roles that are directly related to the tasks of planning, sourcing, making, delivering, returning, and enabling in a supply chain:

>> Associates

>> Technicians

>> Planners and analysts

>> Engineers

>> Supervisors

>> Managers

>> Sales representatives

>> Information technology managers

>> Project managers

>> Executives

Two other important job categories are often ignored:

>> Journalists

>> Educators

You can think of these job categories in terms of the framework in Figure 19-3. In general, the higher you go on this chart, the more money you'll be paid, but the fewer job openings you're likely to find.

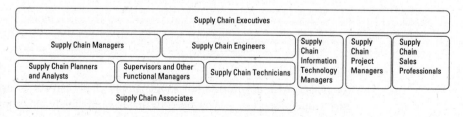

FIGURE 19-3: Supply chain careers framework.

The rest of this chapter describes these categories. As you read about the jobs, you see why some positions are considered to be supply chain jobs even though that fact isn't always clear from the job titles.

TIP

The use of the words *logistics*, *purchasing*, or *operations* is a clear sign of a supply chain job.

Associates

Supply chain associate jobs usually don't require in-depth education and training, but you may have to get a license to operate specific kinds of equipment or take training on the information systems related to the job in a particular company. These jobs are often hourly, and many are seasonal.

The work of supply chain associates has a huge effect on the flow of the entire supply chain. Not much happens without the help of buyers, truck drivers, warehouse workers, and equipment operators. These roles can be great places to learn the ropes and get firsthand experience with many practical challenges that affect supply chain performance. Here are some jobs that are considered to be supply chain associate positions:

>> **Procurement clerks:** Buy stuff from suppliers, and make sure that all the paperwork is in order. Common job titles for procurement clerks include buyer, procurement assistant, procurement officer, procurement specialist, procurement technician, purchasing assistant, purchasing associate, purchasing clerk, purchasing specialist, and warehouse clerk.

>> **Stock clerks:** Handle the shipping and receiving of inventory in a factory or distribution center. Common job titles for stock clerks include bay stocker, material handler, receiver, receiving lead, stock clerk, stocker, stockroom clerk, warehouse clerk, warehouse representative, and warehouse worker.

>> **Weighers, measurers, checkers, and samplers:** Collect data and metrics throughout the supply chain. Common job titles for these roles include cycle counter, inventory specialist, lab technician, material control manager, quality assurance lab technician, quality control lab technician, quality control operator, quality control technician, scale operator, and supply clerk.

>> **Laborers and freight, stock, and material movers:** Move products or packages from one place to another manually (without a forklift). Common job titles for these roles include dock worker, laborer, line tender, loader, material handler, merchandise pickup/receiving associate, receiver, receiving associate, shipping and receiving materials handler, and warehouse worker.

- » **Machine feeders and offbearers:** Support the machines in a supply chain by loading products on them and unloading products from them. Job titles for these roles include feeder, line operator, lug loader, machine feeder, off-bearer, sawmill worker, and tube puller.

- » **Packers and packagers:** Put products in the proper packaging to ensure that the products are protected. Job titles for these roles include bagger, inspector packer, mini shifter, pack-out operator, packager, packer, picker and packer, sacker, selector packer, and shipping clerk.

- » **Industrial truck and tractor operators:** Move materials around a distribution center or storage yard, using a fork truck. Common job titles for these roles include checker loader, forklift technician, fork truck driver, forklift driver, forklift operator, lift truck operator, shag truck driver, spotter driver, tow motor operator, and truck driver.

- » **Light truck or delivery services drivers:** Drive small delivery trucks to pick up parts from suppliers or drop off packages to customers. Common job titles for these roles include bulk delivery driver, delivery driver, driver, driver/merchandiser, package car driver, package delivery driver, route driver, route supervisor, service provider, and truck driver.

- » **Heavy and tractor-trailer truck drivers:** Drive big rigs — the semis that move freight across the country. Common job titles for these roles include delivery driver, driver, line haul driver, log truck driver, over-the-road driver, production truck driver, road driver, semi-truck driver, tractor-trailer operator, and truck driver.

Table 19-1 lists the O*NET codes for some supply chain associate positions.

TABLE 19-1: **O*NET Codes for Supply Chain Associate Positions**

Job Categories	Codes
Procurement clerk	43-3061.00
Stock clerks: stockroom, warehouse, or storage yard	43-5081.03
Weighers, measurers, checkers, and samplers, record keepers	43-5111.00
Laborers and freight, stock, and material movers	53-7062.00
Machine feeders and offbearers	53-7063.00
Packers and packagers	53-7064.00
Industrial truck and tractor operators	53-7051.00
Light truck or delivery services drivers	53-3033.00
Heavy and tractor-trailer truck drivers	53-3032.00

Technicians

Supply chain technicians operate, maintain, install, and upgrade the automation technologies that have become critical to most supply chains. These jobs generally require specialized technical training in areas such as electronics, machining, computer programming, and welding. As automation and drones become more critical for supply chains, the need for technicians who can support these new tools is likely to increase. Following are some job titles that fall into the supply chain technician category.

>> **Electromechanical technicians:** Operate, test, maintain, or calibrate unmanned, automated, servomechanical, or electromechanical equipment. These technicians may operate unmanned submarines, aircraft, or other equipment at worksites. Even though it isn't obvious from the name, this job category includes drone operators. Electromechanical technicians may assist engineers in testing and designing robotics equipment. Job titles for this category include electromechanic, electromechanical technician, electronic technician, engineering technician, laboratory technician, maintenance technician, mechanical technician, product test specialist, test technician, and tester.

>> **Robotics technicians:** Build, install, test, or maintain robotic equipment or related automated production systems. Job titles for this category include automation technician, electrical and instrumentation technician, electronics technician, field service technician, instrument specialist, and instrumentation technician.

>> **Industrial engineering technologists:** Assist industrial engineers in such activities as quality control, inventory control, and material flow methods. These workers may conduct statistical studies or analyze production costs. Job titles in this category include associate product integrity engineer, head of operation and logistics, liaison engineer, manager, asset management, materials planner/ production planner, planner/scheduler, production control supervisor, quality management coordinator, quality tech, and senior quality methods specialist.

>> **Industrial machinery mechanics:** Repair, install, adjust, or maintain industrial production and processing machinery or refinery and pipeline distribution systems. Job titles in this category include fixer, industrial machinery mechanic, industrial mechanic, loom fixer, machine adjuster, maintenance mechanic, maintenance technician, master mechanic, mechanic, and overhauler.

>> **Conveyor operators and tenders:** Control or tend conveyors or conveyor systems that move materials or products to and from stockpiles, processing stations, departments, or vehicles. These workers may control the speed and routing of materials or products. Job titles in this category include assembly line tender, bander, cartoner operator, chain puller, chipper operator,

debarker operator, packing line operator, press operator, process line operator, and process operator.

>> **Bus and truck mechanics and diesel engine specialists:** Diagnose, adjust, repair, or overhaul buses and trucks, or maintain and repair any type of diesel engines. These workers include mechanics working primarily with automobile or marine diesel engines. Job titles in this category include bus mechanic, diesel mechanic, diesel technician, fleet mechanic, general repair mechanic, mechanic, service technician, trailer mechanic, transit mechanic, and truck mechanic.

>> **Manufacturing engineering technologists:** Develop tools, implement designs, or integrate machinery, equipment, or computer technologies to ensure effective manufacturing processes. Job titles in this category include business process analyst, manufacturing coordinator, manufacturing technology analyst, product manager, and scientist.

Table 19-2 lists the O*NET codes for some supply chain technician positions.

TABLE 19-2: ## O*NET Codes for Supply Chain Technician Positions

Job Categories	Codes
Electromechanical technicians	17-3024.00
Robotics technicians	17-3024.01
Industrial engineering technologists	17-3029.05
Industrial machinery mechanics	49-9041.00
Conveyor operators and tenders	53-7011.00
Bus and truck mechanics and diesel engine specialists	49-3031.00
Manufacturing engineering technologists	17-3029.06

Planners and Analysts

Planning and analyzing the flow of money, material, and information is an essential part of making any supply chain work. The planners and analysts who do this work typically combine their knowledge of the business with technology savvy and expertise in supply chain information systems. Some of these jobs require an associate's or bachelor's degree, but it's often possible to acquire the skills for these jobs through work experience and/or professional certification programs. Following are some positions that fall into this category:

>> **Logistics analysts:** Analyze product delivery or supply chain processes to identify or recommend changes. These workers may manage route activity, performing tasks such as invoicing, electronic billing, and shipment tracing. Job titles in this category include global logistics analyst, logistics analyst, and supply chain analyst.

>> **Management analysts:** Conduct organizational studies and evaluations, design systems and procedures, conduct work simplification and measurement studies, and prepare operations and procedures manuals to help management operate more efficiently. Job titles in this category include administrative analyst, business analyst, employment programs analyst, leadership development manager, management analyst, management consultant, organizational development consultant, principal consultant, program management analyst, and quality control analyst.

>> **Operations research analysts:** Formulate and apply mathematical modeling and other optimizing methods to develop and interpret information that helps management with decision-making, policy formulation, and other functions. These workers may collect and analyze data, as well as develop decision-support software, services, or products. They may also develop plans to optimize the time and cost for a logistics network. Job titles in this category include analytical strategist, business analytics director, business insight and analytics manager, decision analyst, operations research analyst, operations research group manager, operations research manager, and scientist.

>> **Production, planning, and expediting clerks:** Coordinate and expedite the flow of work and materials within or between departments of an establishment according to a production schedule. Duties include reviewing and distributing production, work, and shipment schedules; conferring with department supervisors to determine progress of work and completion dates; and compiling reports on progress of work, inventory levels, costs, and production problems. Job titles in this category include master scheduler, material coordinator, materials planner, planner, production assistant, production clerk, production controller, production planner, production scheduler, and scheduler.

>> **Cargo and freight agents:** Expedite and route incoming and outgoing cargo and freight shipments in airline, train, and trucking terminals and on shipping docks. These workers take orders from customers and arrange pickup of freight and cargo for delivery to the loading platform. They also prepare and examine bills of lading to determine shipping charges and tariffs. Job titles in this category include cargo agent, documentation clerk, drop shipment clerk, freight broker, intermodal dispatcher, international coordinator, load planner, logistics coordinator, logistics service representative, expeditor, and operations manager.

Table 19-3 lists the O*NET codes for some supply chain planner and analyst positions.

TABLE 19-3: **O*NET Codes for Supply Chain Planner and Analyst Positions**

Job Categories	Codes
Logistics analysts	13-1081.02
Management analysts	13-1111.00
Operations research analysts	15-2031.00
Production, planning, and expediting clerks	43-5061.00
Cargo and freight agents	43-5011.00

Engineers

Supply chains are complex systems, and designing them often requires high-level math and engineering. Most of the following roles for supply chain engineers require a university degree in engineering:

» **Industrial engineers:** Design, develop, test, and evaluate integrated systems for managing industrial production processes, including human work factors, quality control, inventory control, logistics and material flow, cost analysis, and production coordination. Job titles in this category include engineer, engineering manager, industrial engineer, manufacturing specialist, operations engineer, plant engineer, process engineer, production engineer, supply chain engineer, and tool engineer.

» **Logistics engineers:** Design or analyze operational solutions for projects such as transportation optimization, network modeling, process and methods analysis, cost containment, capacity enhancement, routing and shipment optimization, and information management. Job titles in this category include logistics engineer, reliability engineer, and systems engineer.

» **Manufacturing engineers:** Design, integrate, and/or improve manufacturing systems or related processes. These workers may work with commercial or industrial designers to refine product designs in a way that increases productivity and decreases costs. Job titles in this category include advanced manufacturing engineer, advanced manufacturing vice president, facility engineer, manufacturing director, manufacturing engineer, manufacturing engineering director, manufacturing engineering manager, plant engineer, process engineer, and process improvement engineer.

>> **Robotics engineers:** Research, design, develop, or test robotic applications. Job titles in this category include associate professor of automation, automation engineer, engineer, and plant floor automation manager.

Table 19-4 lists the O*NET codes for some supply chain engineer positions.

TABLE 19-4: **O*NET Codes for Supply Chain Engineer Positions**

Job Categories	Codes
Industrial engineers	17-2112.00
Logistics engineers	13-1081.01
Manufacturing engineers	17-2199.04
Robotics engineers	17-2199.08

Supervisors

Supervisory jobs are closely related to the supply chain and are frequent stops for supply chain professionals as their careers develop. Supply chain engineers and managers often serve as first-line supervisors early in their careers so that they get practical experience in the daily operations of a supply chain. A supply chain professional could be a great candidate for a role such as loss prevention manager, for example, because she understands how supply chains function. Following are some jobs that fall into this category:

>> **First-line supervisors of production and operating workers:** Directly supervise and coordinate the activities of production and operating workers such as inspectors, precision workers, machine setters and operators, assemblers, fabricators, and plant and system operators. Job titles in this category include assembly supervisor, department manager, manufacturing supervisor, molding supervisor, production manager, production supervisor, quality assurance supervisor, shift supervisor, supervisor, and team leader.

>> **Dispatchers:** Schedule and dispatch workers, work crews, equipment, or service vehicles for conveyance of materials, freight, or passengers, or for normal installation, service, or emergency repairs rendered outside the place of business. Duties may include using a radio, telephone, or computer to transmit assignments, as well as compiling statistics and reports on work progress. Job titles in this category include aircraft dispatcher, city dispatcher,

dispatch manager, dispatcher, operations dispatcher, rail operations controller, train dispatcher, and truck dispatcher.

>> **Loss prevention managers:** Plan and direct policies, procedures, or systems to prevent the loss of assets. These workers try to protect the supply chain from theft by determining risk exposure or potential liability and then developing risk control measures. Job titles in this category include loss prevention manager, logistics loss prevention manager, loss prevention operations manager, manager of loss prevention operations, and market asset and protection manager.

Table 19-5 lists the O*NET codes for some supply chain supervisor positions.

TABLE 19-5:

O*NET Codes for Supply Chain Supervisor Positions

Job Categories	Codes
First-line supervisors of production and operating workers	51-1011.00
Dispatchers (except police, fire, and ambulance)	43-5032.00
Loss prevention managers	11-9199.08

Managers

Supply chain managers are business leaders who make decisions about how a supply chain will operate. They may have end-to-end responsibility for purchasing, logistics, and operations, or their scope of duties may be narrower. These roles generally require a bachelor's degree, and for many of them, a master's degree is beneficial. Following are some examples of supply chain manager positions:

>> **Supply chain managers:** Direct or coordinate production, purchasing, warehousing, distribution, or financial forecasting services and activities to limit costs and improve accuracy, customer service, or safety. These workers analyze procedures and identify opportunities for streamlining activities to meet product distribution needs, as well as direct the movement, storage, or processing of inventory. (In other words, they focus on process improvement.) Job titles in this category include global supply chain director, supply chain director, supply chain manager, and supply chain vice president.

>> **Transportation managers:** Plan, direct, or coordinate the transportation operations within an organization or the activities of organizations that

provide transportation services. Job titles in this category include director of operations, fleet manager, freight coordinator, global transportation manager, traffic manager, train operations manager, trainmaster, transportation director, transportation manager, and transportation supervisor.

» **Storage and distribution managers:** Plan, direct, or coordinate the storage or distribution operations within an organization or the activities of organizations that store or distribute materials or products. Job titles in this category include cold storage supervisor, customer service manager, distribution center manager, distribution manager, distribution operation manager, load-out supervisor, shipping manager, shipping supervisor, stores supervisor, and warehouse manager.

» **Logistics managers:** Plan, direct, or coordinate purchasing, warehousing, distribution, forecasting, customer service, or planning services. These workers manage logistics personnel and logistics systems, as well as direct daily operations. Job titles in this category include global logistics manager, integrated logistics programs director, logistics manager, logistics solution manager, and supply chain logistics manager.

» **Logisticians:** Analyze and coordinate the logistical functions of a firm or organization. These workers are responsible for the entire life cycle of a product, including acquisition, distribution, internal allocation, delivery, and final disposal of resources. Job titles in this category include client services administrator, logistician, logistics director, logistics team lead, logistics vice president, operations vice president, production planner, program manager, supervisory supply management specialist, and supportability engineer.

» **Purchasing managers:** Plan, direct, or coordinate the activities of buyers, purchasing officers, and related workers involved in purchasing materials, products, and services. Job titles in this category include commodity manager, director of materials, director of purchasing, director of strategic sourcing, materials manager, procurement manager, procurement officer, purchasing director, purchasing manager, purchasing supervisor, wholesale or retail trade merchandising managers, and procurement managers.

» **General and operations managers:** Plan, direct, or coordinate the operations of public or private-sector organizations. Duties and responsibilities include formulating policies, managing daily operations, and planning the use of materials and human resources. Job titles in this category include business manager, facility manager, general manager, operations director, operations manager, plant manager, plant superintendent, production manager, and store manager.

Table 19-6 lists the O*NET codes for some supply chain manager positions.

TABLE 19-6: ## O*NET Codes for Supply Chain Manager Positions

Job Categories	Codes
Supply chain managers	11-9199.04
Transportation managers	11-3071.01
Storage and distribution managers	11-3071.02
Logistics managers	11-3071.03
Logisticians	13-1081.00
Purchasing managers	11-3061.00
General and operations managers	11-1021.00

Sales Representatives

For businesses that sell supply chain products and services, revenue is driven by salespeople. To sell this stuff, you need to understand the business. Supply chain software companies, for example, need sales representatives who understand how their product can solve problems for their customers, which means that their salespeople need to understand both the technology and the customers' businesses. Education and training requirements for supply chain sales professionals vary widely, but sales jobs are available in virtually every company that provides supply chain solutions.

The general description of sales representatives (O*NET code 41-4012.00) is those who sell goods for wholesalers or manufacturers to businesses or groups of people. The work requires substantial knowledge of the items being sold. Job titles in this category include account executive, account manager, outside sales representative, sales consultant, sales director, sales representative, and salesperson.

Information Technology Managers

Supply chains have become heavily dependent on information systems, which are in a constant state of change. Consequently, professionals who have both the IT savvy and the supply chain knowledge to manage these systems successfully are in high demand. A career as a supply chain IT professional often requires both a college degree and professional certifications. For example, IT professionals may need certifications for the hardware or software that they maintain or for the programming languages that they use. They may also need to be certified in project management or in a software development framework such as Scrum. Supply chain IT positions include the following:

>> **IT project managers:** Plan, initiate, and manage IT projects. These workers lead and guide the work of technical staff, and serve as liaisons between the business and technical aspects of projects. They also plan project stages; assess business implications for each stage; and monitor progress to ensure that deadlines, standards, and cost targets are met. Job titles in this category include IT manager, IT project manager, program manager, project manager, team coach, project leader, team leader, technical project lead, project management office (PMO) leader, and transition manager.

>> **Software developers:** Research, design, develop, and test operating-system software, compilers, and network distribution software for industrial, business, and general computing applications. These workers set operational specifications and formulate and analyze software requirements; they may design embedded systems software. They also apply principles and techniques of computer science, engineering, and mathematical analysis. Job titles in this category include developer, infrastructure engineer, network engineer, publishing systems analyst, senior software engineer, software architect, software developer, software engineer, systems coordinator, and systems engineer.

>> **Computer and information systems managers:** Plan, direct, or coordinate activities in such fields as electronic data processing, information systems, systems analysis, and computer programming. Job titles in this category include application development director, computing services director, data processing manager, information systems director, information systems manager, information systems supervisor, information technology director, IT manager, management information systems director, and technical services manager.

Table 19-7 lists the O*NET codes for some supply chain IT manager positions.

TABLE 19-7: ## O*NET Codes for Supply Chain IT Manager Positions

Job Categories	Codes
IT project managers	15-1199.09
Software developers, systems software	15-1133.00
Computer and information systems managers	11-3021.00

Project Managers

Supply chains are in a continuous state of change, which means that lots of projects need to be managed. Managing projects well requires two different skill sets: knowledge of how supply chains work and expertise in project management. Combining these two professions is a bridge too far for the government classification system, so you'll have a tough time finding official guidance about how many jobs in this category are available. But you can do an Internet search to find these jobs around the world.

Job titles include project manager, program manager, project specialist, project leader, program administrator, project management office manager, center of excellence leader, and black belt.

Journalists

The community of supply chain journalists is small, but these people play a critical role in the industry. Understanding what's happening and explaining it to others take work and practice. Trade magazines, business news services, and online platforms need accurate, insightful, well-written content.

If you want to know how supply chains are changing and you like to write, a job as a supply chain journalist could be an excellent fit for you. Job titles in this category include contributor, editor, editorial director, publisher, author, and technical writer.

TIP

No matter what your area of expertise is, writing books and submitting articles for trade journals and magazines is a great way to build your brand and grow your professional network. Building relationships with writers and editors also increases the likelihood that they'll reach out to you for interviews or story ideas.

Executives

More roles are available all the time for supply chain executives. Many companies now have a chief supply chain officer (CSCO) who oversees the entire supply chain, and reports directly to the CEO, and some CSCOs have been promoted to CEOs. Supply chain executive jobs usually require a bachelor's degree, and a large percentage of executive positions require a master's degree. In O*NET, all the chief executive jobs are lumped into a single job category with the code 11-1011.00.

Chief executives determine and formulate policies and provide overall direction of companies or private and public-sector organizations within guidelines set up by a board of directors or similar governing body. These workers plan, direct, or coordinate operational activities at the highest level of management with the help of subordinate executives and staff managers. Job titles in this category include chief executive officer, chief operating officer, chief supply chain officer, chief procurement officer, chief purchasing officer, chief logistics officer, executive director, executive vice president, operations vice president, president, and vice president.

Educators

Where do people learn the tools, rules, and language required to do supply chain jobs? From teachers, of course. If you have a strong background in supply chain, and you like sharing your knowledge and experience with others, you might consider a career as a supply chain educator. Following are a few jobs in this category:

>> **Vocational education teachers:** Teach or instruct vocational or occupational subjects at the postsecondary level (but at less than baccalaureate level) to students who have graduated or left high school. These workers include correspondence-school, industrial, and commercial instructors, as well as adult-education teachers and instructors who prepare people to operate industrial, transportation, and communications equipment. Jobs may be in public or private schools or in organizations engaged in a primary business other than education. Job titles in this category include mentor, coach, instructor, professor, adjunct professor, and teacher.

>> **Career/technical education teachers:** Teach occupational, career and technical, or vocational subjects at the secondary-school level in public or private schools. Job titles in this category include business education teacher, instructor, marketing education teacher, and technology education teacher.

>> **Business teachers:** Teach courses in business administration and management, such as accounting, finance, human resources, labor and industrial relations, marketing, and operations research. These workers includes teachers who are primarily engaged in teaching and those who do a combination of teaching and research. Job titles in this category include associate professor, business administration professor, business instructor, business office technology instructor, business professor, faculty member, instructor, management professor, marketing professor, and professor.

Table 19-8 lists the O*NET codes for some supply chain educator positions.

TABLE 19-8: ## O*NET Codes for Supply Chain Educator Positions

Job Categories	Codes
Vocational education teachers, postsecondary	25-1194.00
Career/technical education teachers, secondary school	25-2032.00
Business teachers, postsecondary	25-1011.00

Humanitarian Supply Chain Professionals

When a major crisis occurs — such as hurricane, a flood, earthquake, or tornado — it often disrupts supply chains for essential items like food, water, and clothing. There is a growing community of volunteers and full-time professionals who specialize in humanitarian supply chain management; these people create temporary supply chains to receive and deliver relief supplies while permanent supply chains are being repaired. For example, a humanitarian supply chain team might set up a temporary distribution center in a vacant warehouse near a community that was flooded, and they could use this facility to receive the donations that are shipped in from out-of-state charities. Because they streamline the flow of relief supplies to victims of a disaster, humanitarian supply chain professionals play a critical role in the recovery. The job titles for humanitarian supply chain professionals can come from any of the categories in this chapter, but the employers are usually nonprofit organizations (such as the American Red Cross) or government agencies (such as the Federal Emergency Management Agency). There is also a nonprofit organization called American Logistics Aid Network (www.alanaid.org) that specializes in meeting the supply chain needs of communities that are victims of a disaster.

Chapter **20**

Pursuing Supply Chain Education

To advance through your career as a supply chain professional, you'll probably need a combination of degrees and certifications, along with a regular dose of online learning and continuing education. This chapter provides information about the most popular supply chain certifications from professional societies like APICS, ISM, CSCMP, and PMI. It also talks about degrees and other credentials that you can earn from traditional community colleges and universities. Finally, the chapter introduces you to online learning options that are now available and two games that can be useful teaching tools.

Earning Certificates and Certifications

Credentials such as a certificate or a certification tells your boss, your colleagues, and recruiters that you are knowledgeable about a subject. Many universities, community colleges, professional societies, and online training providers offer certifications in supply chain management. *Supply Chain Management Review* has published a long list of these programs at www.scmr.com/images/site/SCMR1607_Certification_download1a.pdf.

This section focuses on the most popular supply chain certifications from professional societies because these certifications are the most widely recognized in industry.

APICS

APICS is one of the oldest, best-known supply chain management associations. Originally the American Production and Inventory Control Society, the organization became more global and expanded beyond inventory and production control, so it dropped the long name. You can find information about APICS certifications at www.apics.org.

Certified Professional in Inventory Management (CPIM)

CPIM is a preferred qualification for supply chain planners and analysts, consisting of five modules:

>> Basics of Supply Chain Management

>> Master Planning of Resources

>> Detailed Scheduling and Planning

>> Execution and Control of Operations

>> Strategic Management of Resources

These five modules are broken into two exams: one exam for the first module (Basics of Supply Chain Management) and a second exam that covers the other four modules. You take the tests at an authorized testing center. You don't need to take the two exams at the same time, and you can take them in any order, but you need to complete both to become certified. Each exam of 150 questions is administered on a computer, and you have three and a half hours to complete each test. You receive your score as soon as you complete the exam.

There are no perquisites for CPIM. You can prepare for the exam by studying on your own, by taking classes, or by using online study tools. You get a discount on the materials by joining APICS as a PLUS member, which costs $220. Then you can purchase all of the books and the two exam vouchers for $1,680.

If you want to take an instructor-led class, check with your local APICS chapter or a local college. If you register for a class, make sure you look at the fine print: Some training providers include the cost of books and exam vouchers in the tuition fee, but others make you buy the materials on your own.

TIP

APICS members get access to the Exam Content Manuals for each certification, which include sample test questions.

For more information, check out www.apics.org/credentials-education/credentials/cpim/exams.

Certified in Logistics, Transportation and Distribution (CLTD)

CLTD, one of the newest supply chain certifications, has eight modules:

» Logistics and Supply Chain Overview

» Capacity Planning and Demand Management

» Order Management

» Inventory and Warehouse Management

» Transportation

» Global Logistics Considerations

» Logistics Network Design

» Reverse Logistics and Sustainability

These eight modules are all covered by one exam that you take at an approved testing center. It is a computer-based exam with 150 questions, and you have three and a half hours to complete it. You'll receive your score as soon as you complete the test.

To be eligible for the CLTD exam you need to have three years of related experience, a bachelor's degree, or another supply chain certification from APICS or the Institute for Supply Management. To document that you have met one of these requirements you need to complete the Certification Eligibility application on the APICS website (www.apics.org/credentials-education/credentials/eligibility) before you'll be allowed to register for the exam.

You can prepare for CLTD on your own, or you can take a class from your APICS chapter or a local college. If you decide to take a class, make sure you read the fine print: The cost of books and exam vouchers is not always included in the price.

You get a discount on the materials by joining APICS as a PLUS member, which costs $220. Then you can purchase all of the books and the exam voucher for $1,370. For more information, check out www.apics.org/credentials-education/credentials/cltd/exam-process.

Complete the Certification Eligibility application at least two weeks before you plan to register for the exam.

APICS exams are administered by Pearson Vue, which has testing centers around the world. You can find the testing center closest to you at www.pearsonvue.com/apics/locate/.

Certified Supply Chain Professional (CSCP)

CSCP covers a range of supply chain topics and breaks the material into three modules:

>> Supply Chain Design

>> Supply Chain Planning and Execution

>> Supply Chain Improvement and Best Practices

These three modules are all covered by one exam that you take at an approved testing center. It is a computer-based exam with 150 questions, and you have three and a half hours to complete it. You'll receive your score immediately.

You can prepare for the CSCP on your own, or you can take a class from your APICS chapter or a local college. If you decide to take a class, make sure you read the fine print: The cost of books and exam vouchers is not always included in the price.

To be eligible for the CSCP exam you need to have three years of related experience, a bachelor's degree, or another supply chain certification from APICS or the Institute for Supply Management. To document that you have met one of these requirements you need to complete the Certification Eligibility application on the APICS website (www.apics.org/credentials-education/credentials/eligibility) before you'll be allowed to register for the exam.

You get a discount on the materials by joining APICS as a PLUS member, which costs $220. Then you can purchase an exam voucher for $695 and purchase the learning system for $995. For more information, check out www.apics.org/credentials-education/credentials/cscp/.

Some universities offer college credits for CPIM and CSCP certifications. Check with the National College Credit Recommendation Service for more information: www.nationalccrs.org/

You can sometimes find used copies of APICS study materials online, but they may be illegal copies. Buying or selling APICS materials illegally is a violation of the APICS ethics rules and can lead to having your certification revoked.

Supply Chain Operations Reference-Professional (SCOR-P)

SCOR-P isn't a certification but an endorsement you earn by attending a three-day class. The class explains the SCOR model (see Chapter 5) and discusses how the metrics work and how to implement projects based on SCOR.

If you need to implement the SCOR model in your company, taking the SCOR-P class helps you build a deeper understanding of the steps to follow. There is a list of SCOR-P classes at www.apics.org/credentials-education/education-programs/scor-professional-training. If you have several people who need to be trained, you can schedule private SCOR-P classes through your local APICS chapter.

TIP

There is a free APICS Dictionary app that includes study tools to help you prepare for exams. You can download the app onto your mobile device from the App Store or the Google Play Store.

Project Management Institute

The Project Management Institute (PMI) is an association for project managers. It maintains a document called the Project Management Body of Knowledge (PMBOK) that serves as a framework for projects. Many supply chain management jobs include project management responsibilities, so it is common for employers to seek out experienced supply chain candidates who also have PMI credentials. You can find the complete list of PMI certifications at www.pmi.org, but the organization's most popular certification is the Project Management Professional (PMP).

The PMP certification demonstrates your understanding of the five processes in the PMBOK:

>> Initiating

>> Planning

>> Executing

>> Monitoring and Controlling

>> Closing

To earn the PMP designation, you need to meet minimum requirements for education and experience. If you have a bachelor's degree then you need to have 4,500 hours of experience as a project manager and 35 hours of project management education. If you have a high school diploma or an associate's degree, then the required amount of project management experience increases to 7,500 hours.

After you meet the experience and education requirements you need to take the PMP exam. You get a $150 discount on the exam if you are a member of PMI; membership is $129. The 200-question test costs $405, and you are allowed two hours to complete it. If you want all the details about the PMP certification process you can download the free PMP Handbook from www.pmi.org/-/media/pmi/documents/public/pdf/certifications/project-management-professional-handbook.pdf?la=en.

TIP

I teach two online courses at LinkedIn Learning that can count toward your PMI education requirements. You can find them at www.linkedin.com/learning/instructors/daniel-stanton.

Council of Supply Chain Management Professsionals

The Council of Supply Chain Management Professionals (CSCMP) has changed its name a few times, which sometimes causes confusion. You may run across references that were published under an old name such as the National Council of Physical Distribution Management or Council of Logistics Management. You can find information about how to get CSCMP credentials at http://cscmp.org.

CSCMP's SCPro certification is designed around eight pillars:

>> Integrated Supply Chain Management

>> Demand and Supply Integration

>> Supply Management and Procurement

>> Manufacturing and Service Operations

>> Transportation

>> Inventory Management

>> Warehousing

>> Order Fulfillment and Customer Service

SCPro provides certifications on three levels:

>> **Cornerstones of Supply Chain Management (Level 1):** To earn this certification, you take a 160 question multiple-choice online exam about the material in the eight pillars of supply chain management. You are given four and a half hours to finish the test. The cost of the exam for CSCMP members is $650. It costs $325 to join CSCMP.

>> **Analysis and Application of Supply Chain Challenges (Level 2):** Level 1 certification is required. The certification process for Level 2 involves reading case studies and answering questions about them in a four-hour exam. The cost of the exam is $1,095 for CSCMP members.

>> **Initiation of Supply Chain Transformation (Level 3):** Level 2 certification is required. The certification process for Level 3 involves developing a plan to implement a supply chain transformation in a real organization. The goal is to demonstrate that you know the concepts and can apply them in a real-world situation. Contact CSCMP for more information about the cost of completing SCPro Level 3 (scpro@cscmp.org or 1-630-574-0985).

Institute for Supply Management

You may be familiar with ISM because business reporters often cover data that is released by the Institute for Supply Management (ISM), which track how much money companies are spending.

ISM has two certifications: one that covers supply chain management with a focus on procurement and a second that focuses on supplier diversity. You can get details about the ISM certifications at www.instituteforsupplymanagement.org.

Certified Professional in Supply Management (CPSM)

The CPSM certification, for people who develop and execute purchasing strategy for organizations, groups supply chain content into three exams:

>> Foundation of Supply Management

>> Effective Supply Management Performance

>> Leadership in Supply Management

It costs $210 to join ISM, and then it costs $229 for each exam. The first two exams have 165 questions each, and you are given two and three-quarters hours to complete each exam. The third exam has 180 questions, and you are have three hours to complete the exam. In addition to passing the exams, you also need to meet education and experience requirements: three years of experience along with a bachelors' degree, or five years of experience if you don't have a degree.

After you have passed all three CPSM exams, you need to submit an application to ISM that includes your score reports, a letter from your employer verifying your experience, and a copy of your university diploma or transcript. You also need to pay an application fee of $119. You can find the application form at www.institute forsupplymanagement.org/files/Certification/CPSMOrgApp.pdf.

TIP

ISM exams are administered by Pearson Vue, which has testing centers around the world. You can find the testing center closest to you at this website: www.pearsonvue.com/ism/locate/.

Certified Professional in Supplier Diversity (CPSD)

The CPSD certification is for people who manage supplier diversity initiatives. To earn the CPSD, you need to meet education and experience requirements and pass two exams:

» Foundation of Supply Management

» Essentials in Supplier Diversity Exam

The first exam has 165 questions that you need complete in two and three-quarters hours. The second exam has 120 questions, and you need to complete it in two hours. The cost for each exam is $229 for ISM members. In addition to passing the exams, you also need to meet education and experience requirements: three years of experience along if you have a bachelors' degree, or five years of experience if you don't have a degree.

After you have passed both CPSD exams, you need to submit an application to ISM that includes your score reports, a letter from your employer verifying your experience, and a copy of your university diploma or transcript. You also need to pay an application fee of $119. You can find the application form at www.institute forsupplymanagement.org/files/Certification/CPSDOrigApp.pdf.

TIP

Because the Foundation of Supply Management exam is required for both the CPSM and CPSD certifications, many people get both certifications.

International certifications

Certifications are available in many countries, and supply chain professionals who work outside the United States may want to explore these programs.

Chartered Institute for Logistics and Transport (CILT)

CILT is the UK association for logistics and operations professionals. It costs £143 to join CILT. As you achieve more education and progress in your career, you can advance your status within CILT. The four grades of CILT membership are

- » Affiliate
- » Member
- » Chartered Member
- » Chartered Fellow

You can get more information about CILT credentials at www.ciltuk.org.uk.

Chartered Institute for Procurement and Supply (CIPS)

CIPS is the UK association for procurement professionals, offering certificates and diplomas. It costs £234 to become a member of CIPS. When you start a career in operational procurement roles, you can get these certificates:

- » Certificate in Procurement and Supply Operations
- » Advanced Certificate in Procurement and Supply Operations

When you get advanced education or move into management roles, you can pursue these diplomas:

- » Diploma in Procurement and Supply
- » Advanced Diploma in Procurement and Supply
- » Professional Diploma in Procurement and Supply

You can find more details about CIPS credentials at www.cips.org.

Earning Degrees and Diplomas

The best way to prepare for many supply chain management jobs is to get a formal degree or diploma. The right school and the right course of study depend on what you want to do when you finish your education.

Supply chain jobs require business, engineering, and technology skills. When you look at degree options, think about how each one can help you develop in all three areas. If you plan to become a supply chain analyst, for example, you'll probably benefit most from a business degree, but your classes should give you the opportunity to see how logistics networks are engineered and expose you to technologies that drive the data you'll be analyzing.

Undergraduate degrees

Many community colleges offer supply chain management courses and allow you to earn an associate's degree in about two years. With this kind of degree, you would be qualified for an entry-level job as a supply chain analyst or technician.

For more senior jobs, such as supply chain manager, you probably need a four-year degree in supply chain management. Undergraduate programs in supply chain management have become popular in the past few years and are offered in business schools at public and private universities around the United States.

If you're interested in jobs involving supply chain technology or engineering, look at degrees in those areas. A degree in industrial engineering, industrial distribution, or industrial technology could be a good choice. Some universities offer certificates to students who take a certain number of supply chain classes as part of their engineering or technology degree. At Bradley University, for example, you can earn a Bachelor of Science in Industrial Engineering degree with a concentration in Global Supply Chain Management.

Graduate degrees

As you move farther up the management ladder, you'll probably need a master's degree. If your undergraduate degree is in a field other than supply chain management, you need a master's degree with a supply chain focus. A few schools offer master's degrees in supply chain management, but many more offer Master of Business Administration (MBA) degrees with a concentration in supply chain management.

Currently, only four universities in the United States offer graduate degrees in supply chain engineering: Massachusetts Institute of Technology (MIT), Georgia Institute of Technology, North Carolina State University, and New Jersey Institute of Technology. Many graduate programs in industrial engineering and industrial technology, however, have courses that also apply to supply chain careers.

Exploring Online Education Options

Online supply chain education programs range from free videos to paid subscription programs to full-blown graduate courses. It's hard to say what long-term effect these online programs will have on traditional college programs and certifications, but these programs are making supply chain education cheaper and easier to access for people around the world.

Traditional online programs

Many universities offer online versions of their courses and even online degrees. In most cases, the curriculum is identical to that of a traditional degree program, but the way in which the online material is delivered can vary among schools and even among professors. Some online courses use videoconferences that offer live interaction with the professor and other students; others use video recordings of a lecture; still others ask students to read course materials, write their homework, and interact via email.

MITx MicroMasters in Supply Chain Management

MIT's supply chain master's degree program is ranked among the top programs in the world. Recently, the school combined some of that program's content in a new program called MITx MicroMasters in Supply Chain Management.

This program consists of five online courses, which anyone can take for free. If you pay a fee of $1,200, however, MIT validates your identity and allows you to take exams at the end. If you complete all five courses and pass the exams, you receive a MicroMasters credential in Supply Chain Management. Later, if you're accepted at MIT as a graduate student, you get credit for your MicroMasters courses.

The five courses are

>> Supply Chain Analytics

>> Supply Chain Fundamentals

>> Supply Chain Design

>> Supply Chain Dynamics

>> Supply Chain Technology and Systems

You can find more information about this program at www.edx.org/micro masters/mitx-supply-chain-management.

Coursera

Coursera is a website that allows many universities to share their courses online. The site currently offers supply chain management courses from a few schools, including Rutgers University.

The costs vary (from $15 to $25,000) depending on how you use the website. You pay a subscription fee every month to access the Coursera library.

To search the library and find out how much a given course of study costs, visit www.coursera.org.

LinkedIn Learning

LinkedIn Learning (formerly Lynda.com) is an online library of courses taught by university professors and industry experts. Several good courses on supply chain management are available, as well as courses on useful topics such as project management, Lean, and Six Sigma. When you complete a course on LinkedIn Learning, you can have that information added to your LinkedIn profile.

You can get access to the entire LinkedIn Learning library for a subscription fee of $35 per month. Visit www.linkedin.com/learning for more information.

TIP

If you're active-duty military or a military veteran, you can request a one-year free subscription to LinkedIn Learning. For details, visit linkedinforgood. linkedin.com/programs/veterans.

YouTube

You can find a lot of great supply chain management content on YouTube; you just have to look among the millions of funny cat videos to find it. Videos from universities and associations explain supply chain management in many ways and in many languages. You can also find corporate videos that provide examples of supply chains in action. To find these videos, visit www.youtube.com and search for "supply chain."

TIP

You might like this MIT video that uses a lemonade stand to illustrate the challenges of managing a supply chain: www.youtube.com/watch?v=gBRrG0-SA1I.

Playing Supply Chain Games

Supply chains often behave in unpredictable ways, and it can be difficult to explain why. Rather than using traditional teaching methods, such as books and lectures, it is easier (and more fun!) to demonstrate these behaviors by playing simulation games. There are two games in particular that are highly effective teaching tools for supply chain management: The Beer Game and The Fresh Connection.

The Beer Game

One of the first people to teach and research supply chain management was an MIT professor and electrical engineer named Jay Forrester. Forrester noticed that when businesses exchange money, material, and information, they behave like electrical circuits. He created a technique for modeling businesses that was similar to the technique he used to analyze circuits, and he called his approach system dynamics.

To explain how system dynamics works, he created The Beer Game. Players are divided into four teams: customer, retailer, distributor, and brewery. In this simulated beer supply chain, you see how small variations in demand can quickly create inventory stockpiles and stockouts. The game is used in university classes and executive education programs around the world.

You can order the game from the System Dynamics Society (`www.systemdynamics.org/products/the-beer-game`) for $125. Several online versions of the game are available, and some are free. I find that playing the original version of the game is a more effective way to teach people about system dynamics and introduce them to the unpredictability of supply chains.

TIP

If you want to see The Beer Game in action, check out this old video of MIT Professor John Sterman on YouTube: `www.youtube.com/watch?v=vQQUxgLfY-g`.

The Fresh Connection

If you're looking for an online supply chain game, check out The Fresh Connection, a simulation created by a group of supply chain experts in the Netherlands.

To play the game, divide people into teams of four players each. These players are assigned to key supply chain roles for a fruit-juice company called The Fresh Connection, which is struggling financially. The vice presidents of purchasing, operations, sales, and supply chain management need to analyze metrics and make decisions that improve return on investment for the entire company. In addition to providing hands-on experience with the tools, rules, and language of supply chain management, the game shows how hard it can be for people to communicate and make decisions as a team.

Most people who play the game do so through their companies or universities, or as part of a professional development program.

For more information on The Fresh Connection, visit www.thefreshconnection.biz/en_us.

REMEMBER

The game was created in the Netherlands, local suppliers are those suppliers in Central Europe, which can be disorienting for Americans when they first play the game.

6

The Part of Tens

Discover ten important questions that you should ask about your own supply chain.

Chapter **21**

Ten Questions to Ask About Your Supply Chain

One of the most exciting and challenging aspects of supply chain management is how quickly things change. New customers, new suppliers, and new technologies are added to supply chains every day. In order for supply chain managers to meet their goals of delivering value to customers while maximizing profits, they need to always be looking for ways to improve. This chapter provides ten questions that you should ask to make sure your supply chain is meeting your customers' needs, giving your company a competitive advantage, and keeping pace with technology trends.

Who Are Your Key Customers?

One big challenge for supply chain managers is that they're often disconnected from the company's customers. Sales and marketing departments make deals and entice customers to buy; then it's up to the supply chain folks to make the products and deliver them on time. Although supply chain managers have a set of production targets, they often have no idea who their customers are.

Although all of your customers are important, your key customers are the ones that are most important for your supply chain. Key customers buy in large quantities, are expected to buy more in the future, or are influential in your industry. As a supply chain manager, you should learn who these key customers are and what makes them important to your business so that you can focus your improvement efforts on profitably meeting their needs.

TIP

Two common ways for supply chain managers to collaborate directly with key customers are through routine meetings and process improvement projects (see Chapter 4).

What Do Your Key Customers Value?

Your supply chain creates value by addressing your customers' needs. There are many ways to gather data about the things that your key customers expect and are willing to pay for including:

>> Analyzing industry trends

>> Conducting surveys

>> Interviewing customers

>> Attending conferences

>> Sponsoring focus groups

As you gain new insights about what your customers value, use this information to improve the metrics for your supply chain (see Chapter 16). Ensuring that your supply chain is performing in terms of metrics that matter to your key customers helps you capture new customers, sell more to your existing customers, and introduce new products and services that address needs that aren't being met.

How Could Your Supply Chain Create More Value?

Companies can become comfortable — even complacent — about the relationship they have with their customers. This attitude is dangerous, of course, because what customers want and how much they are willing to pay will change over time.

There is often pressure to lower your prices to make your products more competitive. You should always be looking for ways to improve supply chain efficiency because this can allow you to lower prices without sacrificing profits. However, you should also be looking for opportunities to increase revenue by reaching new customers or making your product or service more valuable to your current customers. For example, selling products online can be a good way to connect with new customers, and profitably fulfilling to online sales often involves significant changes to a supply chain.

How Do You Define Supply Chain Management?

Many people use the term "supply chain management" when they are really talking about the procurement, logistics, or operations functions. To be effective in improving your company's supply chain, you need to have a broader perspective. For example, a project that reduces procurement costs can end up increasing costs for logistics and operations. As a supply chain manager you should look across all three of these functions and identify the best end-to-end solution. You should also look beyond your own company and understand the effects that a change could have on your suppliers and your customers.

Driving down costs and improving performance in a supply chain requires alignment across functions and between companies, and that means everyone needs to think about how their decisions affect the rest of the supply chain. Supply chain management should be viewed as the process of synchronizing the activities within your company and aligning them with your customers and suppliers.

What Information Do You Share with Suppliers?

Your suppliers need to get certain information from you to maximize their value in your supply chain. Many companies try to position themselves as strategic partners with their customers but then maintain a guarded, arms-length relationship with their own suppliers. It's also important to make sure that you are sharing information in a useful way. If the data you share is hard to interpret or changes too frequently, it can cause confusion.

Here are two tips for successfully sharing information with your suppliers:

>> **Share all the information you can.** Decide what information to share with suppliers and what information to hold back. Some business information certainly needs to be protected, but not all of it requires the security of state secrets. In fact, you're probably better off to share every piece of information that could be useful for a supplier unless you can identify a genuine risk from disclosing it.

>> **Ask suppliers what they want.** Talk with your suppliers to find out what information they want from you and how (and whether) they're able to get it. In many supply chains, one company assumes that another company is getting the information that it needs, but that may be incorrect. The information could be hard to find or interpret, or it could be going to the wrong person in the company. The easiest way to identity and resolve gaps is to have a conversation with the supplier.

Sharing information with suppliers can help both your company and the supplier create more value.

TIP

Many retailers have begun sharing sales and inventory information with their suppliers in order to reduce the bullwhip effect (see Chapter 2). When suppliers have access to information about supply and demand in retail stores they can do a better job of planning for future needs.

How Do You Compare with Competitors?

You can find out a lot about how well your own supply chain is doing by benchmarking against other companies, including your competitors (see Chapter 2). You can do benchmarking informally by researching public information about your competitors. You also can do formal benchmarking by sharing data between companies or working with a research firm that collects data from many companies and provides them all with benchmarking reports. One advantage to participating in a multi-company benchmarking study is that it can allow participants to see how they're performing relative to other companies without having to reveal their identities.

WARNING

Although sharing non-financial data with other companies for benchmarking studies is usually perfectly legal, it's illegal to share some information that could stifle competition. For example, you probably can share information about your inventory turns, but you probably can't share information about your prices. Before sharing any information with someone who works for one of your competitors, make sure that you understand what you can and can't discuss.

What Changes Could Increase Revenue?

There are basically only three ways to increase revenue, and each of them depends on effective supply chain management:

>> Raise prices.

>> Sell more stuff to current customers.

>> Attract new customers.

To raise prices, you need to be providing more value than your competitors. As long as you can deliver the product your customers want, when they want it, and where they want it better than your competitors, then you can charge more money.

If you are looking for ways to increase revenues by selling more stuff to current customers and attracting new customers, here are some specific goals that supply chain management can pursue:

>> Distribute your products through new channels.

>> Improve customer experience and increase brand loyalty.

>> Adapt your product, package, and processes to the needs of new customers.

Think about ways to increase revenue for your company and then get your supply chain team on board with those initiatives.

What Changes Could Lower Costs?

Supply chain management decisions drive most of the costs for every company, so be on the lookout for opportunities to reduce the amount of money that you spend. Following are some supply chain savings to look for:

>> **Increase transportation capacity utilization.** By squeezing more valuable products into every shipment, you make better use of the money that you spend on transportation and lower your overall costs.

>> **Increase supply chain velocity.** By increasing the rate at which products move through your supply chain, you increase your return on investment. Inventory velocity can be measured with inventory turns. Shipment velocity can be measured with order lead times or transportation lead times.

End-to-end supply chain velocity — how long it takes for a product to get to your customer — can provide important insights about where your products get stuck along the way.

>> **Reduce order variability.** Variability in order patterns is a well-known driver of costs in supply chains. Variability causes companies to build up inventory, which is expensive. Inventory swings amplify as they move up the supply chain, causing the bullwhip effect (see Chapter 2). Finding ways to make smaller orders more frequently and reduce variability can translate into significant savings by reducing both inventory and the chance of lost sales from stockouts.

Efforts that you make in each of these areas have direct and indirect benefits. The direct benefits are money added to your bottom line. The indirect benefits are reductions in waste and a better utilization of the capacity throughout the supply chain.

REMEMBER

Often, 80 percent of a company's expenses are tied directly to supply chain decisions. Every dollar saved in the supply chain becomes profit for your company.

What Affects Your Supply Chain Now?

Supply chain technology is evolving quickly, and no supply chain manager can afford to ignore it. To stay competitive, keep your finger on the pulse of supply chain technology. Here are a few good ways to stay informed:

>> Read supply chain magazines and blogs.

>> Attend supply chain conferences and trade shows.

>> Subscribe to reports by supply chain consultants and analysts.

>> Stay active in a professional association.

>> Maintain communications with technology vendors.

You may not need to learn the ins and outs of every new technology that comes down the pike, but you need to have a sense for how new technologies can help you deliver more value to your customers, either by increasing revenue or reducing costs.

What Will Affect Your Supply Chain in the Future?

You may have heard the saying "A leader needs to have a microscope in one eye and a telescope in the other." Using your telescope to look at the future of supply chain management can make the field fun and exciting or terrifying and risky.

Imagine telling your wristwatch that you want a taco, and a few minutes later, a drone will deliver that taco. That scenario sounds silly, but all of the technology that you'd need for that supply chain is available today. All it would take to make that supply chain a reality is a viable business plan.

There will be lots of opportunities to transform supply chains using technology in the next few years, and by recognizing those opportunities early you can get a competitive advantage. Try to imagine ways that each step in your supply chain could be done differently using technology, and look for opportunities to create value in new ways.

In many cases, the technology doesn't change what is happening, but it does change how it happens. For example, right now you probably go to the grocery store and pick out your bananas. However, many grocery stores will allow you to place orders through a website and pick them up at the curb. You are still buying bananas, but how you buy them is starting to change. The time that your customers save by ordering online instead of shopping in the store is valuable to those customers.

In other cases, new technologies could make an existing supply chain obsolete. For example, imagine a world of autonomous cars that are shared or rented on demand. Rather than buy cars from a dealership, customers may sign up for subscriptions to a car-on-demand service through a website. This new technology could make car dealerships, and their supply chains, obsolete.

The only way to measure risks and identify opportunities that come from technological innovation is to stay in touch with trends. Understand the value your supply chain provides to your customers and what additional needs aren't being met; then keep an eye out for new technologies that could help you meet those needs.

Index

A

A-B Testing, 32
Aberdeen (website), 195
accepting the risk, 101, 255
accounts payable metrics, 241
Adelante SCM (website), 195
administrator, 24
advance ship notice (ASN), 179
advanced manufacturing
  about, 197–198
  automated manufacturing, 199–200
  automated mobile robots, 203–204
  computer-aided design, 200
  obsolescence and, 198–199
  3D printing, 200–202
  unmanned/autonomous vehicles, 204–205
agility, as a SCOR attribute, 236, 237–238
AI (artificial intelligence), 214
air transportation, 133–134
Alexander, Michael (author)
  Excel Dashboards & Reports For Dummies, 273
Amazon, 205
American Logistics Aid Network (website), 294
American Production and Inventory Control Society (APICS), 296–299
analysis paralysis, 63, 231
analysts, 284–286
analytics. *See* supply chain analytics
Analyze, as step in Six Sigma, 52
ANN (artificial neural network), 203
anyLogistix (website), 191
APICS (American Production and Inventory Control Society), 296–299
APICS Dictionary (website), 108
ARC Advisory Group (website), 195
Arena (website), 191
Ariba (website), 189
artificial intelligence (AI), 214

artificial neural network (ANN), 203
ASN (advance ship notice), 179
AS/RS (automated storage and retrieval systems), 144
asset-based 3PL, 147
assets, 160–161, 236, 238
associates, 281–282
authority, cross-functional project teams and, 56
automated manufacturing, 199–200
automated mobile robots, 203–204
automated storage and retrieval systems (AS/RS), 144
autonomous vehicles, 204–205
avoiding the risk, 101, 256
Ayers, James B. (author)
  Handbook of Supply Chain Management, 2nd Edition, 15

B

balancing a line, 116
balancing loops, 28
batch sizes, 230
The Beer Game, 307
benchmarking, 30
BI (business intelligence) software, 192–193
biased error, 42
Big Data, 212–213, 260–261
bill of lading (BoL), 140
bimodal innovation, as a principle of supply chain management, 12–13
blockchains, 211–212
BluJay (website), 179
BoL (bill of lading), 140
Box, George (statistician), 192
boxcars, 129
BravoSolution (website), 189
brick-and-mortar channel, 215
bulk carriers, 129

H

Handbook of Supply Chain Management, 2nd Edition (Ayers), 15

heavy truck drivers, 282

"hierarchical" culture, 25

HighJump (website), 181, 187

HMI (human-machine interface), 203

honesty, in supplier relationships, 96

hopper cars, 129

house of quality (HOQ), 32

human resources, leveraging, 167–169

humanitarian supply chain professionals, 294

human-machine interface (HMI), 203

I

IBM (website), 193

icons, explained, 2

identification and control equipment, 144

IFS (website), 185

igloos, 133

Improve, as step in Six Sigma, 52–53

inbound logistics, 22

Incoterms (International Commercial Terms), 140

indefinite delivery contract, 97

industrial automation, 199–200

industrial engineer, 286

industrial engineering technologist, 283

industrial machinery mechanic, 283

Industrial Revolution, 261

industrial truck/tractor operators, 282

Infor (website), 181, 183, 185, 186, 188, 190

information technology (IT), 166–167

information technology managers, 290–291

information value chain, 166

innovation, 49–55

input costs, minimizing, 91–92

inputs, 71, 92–93

Insight Maker (website), 29

insourcing, 94–95

Institute for Supply Management (ISM), 105, 301–302

integrator, 24

Intelligrated (website), 187

interface, 203

interlock, 203

internal collaboration, 17

international certifications, 302–303

International Commercial Terms (Incoterms), 140

Internet of Things (IoT), 212–213, 260–261

interpolation, 265–268

inventory

vs. customer service, 41–43

vs. downtime, 43–44

managing, 135–141

as Muda in Lean approach, 49

optimizing, 224–225

vendor-managed, 226

inventory costs, 36

inventory counts, 138

inventory ordering policies, 141–142

IoT (Internet of Things), 212–213, 260–261

ISM (Institute for Supply Management), 105, 301–302

ISO 9001 certification, 124

IT project manager, 291

J

JDA (website), 179, 181, 187

JIT (Just In Time), 111, 142

Jobs To Be Done Theory, 33

John Gait (website), 183

journalist, 292

Just In Time (JIT), 111, 142

K

kaizen, 50

Kanban strategy, 44, 142

Kay, Michael (industrial engineering expert), 143

key performance indicators (KPIs), 30

Kinaxis (website), 183

KPIs (key performance indicators), 30

L

labor management system (LMS), 186–187

laborers, 281

Lapide, Larry (professor), 39

last mile, 214

LCL (less than container load), 130

lean manufacturing, 111

Lean Manufacturing, 44, 49–51

less than container load (LCL), 130

less than truckload (LTL), 131–132, 178

leveling a line, 116

life cycle costs, 90–95

light truck drivers, 282

LinkedIn Learning, 306

live load/unload, 140

Llamasoft (website), 192

LMS (labor management system), 186–187

loading dock, 137

local risks, 253

Logility (website), 183

logistician, 289

logistics, 22–23, 44–45

logistics analyst, 285

logistics engineer, 286

logistics manager, 289

loss prevention manager, 288

lost time incident rate, 244

lot sizes, 230

LTL (less than truckload), 131–132, 178

luxury goods, 34

M

machine feeders, 282

Magic Quadrant, 194

Make process

about, 69–71

choosing production environment, 118–121

defined, 107

identifying manufacturing process types, 115–117

implementing quality control and quality assurance, 121–124

planning and scheduling production, 108–114

reducing manufacturing waste, 124–125

make-to-order approach, 78–79, 118, 119–120

make-to-stock approach, 78–79, 118, 119

management analyst, 285

managers, 288

Manhattan Associates (website), 181, 187

manufacturing, 115–117. *See also* advanced manufacturing

manufacturing cell, 116

manufacturing engineer, 286

manufacturing engineering technologist, 284

manufacturing resource planning, 185

manufacturing stall, 116

manufacturing waste, 124–125

MAPE (mean absolute percentage error), 43

Master Demand Schedule (MDS), 110

Master Production Schedule (MPS), 110

material handling equipment, 143–144

material movers, 281

material requirements planning (MRP) system, 182, 183–185

MDS (Master Demand Schedule), 110

mean absolute percentage error (MAPE), 43

Measure, as step in Six Sigma, 52

measurers, 281

Mentzer, John T. (author)

The New Supply Chain Agenda, 16

MercuryGate (website), 179

metrics

about, 233–235

aligning with customers, 159–160

financial, 241–242

identifying performance attributes, 235–236

operational, 238–240

people, 242–244

process, 72–73

SCOR, 236–238

sharing with suppliers, 160

sustainability, 245–246

Microsoft (website), 185, 186, 188, 190, 193

Microsoft Excel, 273

minor wear and tear, 151–152

Project Management Institute (PMI), 169–170, 299–300

project management office (PMO), 171

project managers, 292

project scorecards, 61–62

projects, 55–64

promotions, managing, 230

pull strategy, 44

purchase orders (POs), 145

purchasing
about, 21–22, 87
establishing ethics, 104–105
segmenting supply chains, 88–90

purchasing manager, 289

put-away, 137–138

Q

QFD (quality functional design), 32

Qlik (website), 193

qualitative metrics, 30, 234

quality, 36–37, 122–124

quality assurance (QA), 121–124

quality control (QC), 121–124

quality functional design (QFD), 32

quantitative metrics, 30, 234

querying data, 264

R

RACI Matrix, 59–60

rail spurs, 131

rail transportation, 129–131

random variability, 123

"rational" culture, 25

reasonableness, in supplier relationships, 96

receiving, 137

recruiting, 167–168

recycling, 125

refrigerated boxcars, 129

refrigerated trailers, 133

regional sourcing, 222

regulatory compliance, 164–165

reinforcing loops, 28

relationships, supplier, 95–96

reliability, as a SCOR attribute, 236–237

remanufacturing, 153

Remember icon, 2

rent option, 177

requirements, aligning resources with, 79–80

researching, for careers, 277–278

resilience, building, 249–250

Resilient Enterprise (Sheffi), 252

resources, aligning with requirements, 79–80

responsiveness, 74–75, 236, 237

retail, 146

retaining people, 168

return on supply chain fixed assets metric, 238

return on working capital (ROWC), 238

Return process, 69–71

returns, planning for, 85–86

revenues, 8, 150–151, 315

reverse supply chain
about, 85–86, 149
growing revenues, 150–151
managing closed-loop supply chains, 153–154
managing fraudulent products, 154–155
managing trade-ins, 155
managing unauthorized returns, 154–155
processing returns of new/excess products, 151–152
processing returns of used/defective products, 152–153

RFID tags, 144, 161

risk management, as a principle of supply chain management, 14

risk register, 101

risk scorecard, 101

risks
about, 247
building resilience, 249–250
classifying, 252–253
considerations, 122
dealing with, 101–102
effects and, 104

unmanned vehicles, 204–205

untapped skills/employee creativity, as Muda in Lean approach, 49

upside supply chain adaptability metric, 237

upside supply chain flexibility metric, 237

upstream, 87

U.S. Federal Reserve (website), 113

utilization rates, 113

V

value
  creating more, 312–313
  defined, 8
  for key customers, 312
  what customers, 32

value creation, as a principle of supply chain management, 15

value-added service, 147

value-stream mapping (VSM), 48

variability, controlling, 122–124

vendor-managed inventory (VMI), 226

vendors. *See* suppliers

visibility, 15, 209–210, 219–220

VMI (vendor-managed inventory), 226

vocational education teacher, 293

VSM (value-stream mapping), 48

W

waiting, as Muda in Lean approach, 49

Walmart, 222

warehouse execution system (WES), 139, 180–181

warehouse management system (WMS), 137, 180–181

warehousing, managing, 135–141

Warning icon, 2

waste, manufacturing, 124–125

waste metrics, 245, 246

wear and tear, 151–152

websites. *See also specific websites*
  certificates/certifications, 295
  material handling equipment taxonomy, 144
  system dynamics modeling, 29
  utilization rates, 113

weighers, 281

WES (warehouse execution system), 139, 180–181

What's In It For Me? (WIFM), 96

What's In It For Them? (WIFT), 96

WMS (warehouse management system), 137, 180–181

workforce augmentation service, 147

work-in-process inventory (WIP), 84

Y

yard management, 140–141

yield improvement metric, 242

yield metric, 240

YouTube, 306

Z

Zappos.com, 150

zero cash conversion cycle, 99

About the Author

Daniel Stanton, M. Eng., MBA, SSBB, PMP, CSCP, is passionate about supply chains and the role that they play in our everyday lives. He has developed supply chain strategies, coached executives, and led supply chain projects for companies including Caterpillar, APICS, and MHI. These days, he devotes his time to teaching, conducting research serving on boards, and helping startup companies develop cool new supply chain technologies.

You'll often find Daniel speaking at supply chain management events around the world. He's also created several online courses for LinkedIn Learning. He holds a master of engineering in logistics from MIT's Supply Chain Management program, is an adjunct professor at Bradley University, and is a doctoral researcher at Cranfield University.

You can visit Daniel's website (www.danielstanton.com), or follow him on social media for more insights about supply chain management, project leadership, and the other things that he grooves on:

Twitter: @stanton_daniel

LinkedIn: www.linkedin.com/in/danielstanton/

Dedication

To my wife Ruth, my partner in everything that matters. And to our daughters, our parents, and our families. What a team!

To my colleagues from CSCMP, APICS, ISM, SCC, WERC, ASTL, PMI, ALAN, DMSCA, and MHI who have contributed so much to the development of supply chain management as a profession.

To my professors, colleagues, and classmates at MIT, Cranfield, SDSMT, Bradley, and throughout the academic community who have challenged my thinking and expanded my horizons.

To my many friends from Caterpillar and the U.S. Navy, where I've had incredible opportunities to experience the challenge of managing a supply chain at a global scale.

To the staff and volunteers from the American Logistics Aid Network who unite supply chain professionals and support communities during natural disasters.

And to Nani, Ruby, Rooney, and Bear — our furry family members.

Acknowledgments

Writing this book has been a blast, but I definitely didn't do it alone. I owe a huge debt to many friends, colleagues, students, and professors who have encouraged me and who make the world a better place every day by teaching, learning, researching, and applying supply chain management. Thank you!

This book would have remained 80 percent complete forever if it weren't for the help and sacrifice of my whole family, giving me the support and the time to do it. Yes, children. . . I can play with you now! For Mom, Mamacita, and Papa — thank you for always being ready to help. For my business partners — Ruth, Dan, Rick, Jeevan, and Tom — thank you for sticking with me as I juggled multiple commitments. For Rob, Jim, Michael, Scott, Jeff, Muthu, Kathy, Susie, Sharon, Jonathan, Nick, Steve, Angela, Teresa, and Andrew — thank you for standing at the ready when I needed to talk things out. And for Amy, Charlotte, and Beth, thank you for believing in me and helping me at every step along the way.

Publisher's Acknowledgments

Acquisitions Editor: Amy Fandrei

Project Editor: Charlotte Kughen

Copy Editor: Kathy Simpson

Technical Editor: Elizabeth Rennie

Editorial Assistant: Matthew Lowe

Sr. Editorial Assistant: Cherie Case

Production Editor: Antony Sami

Cover Image: ©enot-poloskun/Getty Images

Leverage the power

Dummies is the global leader in the reference category and one of the most trusted and highly regarded brands in the world. No longer just focused on books, customers now have access to the dummies content they need in the format they want. Together we'll craft a solution that engages your customers, stands out from the competition, and helps you meet your goals.

Advertising & Sponsorships

Connect with an engaged audience on a powerful multimedia site, and position your message alongside expert how-to content. Dummies.com is a one-stop shop for free, online information and know-how curated by a team of experts.

- Targeted ads
- Video
- Email Marketing
- Microsites
- Sweepstakes sponsorship

20 **MILLION**
PAGE VIEWS
EVERY SINGLE MONTH

15
MILLION
UNIQUE
VISITORS PER MONTH

43%
OF ALL VISITORS
ACCESS THE SITE
VIA THEIR MOBILE DEVICES

700,000 NEWSLETTER
SUBSCRIPTIONS
TO THE INBOXES OF
300,000 UNIQUE INDIVIDUALS
EVERY WEEK

# of dummies

PERSONAL ENRICHMENT

9781119187790
USA $26.00
CAN $31.99
UK £19.99

9781119179030
USA $21.99
CAN $25.99
UK £16.99

9781119293354
USA $24.99
CAN $29.99
UK £17.99

9781119293347
USA $22.99
CAN $27.99
UK £16.99

9781119310068
USA $22.99
CAN $27.99
UK £16.99

9781119235606
USA $24.99
CAN $29.99
UK £17.99

9781119251163
USA $24.99
CAN $29.99
UK £17.99

9781119235491
USA $26.99
CAN $31.99
UK £19.99

9781119279952
USA $24.99
CAN $29.99
UK £17.99

9781119283133
USA $24.99
CAN $29.99
UK £17.99

9781119287117
USA $24.99
CAN $29.99
UK £16.99

9781119130246
USA $22.99
CAN $27.99
UK £16.99

PROFESSIONAL DEVELOPMENT

9781119311041
USA $24.99
CAN $29.99
UK £17.99

9781119255796
USA $39.99
CAN $47.99
UK £27.99

9781119293439
USA $26.99
CAN $31.99
UK £19.99

9781119281467
USA $26.99
CAN $31.99
UK £19.99

9781119280651
USA $29.99
CAN $35.99
UK £21.99

9781119251132
USA $24.99
CAN $29.99
UK £17.99

9781119310563
USA $34.00
CAN $41.99
UK £24.99

9781119181705
USA $29.99
CAN $35.99
UK £21.99

9781119263593
USA $26.99
CAN $31.99
UK £19.99

9781119257769
USA $29.99
CAN $35.99
UK £21.99

9781119293477
USA $26.99
CAN $31.99
UK £19.99

9781119265313
USA $24.99
CAN $29.99
UK £17.99

9781119239314
USA $29.99
CAN $35.99
UK £21.99

9781119293323
USA $29.99
CAN $35.99
UK £21.99

dummies.com

dummies
A Wiley Brand

Learning Made Easy

ACADEMIC

9781119293576
USA $19.99
CAN $23.99
UK £15.99

9781119293637
USA $19.99
CAN $23.99
UK £15.99

9781119293491
USA $19.99
CAN $23.99
UK £15.99

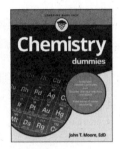

9781119293460
USA $19.99
CAN $23.99
UK £15.99

9781119293590
USA $19.99
CAN $23.99
UK £15.99

9781119215844
USA $26.99
CAN $31.99
UK £19.99

9781119293378
USA $22.99
CAN $27.99
UK £16.99

9781119293521
USA $19.99
CAN $23.99
UK £15.99

9781119239178
USA $18.99
CAN $22.99
UK £14.99

9781119263883
USA $26.99
CAN $31.99
UK £19.99

Available Everywhere Books Are Sold

dummies.com

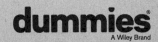